Research on Teacher Identity

Paul A. Schutz • Ji Hong • Dionne Cross Francis
Editors

Research on Teacher Identity

Mapping Challenges and Innovations

 Springer

Editors
Paul A. Schutz
University of Texas
San Antonio, TX, USA

Ji Hong
University of Oklahoma
Norman, OK, USA

Dionne Cross Francis
Indiana University
Bloomington, IN, USA

ISBN 978-3-319-93835-6   ISBN 978-3-319-93836-3   (eBook)
https://doi.org/10.1007/978-3-319-93836-3

Library of Congress Control Number: 2018948730

This Springer imprint is published by Springer Nature, under the registered company Springer International Publishing AG
The registered company address is: Gewerbestrasse 11, 6330 Cham, Switzerland

Contents

Part III   Teacher Identity Development in Various Learning Contexts

Part IV   Teacher Identity Development in the Content Areas

Part V   Social Historical Contextual Influences on Teacher
**   Identity Development**

Contributors

Sanne F. Akkerman Department of Education, Utrecht University, Utrecht, The Netherlands

Janet Alsup Department of Curriculum and Instruction, Purdue University, West Lafayette, IN, USA

Lucy Avraamidou Institute for Science Education and Communication, University of Groningen, Groningen, The Netherlands

Larike H. Bronkhorst Department of Education, Utrecht University, Utrecht, The Netherlands

Rebecca Buchanan School of Learning and Teaching, University of Maine, Orono, ME, USA

Grace A. Chen Department of Teaching and Learning, Vanderbilt University, Nashville, TN, USA

Sharon Chubbuck Department of Educational Policy and Leadership, Marquette University, Milwaukee, WI, USA

Matthew Clarke School of Education, York St John University, York, UK

Dionne Cross Francis Department of Curriculum and Instruction, Indiana University, Bloomington, IN, USA

Christopher Day Faculty of Social Science, School of Education, University of Nottingham, Nottingham, UK

Vesna Dimitrieska School of Education, Indiana University, Bloomington, IN, USA

Ayfer Eker Department of Curriculum and Instruction, Indiana University, Bloomington, IN, USA

Joanna K. Garner   Center for Educational Partnerships, Old Dominion University, Norfolk, VA, USA

Ji Hong   Department of Educational Psychology, University of Oklahoma, Norman, OK, USA

Ilana S. Horn   Department of Teaching and Learning, Vanderbilt University, Nashville, TN, USA

Mahsa Izadinia   School of Education, Edith Cowan University, Joondalup, Australia

Tambra O. Jackson   Department of Teacher Education, Indiana University – Purdue University Indianapolis, Indianapolis, IN, USA

Wayne Journell   Department of Teacher Education and Higher Education, University of North Carolina at Greensboro, Greensboro, NC, USA

Avi Kaplan   Department of Psychological Studies in Education, Temple University, Philadelphia, PA, USA

Geert Kelchtermans   Faculty of Psychology and Educational Sciences, University of Leuven, Leuven, Belgium

Jinqing Liu   Department of Curriculum and Instruction, Indiana University, Bloomington, IN, USA

Paulien C. Meijer   Radboud Teachers Academy, Radboud University Nijmegen, Nijmegen, The Netherlands

Sharon L. Nichols   Department of Educational Psychology, University of Texas at San Antonio, San Antonio, TX, USA

Susan Bobbitt Nolen   Learning Sciences & Human Development, University of Washington, Seattle, WA, USA

Brad Olsen   Education Department, University of California-Santa Cruz, Santa Cruz, CA, USA

Ida E. Oosterheert   Radboud Teachers Academy, Radboud University Nijmegen, Nijmegen, The Netherlands

Paul W. Richardson   Faculty of Education, Monash University, Melbourne, Australia

Martine M. van Rijswijk   Department of Education, Utrecht University, Utrecht, The Netherlands

Maria Ruohotie-Lyhty   Department of Language and Communication Studies, University of Jyväskylä, Jyväskylä, Finland

Paul A. Schutz Department of Educational Psychology, University of Texas at San Antonio, San Antonio, TX, USA

Samantha Schwenke Department of Educational Leadership and Policy Studies, University of Texas at San Antonio, San Antonio, TX, USA

Jan van Tartwijk Department of Education, Utrecht University, Utrecht, The Netherlands

Helen M. G. Watt School of Education and Social Work, The University of Sydney, Camperdown, Australia

Michalinos Zembylas Program of Educational Studies, Open University of Cyprus, Latsia, Cyprus

About the Authors

Sanne F. Akkerman is a Professor of Educational Sciences at Leiden University. In her research, she focuses on transitions of students and collaborations between professionals across disciplinary, educational, and organizational contexts and the impact of such multi-systemic participations on interest and identity development.

Janet Alsup is a Professor of Literacy and Language Education and Head of the Curriculum and Instruction Department at Purdue University. Professor Alsup's research centers on teacher professional identity development, secondary literacy pedagogies, narrative and teacher research, and adolescent literature and identity formation. She has published five books, including *Teacher Identity Discourses: Negotiating Personal and Professional Spaces* (Routledge, 2005).

Lucy Avraamidou holds a PhD in Science Education from the Pennsylvania State University and she works as an Associate Professor of Science Education at the University of Groningen in the Netherlands. Prior to her appointment, she worked at the University of Nicosia in Cyprus and at King's College London. Her research is associated with theoretical and empirical explorations of beginning teachers' learning and development with the use of interpretive approaches. She has authored more than 50 publications and edited two book volumes with titles: *Studying Science Teacher Identity* (2016) and *Intersections of Formal and Informal Science* (2016, co-edited).

Larike H. Bronkhorst is an Assistant Professor of Educational Sciences at Leiden University Graduate School of Teaching in the Netherlands. Her research explores students' and professionals' learning across contexts, specifically focusing on understanding the connections, or lack thereof, between different contexts of learning.

Rebecca Buchanan is an Assistant Professor of Curriculum, Assessment, and Instruction at the University of Maine. Her research examines contextually situated teacher learning. She is interested in the intersection of personal identity, professional development, school reform, literacy, and language. She employs qualitative methods and discourse analysis to investigate how teachers learn in and across multiple contexts by connecting their own personal and professional pasts with the present.

Grace A. Chen is a doctoral student in Learning, Teaching, and Diversity at Vanderbilt University. A former secondary mathematics teacher, she is interested in the influence of teacher identity on pedagogical practice, particularly as it relates to teachers' conceptions of equity and justice.

Sharon Chubbuck is an Associate Professor in the College of Education at Marquette University. Her research interests are focused on the nature of socially just teaching, in pre-service teacher preparation, and in-service teacher practice. She is currently studying systemic reform to increase equitable access to educational quality for students of color.

Matthew Clarke is a Professor of Education at York St John University in England. Prior to taking up his current position, he worked in universities in Australia, Hong Kong, and the United Arab Emirates. His research interests focus on education policy and politics, particularly their implications for teachers, and his work draws on psychoanalytic, political, and social theories.

Dionne Cross Francis is an Associate Professor of Mathematics Education in the Department of Curriculum and Instruction at Indiana University and the Director of the Center for P-16 Research and Collaboration. Her research interests include investigating the relationships among psychological constructs such as beliefs, identity, and emotions and how the interplay between these constructs influence teachers' instructional decision-making prior to and during the act of teaching (mathematics).

Christopher Day is a Professor of Education at the University of Nottingham. His research and publications focus on teachers' work, lives, and effectiveness and school leadership. He is Editor-in-Chief of *Teachers and Teaching: Theory and Practice* and a Fellow of the Academy of Social Sciences. His latest book is *Teachers' Worlds and Work: Understanding Complexity, Sustaining Quality* (2017), Routledge: London & New York.

Vesna Dimitrieska holds a PhD in Literacy, Culture, and Language Education and has worked as an EFL/ESL language teacher and language teacher educator in Europe, Asia, and North America. She has conducted research on English language teaching, pedagogies of less commonly taught languages and dual language immersion, teacher talk and teacher educator reflexive practices. She currently works on various global education initiatives in K-16 education.

Ayfer Eker is a graduate student in the Department of Curriculum and Instruction at Indiana University. Her research interests include in-service mathematics teachers' professional development with an emphasis on the relationships among their mathematical knowledge for teaching, beliefs, and teaching practices in addition to student learning and cognition in mathematics.

Joanna K. Garner holds a Ph.D. in Educational Psychology from The Pennsylvania State University. She is currently a Research Associate Professor and the Executive Director of The Center for Educational Partnerships at Old Dominion University in Norfolk, Virginia. Her design-based research on educators' learning, motivation, and identity forms an integral component of the Center's collaborations across the university, in schools, and in informal educational contexts. Garner is an active member of AERA Division C and is currently a Section Editor for *The Journal of Experimental Education*.

Ji Hong is an Associate Professor of Educational Psychology at the University of Oklahoma. Her research focuses on pre-service and in-service teachers' professional identity development, motivation to teach, emotions, and resilience in relation to teacher retention and teacher effectiveness. She is an Associate Editor of *Teachers and Teaching: Theory and Practice* and an Editorial Board member of *Contemporary Educational Psychology*.

Ilana S. Horn is a Professor of Mathematics Education at Vanderbilt University. She uses interpretive methods to study secondary mathematics teachers' learning, seeking to improve education for students and supports for teachers, particularly in urban schools. Her current research project investigates mid-career mathematics teachers' learning in a rich professional development program.

Mahsa Izadinia completed her BA and MA in Teaching English as a Foreign Language in Iran and conducted her PhD in Education at Edith Cowan University, Australia. Currently, she undertakes private research on her areas of interest including teacher education, mentoring programs, and teacher professional identity. Mahsa has published several papers on mentoring and teacher identity.

Tambra O. Jackson is an Associate Professor in Teacher Education at Indiana University – Purdue University, Indianapolis. Her research and teaching focus on teacher learning and development across the professional continuum specifically centered on preparing teachers for diverse student populations, preparing teachers to teach for social justice, and culturally responsive teaching and pedagogy. She resides in Indianapolis with her husband, Les, and their son, Kadir.

Wayne Journell is an Associate Professor and Secondary Teacher Education Coordinator at the University of North Carolina at Greensboro. His research focuses on the teaching of politics in K-12 education. He is also the Editor of *Theory & Research in Social Education*, the premier research journal in social studies education.

Avi Kaplan is an Associate Professor of Educational Psychology at Temple University in Philadelphia, USA. His research interests focus on student and teacher motivation and identity development. His recent research involves the application of the Complex Dynamic Systems approach identity and motivation, and collaborative design-based interventions that focus on promoting educators' and students' motivation and identity exploration around the curriculum. Avi is a Fellow of the Association for Psychological Science and the American Psychological Association, and is currently the Editor of the *Journal of Experimental Education.*

Geert Kelchtermans studied Philosophy and Educational Sciences at the University of Leuven, where he obtained a PhD in 1993 with a study on teachers' professional development from a narrative-biographical perspective. He is now a Full Professor at the same university and head of the Center for Innovation and the Development of Teacher and School (in the Education and Training Research Unit). His research focuses on the interplay between individual educational professionals (teachers, principals, teacher educators) and their professional development on the one hand and their organizational and institutional working conditions on the other.

Jinqing Liu is a doctoral student of Mathematics Education in the Department of Curriculum and Instruction at Indiana University. Her research interests include students' mathematics mistakes handling, assessment of mathematics knowledge for teaching, comparative studies of the teaching and learning in the USA and East Asian Countries, international large-scale assessment, and evidence-based practice. Her career goal is to contribute the cross-cultural understanding of Mathematics Education practice and theory between Western and Eastern countries, and to devote in narrowing down the gap between educational research and practice in mathematics education field.

Paulien C. Meijer is a Professor in Teacher Education at the Radboud Teachers Academy of Radboud University in Nijmegen, the Netherlands. As scientific director, she heads the Academy's Research program "Cultivating creativity in education: Interactions between teaching and learning." She has published about processes of identity development in young and experienced teachers, and all the struggles and joys associated with that.

Sharon L. Nichols a Professor in the Department of Educational Psychological at the University of Texas at San Antonio. Her research interests focus on the ways educational policies impact teacher identities and practices and student development and motivation. She is the past Chair of the Adolescence Special Interest Group of the American Educational Research Association and past treasurer for Division 15 (Educational Psychology) of the American Psychological Association.

Susan Bobbitt Nolen is a Professor of Learning Sciences and Human Development at the University of Washington. Her research investigates the relationship of engagement, identity, and motivation to learn in and across social contexts.

Brad Olsen is a Professor of Education at the University of California, Santa Cruz. His research focuses on teachers, teaching, and teacher education (with emphases on professional knowledge, identity. and school reform); sociolinguistics; philosophical perspectives on education; and qualitative research methods. His most recent book is *Teaching for Success: Developing Your Teacher Identity in Today's Classroom* (2016, Routledge). His current work examines the role of teachers and teacher education in the contemporary education reform climate of the United States and abroad.

Ida E. Oosterheert is an Associate Professor of Teacher Learning and Development at the Radboud Teachers Academy of Radboud University Nijmegen, The Netherlands. Her expertise and research focus on the quality of (student) teachers' learning and development. Currently, she particularly addresses the question of how (secondary) teachers can be supported to learn to cultivate the creativity of their students.

Paul W. Richardson is a Professor and Associate Dean Research, previously Associate Dean Teaching, Faculty of Education, Monash University. He is engaged in a longitudinal study of teachers' career choice motivations, self-efficacy, and career trajectories for different types of beginning and mid-career teachers (www.fitchoice.org), attracting substantial research funding from three sequential Australian Research Council grants (2006–2016). He has begun theorizing the career motivations of early career university academics. He has edited books including *Teacher Motivation* (Routledge 2014) and *Global Perspectives on Teacher Motivation* (CUP 2017).

Martine M. van Rijswijk is a PhD candidate and teacher educator at the Graduate School of Teaching of Utrecht University. In her research, she focuses on student teacher development sense-making processes, both on intrapersonal and interpersonal levels, and teacher educator identity and expertise.

Maria Ruohotie-Lyhty is a Senior Lecturer in Applied Linguistics (Language Learning and Teaching) at the Department of Languages and Communication, University of Jyväskylä, Finland. Her research is broadly situated in the area of identity, agency, and emotions in learning and teaching. She also has experience of developing teacher education practices through action research.

Paul A. Schutz is currently a Professor in the Department of Educational Psychology at the University of Texas at San Antonio. His research interests include the nature of emotion, emotional regulation, and teachers' understandings of emotion in the classroom. He is a past president for Division 15: Educational Psychology of the American Psychological Association and a former Co-Editor of the *Educational Researcher: Research News and Comment*.

Samantha Schwenke is a graduate student in the Department Educational Leadership and Policy studies (K-12 at The University of Texas at San Antonio. Her research interests include the development of teacher identity, the effects of poverty on students, and human relations.

Jan van Tartwijk is a Professor of Education at Utrecht University and Chair of the university's Graduate School of Teaching. In his research, he focuses, among others, on teacher education and the development of teacher expertise, communication processes between students and teachers in (multicultural) classrooms, and assessment and motivation.

Helen M. G. Watt is a Professor of Educational Psychology at the University of Sydney and Australian Research Council Future Fellow 2017–2021. Her longitudinal programs have implications for supporting career development of beginning teachers (www.fitchoice.org) and redressing gender imbalances in STEM fields (www.stepsstudy.org). Helen is currently Associate Editor for *AERA Open* and on several editorial boards. She has edited books including *Global Perspectives on Teacher Motivation* (CUP 2017), *Teacher Motivation* (Routledge 2014), *Gender and Occupational Outcomes* (APA 2008) and founded Network Gender & STEM: www.genderandSTEM.com.

Michalinos Zembylas is a Professor of Educational Theory and Curriculum Studies at the Open University of Cyprus. He is a Visiting Professor and Research Fellow at the Institute for Reconciliation and Social Justice, University of the Free State, South Africa, as well as Research Associate at the Centre for Critical Studies in Higher Education Transformation at Nelson Mandela University. He has written extensively on emotion and affect in relation to social justice pedagogies, intercultural and peace education, human rights education, and citizenship education.

Part I
Introduction to Research on Teacher Identities

Chapter 1
Research on Teacher Identity: Introduction to Mapping Challenges and Innovations

Paul A. Schutz, Dionne Cross Francis, and Ji Hong

There is little question that teachers matter. As a number of researchers have noted, teachers are the key agents who directly impact students' learning and growth (Harris & Rutledge, 2010; Hattie, 2002; Jennings & Greenberg, 2009). The significance of teachers' roles has been even more emphasized in the current educational climate of increasing and persistent teacher attrition, heightened accountability, and demand for quality teaching in challenging school contexts. Over the past few decades, there has been an increasing interest to understand and advocate teachers' lives through their professional identity development and its impact on the quality of their teaching, motivation to teach, commitment, well-being, and career decision making (Beauchamp & Thomas, 2009; Buchanan, 2015; Cross & Hong, 2009; Day, Kington, Stobart, & Sammons, 2006; Hong, 2010; Nichols, Schutz, Rodgers, & Bilica, 2016; Schutz, Cross, Hong, & Osbon, 2007; Van den Berg, 2002).

However, despite the significance and necessity of broadening our knowledge of teachers' identity development, researchers are still in the early stages of understanding how teacher identities are formed, the factors that influence changes of identities, and the role these identities play in students' and teachers' motivation and learning. For example, one challenge has been the complex and multifaceted nature of teachers' identities, which has consequently generated divergent approaches for understanding and fostering teacher identities both within and across disciplines.

P. A. Schutz (✉)
Department of Educational Psychology, University of Texas at San Antonio, San Antonio, TX, USA
e-mail: paul.schutz@utsa.edu

D. Cross Francis
Department of Curriculum and Instruction, Indiana University, Bloomington, IN, USA
e-mail: dicross@indiana.edu

J. Hong
Department of Educational Psychology, University of Oklahoma, Norman, OK, USA
e-mail: jyhong@ou.edu

© Springer International Publishing AG, part of Springer Nature 2018
P. A. Schutz et al. (eds.), *Research on Teacher Identity*,
https://doi.org/10.1007/978-3-319-93836-3_1

The field has been growing without adequately addressing differences and similarities among diverse approaches, discerning strengths and weaknesses, and evaluating effectiveness, applicability, and the value of various frameworks.

Given the challenges and needs of the field, our aim in this volume is (1) to bring together a broad range of international researchers who approach the study of teacher identity from various theoretical perspectives to discuss their assumptions, frameworks, and contributions to the research on teacher identities; (2) to develop understandings, from those various perspectives, of how teachers' identities are developed, and how those identities transact with students' and teachers' motivation and learning within different social and cultural contexts; and (3) to engender deep appreciation for the social, contextual, and political dimensions of studying teachers' identities and contribute to ongoing debates about the implications of our methodological choices for understanding this construct.

To address these goals, this volume features the work of a number of scholars from around the world who represent a variety of disciplines (e.g., Educational Psychology, Teacher Education, Multicultural Education, Educational Philosophy, Cultural Studies, and Policy Studies), scientific paradigms (e.g., critical race theory, psychoanalytic theory, phenomenological approaches, post-structural and post-positivist perspectives), and research methods (e.g., ethnographic, historical, philosophical, longitudinal, meta-studies, quantitative, qualitative, and mixed methodologies). This comprehensive collection will contribute to advancing the field by unpacking some of the complexity of teacher identity, showcasing current research with data explored from diverse perspectives, and providing cogent discussions of the interplay among macro- (e.g., social discourse, performativity agenda, policy demand) and micro- (e.g., classroom dynamics, relationship with parents) level contexts. This combination of variety and transformative potential makes this edited book unique and a valuable resource for researchers interested in studying teacher identities and teacher development.

Edited Book Overview

In addition to this introduction chapter, this book has five additional sections. In the second section the authors focus on "Theoretical Understandings of Teacher Identity Development". This section features a group of authors who focus on some of the key theoretical foundations of inquiries on teacher identity development. To do so these scholars contextualize some of the key processes involved in identity development such as agency, resilience, efficacy, attributions, and the need for vulnerability.

In Chaps. 2 and 3, Janet Alsup and Maria Ruohotie-Lyhty respectively describes accounts of teachers' journeys as they navigate challenges and conflicts in their development as professional educators. In Chap. 2, by presenting a pre-service teacher's narrative (i.e., Teresa), Alsup clarifies the cognitive conflicts beginning teachers may have while enacting authority as they experience vulnerability.

Through showcasing this narrative, the reader will understand Teresa's efforts to negotiate this important balance. It is through this negotiation that a more complex professional identity emerges. In Chap. 3, Maria Ruohotie-Lyhty further highlights how negotiation, defining and redefining are central processes teachers undergo during identity development. She offers a longitudinal perspective on the processes involved in teachers' identity development. Drawing on examples from two longitudinal research projects where she focuses on pre-service and in-service teachers' identity development, she unpacks identity-agency while illustrating how teachers' efforts to maintain and transform their professional identities involve renegotiation, changing ones' conception of self, and/or work to defend that current conception of self.

Authoring their identities is extremely complex as it involves significant work managing transactions among internal (e.g., emotions, efficacy) and external (e.g., policy, school structure) elements. The remaining chapters in this section enhance our understandings of how these elements transact in the identity development process. In their chapter, Paul W. Richardson and Helen M. G. Watt present their developmental perspective on teacher identity and motivation. They discuss how they have adapted current motivational theories (e.g., self-efficacy, expectancy-value, achievement goal, and self-determination) and applied them to the study of teachers' motivation and identity formation. They propose the SOC (Selection, Optimisation, and Compensation) model of successful ageing as an overarching theoretical lens that allows them to provide important insights and a potentially integrative framework for identity development. In Chap. 5, Paul A. Schutz, Sharon L. Nichols, and Samantha Schwenke also draw on motivational theories in discussing their model of teacher identity development. They focus on transactions among teachers' goals, critical emotional episodes, the attributions teachers make about those emotional episodes and how that process may lead to identity development. They suggest that how teachers experience and talk about critical events and the emotions associated with those events may offer identity-generating pathways for teachers as they reflect upon their role and place in the classroom.

Christopher Day follows with a discussion about the relationship among teachers' beliefs about agency, emotional wellbeing, and resilience and discusses their relationship with and their importance to teacher professional identity. To do so, he conceptualizes teacher identities as a blend of the personal and professional selves that emerges during transactions among workplace structures, cultures, and within the constraints of policy mandates. By incorporating the role of external elements, Day provides insight into the multifaceted nature of identity authoring and shaping. As such, given the psychological and cognitive work involved in teaching, he suggests that maintaining a positive sense of professional identity requires on-going emotional and intellectual energy.

In this chapter, Avi Kaplan, and Joanna K. Garner describe their Dynamic Systems Model of Role Identity (DSMRI). Through the lens of the DSMRI, they discuss teacher identity as a complex, dynamic, contextualized integration of personal and contextual influences. They consider the unit-of-analysis of teacher role identity as residing within the person, but its formation as involving the dialogical relations with the person's other role identities and with the role identities of others (i.e., students, colleagues, supervisors). This chapter provides a snapshot of the micro- and macro- influences on teacher identity development.

In the third section the authors focus on research and theory that capture "Teacher Identity Development in Various Learning Contexts". In section three, a common thread through the work of this group of authors is the changing and transformative nature of teacher identity in relation to their career trajectory or various contextual influences (e.g., clinical simulations, dialogues with supervisors, mentor teacher, creativity training). Authors in this section show the development of teacher identity over time, while foregrounding teacher agency as a key mediator between those contextual influences and the individual.

In Chap. 8 by Grace A. Chen, Ilana S. Horn, and Susan Nolen, the authors capture the identity shaping experiences of students in a teacher education course. They focus on two sets of interpretive case studies to theorize the relationship between teacher identity and teacher learning by examining how pre-service teachers' conceptions of a "good teacher" activate motivational filters through which they construct their emerging teacher identities within the context of clinical simulations. By foregrounding teachers' positional identities, the authors discuss how teacher educators lead novice teachers to revise the way they think about instructional practices, and other tasks involved in the work of teaching, as they develop their understanding of what it means to be a "good teacher".

In the next chapter, Martine M. van Rijswijk, Larike H. Bronkhorst, Sanne F. Akkerman, and Jan van Tartwijk focus on the student-supervisor relationship. They analyze the ways that student teachers and teacher educators explored both sensed continuity and sensed discontinuity within the development of their teacher identities. Using supervisor and student teacher dialogues they focus on balancing time (e.g., past, present, and future), content (e.g., their perceived ability to prepare useful lessons), and salience (e.g., understanding what problems needed to be dealt with when). The authors suggest ways to provide support for student teachers and teacher educators by explicitly discussing balancing processes within the context of teacher education.

In Chap. 10, Edith Mahsa Izadinia, highlights the importance of mentor teachers in shaping preservice teachers' identities. She argues that teacher identity is a complex process requiring the coordination of varied internal and external factors. As such, mentor teachers have the potential to influence preservice teachers' understandings of who they are as teachers and what they can do through the ways they engage in the mentor-teacher relationship. In this chapter, she unpacks how mentor teachers' practices and approaches can shape the identity pathway preservice teachers navigate in the process of becoming a teacher.

In the final chapter in this section, Ida Oosterheert and Paulien Meijer connect teaching for creativity and the process of identity transformation. They present core characteristics of a 'creativity cultivating context' and how the establishment of this context is in many ways, the opposite of what teachers often identify with, such as, being the (only) expert in the classroom. Thus, the challenge in cultivating creativity, has the potential to transform their conceptions of themselves as teacher.

In the fourth section, the authors explore "Teacher Identity Development in the Content Areas". The work of this group of authors focus on exploring the question "What does it mean to be a [subject] teacher?" The authors present critical insights related to constant negotiations between teachers' personal and professional identities and its influence on classroom practice; the tensions generated in negotiating what the field purports as [subject] teacher identity and how teachers see themselves professionally; the ways the structure of teacher education programs and experiences within the program afford or constrain the embodying of a [subject] teacher identity; and, how people, places, and the socio-cultural environment shape the dynamic development of the [subject] teacher. The disciplines of focus in these chapters include science, English as a foreign language, mathematics, and social studies.

In Chap. 12, Dionne Cross Francis, Ji Hong, Ayfer Eker, and Jinqing Liu examine the experiences of 18 elementary teachers who were being challenged to change how they defined themselves professionally as a mathematics teacher. The authors describe four core tensions the teachers experience between being an elementary generalist and a mathematics teacher. They also discuss how and why these identity tensions function as sources of growth, instead of barriers to development, which provide further insights for professional developers, school leaders, and policy makers.

In Chap. 13, Lucy Avraamidou, presents a case study of a typical beginning elementary science teacher's (i.e., Anna) identity trajectory over time and across different contexts. She uses a life-history approach to the critical events that Anna experienced through her participation as a science learner in various contexts and communities. By discussing Anna's life events, the author shows the development of her teacher identity as a woman with a goal to be a science teacher and explore the ways in which those events impacted her science teacher identity trajectory.

In this chapter, Vesna Dimitrieska, discusses how language teacher identity develops through the complex interplay between beliefs about language and current teacher learning. Drawing on Vygotsky's (1978) concepts of mediation and internalization as a framework, she describes how pre-service teachers' uses of mediation and internalization serve as a window into their teacher identity development. She suggests that for training programs to initiate change, language teachers must have access to spaces that allow them to construct and reconstruct their language teaching conceptualizations.

In Chap. 15, Wayne Journell explores the role various identities play in teachers' controversial decisions to discuss politics in the social studies classroom. He describes how this filtering through teachers' various identities (e.g., gender, race, political affiliation) influences what teachers choose to discuss, the stance they take, and how they engage students in conversations. How these conversations unfold appear to be related to the identity that is foregrounded in those contexts.

In the fifth section, the authors focus on research and theory related to the "Social Historical Contextual Influences on Teacher Identity Development". Focusing on the potential impact of various social historical contexts on teacher identity development, this body of work includes examinations of teacher identity of minorities in racially homogenous environments - teachers of Color at predominantly white institutions; tensions at the intersection of identity and politics; identity negotiations in the face of contemporary educational policy; the paradoxical nature of teacher identity; and socio-culturally sensitive alternative conceptions of identity, "professional self-understanding".

In this chapter, Michalinos Zembylas and Sharon Chubbuck develop a conceptualization of teacher identity that focuses on the intersection of identity and politics. They suggest that we need to develop more holistic understandings of teacher identity that acknowledges the influence of power relations and politics in teacher identity formation. In addition, recognizing the prospects of developing a critical and transformative orientation towards the conceptualization of teacher identity will bode well in strengthening our understanding of the construct.

In this chapter, Rebecca Buchanan and Brad Olsen examine the relationship between pre-service teacher identity development and the USA's contemporary policy landscape regarding teacher training. They elaborate on how pre-service teachers must navigate and negotiate the effects of these competing views as they learn to enact their own personal visions and practices they are learning in their teacher education program. Through this examination, they highlight pre-service teachers' identity development as both the process and outcome of this complex dynamic.

In the next chapter, Tambra O. Jackson examines how student teachers navigate the effects of competing expectations. She focuses on the experiences of preservice teachers of Color at predominantly White institutions and the ways in which their developing identities as teachers are influenced by the intersection of their racial/ethnic identities and the context of the environment on their teacher education program. Specifically, she illuminates the experiences of students of color as they manage the knowledge and experiential expectations placed on them by their program and their own academic and professional needs. The author suggests implications and recommendations for attending to the teacher identity development of preservice teachers of Color.

In Chap. 19, Matthew Clarke examines the paradoxical and problematic notion of teacher identity. He draws on psychoanalytic theory to illuminate the complex nature of identity, and the construct's relation to teachers' lives and work. He points out that although sometimes identity is characterized by harmony, completeness, or self-sufficiency in many cases, it is a site of conflict, fragmentation, and alienation. Finally, he explores the implications of this paradoxical as both indispensable and impossible.

In Chap. 20, Geert Kelchtermans questions the concept of teacher identity itself and argues the case that "professional self-understanding" may be a more useful concept. He suggests that one's understanding of oneself can be represented, shared, and constructed at a moment in time as a coherent ongoing biography, while at the same time it continues to change and develop over the lifetime – in other words it is inevitably always a (temporary) product, while at the same time an ongoing process.

In the final section, "Future Directions for Research on Teacher Identity" we synthesize the themes that emerge from the chapters and discuss future directions for inquiry on teacher identity, while discussing practical implications for teachers' professional development, and for educational policy and leadership in organizing schools and educational systems.

As indicated, over the past few decades, teachers' professional identities and their development have emerged as a key focus for researchers' efforts at unpacking teachers' professional lives and understanding the quality of their teaching, motivation to teach, and career decision-making. We hope various theoretical, methodological, and practical approaches presented in this volume initiate active scholarly conversations and extend the boundaries of teacher identity research and practice. This endeavor will contribute to refining our understandings of teacher identity development in today's changing and challenging educational climate, and to provide foundations to meaningfully engage various stakeholders – including teachers themselves, teacher educators, school leaders, professional developers, and policy makers – so that they can make informed decisions, develop collaborative partnerships, and make sustainable changes, all of which will empower teachers and improve their professional lives and overall wellbeing.

References

Beauchamp, C., & Thomas, L. (2009). Understanding teacher identity: An overview of issues in the literature and implications for teacher education. *Cambridge Journal of Education, 39*(2), 175–189.

Buchanan, R. (2015). Teacher identity and agency in an era of accountability. *Teachers and Teaching, 21*(6), 700–719.

Cross, D. I., & Hong, J. Y. (2009). Beliefs and professional identity: Critical constructs in examining the impact of reform on the emotional experiences of teachers. In P. A. Schutz, M. Zembylas, & M. (Eds.), *Advances in teacher emotion research: The impact on teachers' lives* (pp. 273–296). Boston: Springer.

Day, C., Kington, A., Stobart, G., & Sammons, P. (2006). The personal and professional selves of teachers: Stable and unstable identities. *British Educational Research Journal, 32*(4), 601–616.

Harris, D., & Rutledge, S. (2010). Models and predictors of teacher effectiveness: A comparison of research about teaching and other occupations. *Teachers College Record, 112*(3), 914–960.

Hattie, J. A. C. (2002). What are the attributes of excellent teachers? In *Teachers make a difference: What is the research evidence?* (pp. 3–26). Wellington, New Zealand: New Zealand Council for Educational Research.

Hong, J. Y. (2010). Pre-service and beginning teachers' professional identity and its relation to dropping out of the profession. *Teaching and Teacher Education, 26*(8), 1530–1543.

Jennings, P. A., & Greenberg, M. T. (2009). The prosocial classroom: Teacher social and emotional competence in relation to student and classroom outcomes. *Review of Educational Research, 79*(1), 491–525. https://doi.org/10.3102/0034654308325693

Nichols, S., Schutz, P. A., Rodgers, K., & Bilica, K. (2016). Early career teachers' emotion and emerging teacher identities. *Teachers and Teaching: Theory and Practice*, 1–16. https://doi.org /10.1080/13540602.2016.1211099

Schutz, P. A., Cross, D. I., Hong, J. Y., & Osbon, J. N. (2007). Teacher identities, beliefs and goals related to emotions in the classroom. In P. A. Schutz & R. Pekrun (Eds.), *Emotion in education* (pp. 223–241). San Diego, CA: Elsevier.

Van den Berg, R. (2002). Teachers' meanings regarding educational practice. *Review of Educational Research, 72*(4), 577–625.

Vygotsky, L. (1978). *Mind in society*. Cambridge: Harvard

Part II
Theoretical Understandings of Teacher Identity Development

Chapter 2
Teacher Identity Discourse as Identity Growth: Stories of Authority and Vulnerability

Janet Alsup

In 2016, I conducted an interview-based research study exploring the teacher identity development of six female English education pre-service teachers at my university. I had conducted a similar study in 2006, and I was interested in exploring how, 10 years later, contemporary student teachers might be similar or different from their predecessors. In this chapter, I provide a brief review of recent research related to teacher identity, vulnerability and authority, and agency. Then, after describing the study's methodology, I present the stories of one of the six students, who I call Teresa, as she shares her experiences as a student teacher learning to be a professional educator. All names are pseudonyms.

While Teresa is just one of the six students in the study, her stories exemplify one of the key findings: a new generation of student teachers engaged in narrative discourse, and by association identity work, related to their conflicting understandings of professional enactments of authority and vulnerability. In addition to these narratives of opposition, I also include some examples of instances when Teresa engages in meaningful identity work by voicing what I call narratives of balance between these two poles of subjectivity. Through these stories of balance, Teresa begins to negotiate 'conceptions of self and other' that, as a young student teacher, often result in cognitive and affective dissonance. Such negotiation results in more complex and comprehensive understandings of student-teacher and teacher-mentor relationships, and, hence, professional identity growth.

J. Alsup (✉)
Department of Curriculum and Instruction, Purdue University, West Lafayette, IN, USA
e-mail: jalsup@purdue.edu

© Springer International Publishing AG, part of Springer Nature 2018   13
P. A. Schutz et al. (eds.), *Research on Teacher Identity*,
https://doi.org/10.1007/978-3-319-93836-3_2

Literature Review: Identity, Vulnerability and Authority

Psychologists and educators have written of the need to balance 'self and other' to grow and evolve as individuals (see Blos, 1967; Erickson, 1968; Kegan, 1982; Kohlberg, 1969; Loevinger, 1976). Robert Kegan's (1982) view of identity might be most relevant to this study, as he sees identity construction as a constant balancing and re-balancing of 'self and other' in a way that reminds one of a spiral or double helix; in this context, a person revisits similar challenges at different points of his or her life, and within divergent circumstances comes to understand these challenges, and themselves, more deeply. These challenges, in Kegan's view, are usually attributed to a lack of balance between subject and object, or self and other (Kroger, p. 160). Adolescent psychologist Jane Kroger (2004) describes Kegan's view of balance this way:

> We spend much of our lives being developmentally "out of balance," moving from one state of subject-object balance to another, and it is to those who accompany another on such a journey of transition that Kegan's theory speaks particularly well … Rather than "breakdown" in one's meaning-making efforts, Kegan prefers the alternative concept of "breakthrough" to capture the essence of change from an old to a new balance … Transition involves a loss, a mourning of that loss, and experiencing a sense of vacuum prior to rebalance. (Kroger, p. 161–62)

Closely related to issues of identity development are the concepts of agency, authority, and vulnerability. Agency can be defined generally as the ability of individuals to make free choices and act independently, amidst cultural and societal structures that can limit them (see Bandura, 1999). Philosophical and psychological understandings of agency are often contradictory, as the first can emphasize individual free will, while the second can place an emphasis on the influences of social and environmental elements on decision-making. In educational research, with Bandura as the exemplar, the focus tends to be on how the environment affects individual decision making, with the understanding that no decision occurs outside of a social context and no person lives in a cultural vacuum. Speaking of such contextualization, studies like Charteris and Smardon's (2015) emphasizes a 'collaborative' and 'dynamic' type of agency-building through which teachers develop the mechanisms to 'embrace' a professional identity beyond the aforementioned vacuum. The researchers cite Priestly and Robinson's (2013) comprehensive definition of agency, which reads

> Agency … [is not something] that people can have; it is something that people do. It denotes a 'quality' of the engagement of actors with temporal-relational contexts-for-action, not a quality of the actors themselves. (Priestley & Robinson, 2013, p. 189 in Charteris & Smardon, 2015, p. 116)

This understanding of agency as situated and creatively lends itself to explorations of related concepts.

Authority and vulnerability on first glance represent the two seemingly opposite poles of agency and free will: total authority being the ability to make choices without hesitation or repercussion, and vulnerability being anxiety or fear that one's decisions might be incorrect, dangerous, or self-defeating. Lasky (2005) reports on a research study of secondary teacher agency and professional vulnerability during a time of educational reform in their school, specifically looking at initial factors in their identity development and contextual issues that can inform their experiences in such times. She writes,

> Vulnerability is a multidimensional, multifaceted emotional experience that individuals can feel in an array of contexts. It is a fluid state of being that can be influenced by the way people perceive their present situation as it interacts with their identity, beliefs, values, and sense of competence. (p. 901)

Such multiplicity of contexts can include micro-political schooling environments (Kayi-Aydar, 2015) situated within broader socio-cultural and political systems (Kelchtermans, 2005; Lasky, 2005).

Other scholars have identified the importance of recognizing one's own vulnerability as a critical element to move beyond shame, (i.e., shame resilience) (Brown, 2006) and have highlighted "how vulnerability shapes [...] practice" (Cutri & Whiting, 2015, p. 1013) and, as such, should be embraced by teachers who are also learners in this journey (Dale & Frye, 2009). In the case of Teresa, she speaks of both types of vulnerability—the trust-building kind and the type that produces anxiety, uncertainty, and guilt. As new teachers receive advice from mentors and both invited and uninvited comments from their students, it is important to remember, as Brown writes, "vulnerability is at the heart of the feedback process" (p. 201).

Since 2006, there has been much interesting research conducted elucidating teacher identity development, specifically. Much of this literature emphasizes the position that teacher professional identity "is not stable or predetermined (Beauchamp & Thomas, 2009; Beijaard, Meijer, & Verloop, 2004; Maclean & White, 2007), rather, it is dynamic and created and recreated during an active process of learning to teach" (Trent, 2010, p. 695), and that context, experience, and personality play a role in its development.

In 2013, Mahsa Izadinia from New Zealand reviewed 29 empirical studies about student teachers' identity and found that, overall, they addressed four broad factors: (1) reflective activities; (2) learning communities; (3) context; and (4) prior experiences (p. 694). Izadinia further stated that based on the studies reviewed,

> ST [student teacher] identity can be defined as ST's perceptions of their cognitive knowledge, sense of agency, self-awareness, voice, confidence and relationship with colleagues, pupils and parents, as shaped by their educational contexts, prior experiences and learning communities. (p. 708)

Izadinia also summarized how the 29 studies she reviewed characterized the shortcomings in current identity research involving student teachers by stating that "although it appears that there is a general acknowledgement of its significance, there is no clear definition of teacher identity" in the works cited (p. 695). In fact, researchers rarely describe how teacher educators affect student teachers' identity development or summarize the negative effects on identity growth (Izadinia, 2013, pp. 709–710).

My own 2006 book-length research study, *Teacher identity discourses: Negotiating personal and professional spaces*, likewise addressed how narrative and discourse are essential to professional identity growth, which is often highly subjective, changeable, and dependent on both context and the identity themes (Holland, 1975) of the young teachers themselves. I found that the participants often told narratives, or stories, of their development as teachers and that these narratives both reflected and affected their identity growth.

Teresa's Story

Drawing on a larger study on teacher identity narratives with six participants from a large research-intensive institution in Midwest state, this case centers on one pre-service teacher and her experiences and identity negotiations—particularly those related to vulnerability, guilt, and agency—during her student-teaching fieldwork in a local school. I interviewed Teresa twice in the spring of 2016, at the beginning of the semester and at the end of the semester, after she had concluded her field experience. At the time of the first interview, she was taking an English methods course that integrated issues of equity, multiple literacies, and English language learning into the objectives and the course assignments. This is an important distinction as it provides an important contextual element to Teresa's repertoire of knowledge about the changing and diversifying rural Midwest classroom. Both pre- and post- interviews were semi-structured and had slightly different questions (see Appendix A for interview protocols).

Because this study stems from a larger research project, the major research question has been adapted and reads as follows: "What are the self-identified philosophies of teaching English held by a current pre-service English teacher at a major Midwestern university?" Follow up questions prompted the participant to describe her current teaching context and any developments over time and their potential links to her belief system.

Who Is in Control? Teresa's Narratives of Authority Versus Vulnerability

Many studies of identity posit that discourse can be an essential part of identity growth (see Foucault, 1973, 1977; Foucault & Nazzaro, 1972; Berkenkotter & Huckin, 1995; Miller, 1984; Bourdieu, 1991; Geertz, 1973). While in this chapter I focus on the discursive genre of narrative, there are many genres of discourse that might potentially affect identity growth. I understand professional identity discourse to be "any discourse that both reflects and influences the professional identity" (p. 206). I define discourse more generally as a concept similarly to James Gee (1999), as both oral/written language and related types of self-expression such as actions and clothing that individuals use to interact in the world and with other people.

In this chapter, I focus on the discourse of narrative, or story. I define narratives as minimally comprised of "at least two necessarily sequenced clauses of which the second is consequential to the first" (Labov and Waletzky, as quoted in Young, 1999, p. 197). At times, I explicitly asked participants to tell me a story; other times I did not. Many theorists over the years have asserted that the telling of personal stories both reflects and creates our sense of self (Bruner & Weisser, 1991; Fischer-Rosenthal, 1995; Gergen, 1994; Hermans, Rijks, Harry, & Kempen, 1993; McAdams, 1993; Polkinghorne, 1991). The review of recent research about teacher identity likewise provides evidence that many research studies about professional identity identify the telling and hearing of stories as essential to its development.

I begin with a discussion of Teresa's narratives of authority versus vulnerability. Over the two interviews, all six participants told a total of 42 of these narratives. At many points during the interviews, participants told stories of when they felt that they had authority as a teacher, when they did not have authority, when they felt powerful and self-efficacious, and when they did not. They also sometimes spoke of feelings of vulnerability—when they were accepting of their faults and failures and could think of such times as fodder for growth.

Teresa's stories of authority and vulnerability focused both on her relationships with her mentors and with her students. She describes her relationship with her mentor teacher as sometimes fraught due to their differing teaching philosophies:

> Because I had such a huge difference in the way I like to teach from my teacher and we were similar in a lot of ways but our communication was not open because I felt shut down at the beginning and then I couldn't get back to a place where I trusted her enough and I was willing to admit when I was wrong and stuff like that.

This focus on negotiating authority and power with her school colleagues continues, as Teresa discusses how she sometimes compared her own way of approaching students' needs to theirs:

> It's not as if my teacher and my co-teacher were these terrible people who didn't want their students to succeed but I don't think that they were necessarily looking at the personal, actual, individual needs of these students and finding out whether or not they were able to or whether or not there was something else in the way.

These examples show Teresa struggling with how to take feedback from those who are mentoring her and who have authority over her, particularly when she didn't agree with their pedagogies and approaches. In this way, her developing sense of authority as a teacher, which is connected to her agency and self-efficacy, was threatened and became vulnerable. It seems like her sense of confidence and self-efficacy was directly related to how her mentors responded to her teaching and even how they approached their own classroom practice. These struggles with authority were ongoing during her student teaching internship, but seemed to moderate over time as Teresa became more comfortable owing moments of vulnerability:

> "You know when you try something you and your students will go with you on it?" I think is one of the ways that you know your students trust you because there's that basis of

whether or not they feel safe with you, but that actually having them get up and do something different with you or participate in discussions that they're not used to having.

This conversation is both about recognizing her students' moments of vulnerability, as well as her own as new teacher. Here Teresa recognizes how expressions and feelings of vulnerability, even in moments when both teacher and students are unsure of the outcome, can encourage risk taking and therefore increase learning. She also equates vulnerability, risk-taking and trust, both for students and teachers. Allowing vulnerability to happen, trusting another to guide your learning, might require a leap of faith that can be frightening; however, Teresa speaks as if it might also be essential to growth.

The last two examples I will share from Teresa are stories of authority versus vulnerability where she again focuses not on her interaction with teaching colleagues, but with her high school students and how she realizes that revealing her vulnerabilities as a young teacher might be conducive to student learning:

> I'm very candid with my students. I try to put myself on their level as much as possible, because I don't see the point in acting as if I am so much older and so much wiser than them, because I'm really not and I think that works out well for me because I like to talk to my students.

And

> So he went…So I was like "You need to read…we finished this scene. You can read it while we're watching." He's [the student] like "Well I'm not gonna [sic] read it." So I said "Okay, go sit out in the hallway and breathe. I'll check on you but you can't just do that." And then he didn't want to talk to me for about a week. And he perked up. Then he got over it. But I think sometimes when you're so candid and relaxed with your students and they get really mad at you when you actually have to be the teacher and discipline them a little bit…

Here Teresa tells of instances when she actively attempted to change how her adolescent students think of her as an authority figure. In the first narrative, instead of acting like an all-powerful teacher, she opts to put herself "on their level" and try to downplay the power differential between them. This strategy seems very different to the one she uses with her colleagues, with whom she continues to feel a sense of unease and a lack of agency. The second narrative tells the story of her internal reflections about how she creates and shares her teacher persona with her students. She tends to be more "relaxed" but understands that it might be confusing to students when she must act the authoritarian and demand certain types of student performance. These stories show that Teresa is actively thinking about negotiating her teacher identity and related enactments of authority and vulnerability. This cognitive and emotional grappling results in identity growth, as seen in the next section.

Using Discourse to Create a Teacher Identity: Teresa's Narratives of Balance

The second type of narrative in which Teresa engaged is what I call narratives of balance, or narratives that expressed a type of balancing between authority and vulnerability as described above, and, by association, other and self. The first two narratives are both from our second interview, which occurred at the end of her student teaching. The last narrative is from the first interview, at the beginning of the internship. There were ways that Teresa mediated the oppositional experiences and connected narratives describing conflicts between authority and vulnerability. These mediating narratives are what I call "narratives of balance." As quoted from Kegan earlier, key to his conception of identity development, a person is continually in a state of finding balance, experiencing imbalance, and then re-seeking satisfying balance, often as a result of ideological, emotional, and/or cognitive growth. In this study, Teresa did express some narrative examples of seeking, and finding, a type of balance between authority and vulnerability, between strong feelings of agency and instances of insecurity and uncertainty.

In the following example, she begins to merge the personal and the professional, the self with the other, in productive and healthy ways:

> I think that it's important to be transparent with your students. Not so much they need to know my personal life, because I always thought it was weird when your teachers were telling you stories about their significant other or their children which was a bit awkward. I don't care about what you did on the weekend. But being transparent with your students and letting them know that you do care.

Here Teresa is describing both allowing herself to be human in the classroom, but not crossing the line into too much personal sharing. She uses the phrase "be transparent" to describe the ideal state of being honest and real, yet not confessional. She is experimenting with concrete ways to bring her 'self' together with the 'other'—or her personal subjectivities with her professional expectations as she understands them.

In a second example, Teresa discusses balance between authority and vulnerability in a different way—this time not so much about integrating the personal with the professional, but instead about when to choose to make authoritarian decisions that may not be what the students desire:

> It [a professional journal article] was called like "The Culture of Care" or something along those lines and it was about showing your students you do care and trying to find a balance between doing the fun stuff that keeps them super engaged and things to do like going outside and acting out the fight scenes from Romeo and Juliet. But also, buckling down. "All right we need to learn how to do this stuff that's kind of boring at times" and it's fine to be like…to say stuff like "Yes this is rough and this is gonna [sic] be hard to get through and it's not the most fun but it's important for this, this and this."

In this narrative excerpt, Teresa explains how she wants to be "fun" with her students and demonstrate that she is easygoing and carefree as a teacher who wants to excite students; however, simultaneously, she remembers that she is the classroom authority who makes the final decisions about curriculum. However, she realizes that these two extremes should ideally balance to create an exciting, yet rigorous, classroom. Just as a teacher's identity should balance the personal and professional, or the self and the other, a teaching philosophy should balance fun with hard work. Each of these balancing acts is a form of negotiating the opposing subjectivities of authority and vulnerability.

In the last narrative of balance I will share, Teresa is connecting her understanding of the importance of empathy for and with students with her classroom presence as a teacher. She describes how this approach should, ideally, balance teacher as authority figure making curricular decisions with teacher as motivator, helping students to "connect" with English content:

> I think that you need to think about your students as people who have likes and dislikes, and who get bored and get excited and sometimes are apathetic. And that goes a long way in explaining how you want to teach, and what you want to teach, and how you approach it. While I'm still learning about abilities and motivations, I definitely think it is the teacher's role to get their students to be engaged and to care about the classroom. I don't think that it's all on the students, because it is compulsory and they have to be here.

Even early in her student teaching experience Teresa seems quite reflective about her practice and how she is beginning to purposefully strike a balance between rigorous curriculum and promoting motivation, between pedagogy and empathy. In these narratives of balance, Teresa shows that she is finding a new, more complex, way of understanding professional oppositions and realizing their synergistic potential.

Transformative Vulnerability: Implications for Teacher Education

Teresa's narrative discourse in our interviews focused on her grappling with notions of how to be the authority, and when to allow vulnerability to creep in. She admits to having lifetime struggles since her homeschooling days with taking criticism from those in charge, and this challenge remains. As Kegan might argue, it's an area of cyclical balance and imbalance in Teresa's identity, and it has reared its head again. Ironically perhaps, since she chose to become a teacher, Teresa has opted to take on the position of an authority figure herself who makes decisions about discipline, classroom management, and curriculum in a classroom. While she struggles at times accepting feedback from authorities, she is relatively comfortable being one herself--until doubts arise that cause her to reflect, lose her balance, and eventually rebalance.

Since we know from research that not only is teacher identity dependent on acts of discourse (see Alsup, 2006) but also the context and experience of the pre-service teachers (see Beijaard et al., 2004), it seems reasonable to understand Teresa's experiences through the lenses of agency, authority, and vulnerability. At the beginnings of her experience she had trouble experiencing both authority and vulnerability simultaneously, as it seemed they were opposing emotional forces. However, as the student teaching experience continued, and her experience grew, Teresa expressed increasing comfort with letting her personal subjectivities show in the classroom--allowing herself to admit to herself, her mentors, and her students that even though she's a teacher she's also a person with hopes, goals, and plans, both herself and her students. In her own words, she is learning to be more "intentional" about her practice and discovering how authority and vulnerability are not polar opposites, but are instead helpmates, each dependent on the other for the creation, and enactment, of an effective and satisfying teacher identity.

In methods courses it is a common practice for professors to ask pre-service teachers to write reflections about their classroom practice experiences and think about what they see and how they might think about the classroom space if they were the teacher. Only rarely are pre-service teachers asked to reflect critically on their own responses to mentorship and their own conceptualizations of themselves as authorities. Inherent in the definition of 'teacher' is that the person is in charge and makes decisions that govern the workings of the class. But how does a young teacher negotiate that understanding of 'teacher' with many of the pedagogies advocated by teacher education research today, such as critical pedagogies, student centered approaches, and culturally responsive instruction? To engage with students fully, to empathize with their states of being, and to motivate them to truly learn, the teacher must also be able to practice vulnerability--and be comfortable in spaces and places where their role as authoritarian might not be uncontested.

Acknowledgement Special thanks to doctoral research assistant Ileana Cortes Santiago, without whom this could not have been written.

Appendix

Interview Protocols
Each of the six participants was interviewed twice during spring semester 2016:

Interview #1 (Early Semester)

1. What do you believe is important in English teaching? Why? Can you give some classroom examples?
2. How do you describe yourself as a teacher? Why?
3. What are some of your clearest memories of teaching/learning?
4. Can you share some stories of teaching/learning that you remember clearly for whatever reason? Why do you think you remember those stories?
5. If you had to state your philosophy of teaching English, what would it be?

Interview #2 (Late Semester)

1. What do you believe is important in English teaching? Why? Can you give some classroom examples?
2. How do you describe yourself as a teacher? Why?
3. What are some of your clearest memories of teaching/learning?
4. Can you share some stories of teaching/learning that you remember clearly for whatever reason? Why do you think you remember those stories?
5. If you had to state your philosophy of teaching English, what would it be?
6. Can you take a photo that is a metaphorical representation of your teacher identity? Please describe the photo to me, and why you took the image you did.

References

Alsup, J. (2006). *Teacher identity discourses: Negotiating personal and professional spaces*. New York: Routledge.

Bandura, A. (1999). A social cognitive theory of personality. In L. Pervin & O. John (Eds.), *Handbook of personality* (2nd ed., pp. 154–196). New York: Guilford Publications.

Beauchamp, C., & Thomas, L. (2009). Understanding teacher identity: An overview of issues in the literature and implications for teacher education. *Cambridge Journal of Education, 39*(2), 175–189.

Beijaard, D., Meijer, P. C., & Verloop, N. (2004). Reconsidering research on teachers' professional identity. *Teaching and Teacher Education, 20*, 107–128.

Berkenkotter, C., & Huckin, T. (1995). *Genre knowledge in disciplinary communities*. Hillsdale, NJ: Lawrence Erlbaum.

Blos, P. (1967). The second individuation process of adolescence. *Psychoanalytic Study of the Child, 22*, 162–186.

Bourdieu, P. (1991). *Language and symbolic power*. Cambridge, MA: Harvard University Press.

Brown, B. (2006). Shame resilience theory: A grounded theory study on women and shame. *Families in Society: The Journal of Contemporary Social Services, 87*(1), 43–52.

Bruner, J., & Weisser, S. (1991). The invention of self: Autobiography and its forms. In D. R. Olson & N. Torrance (Eds.), *Literacy and orality* (pp. 129–248). Cambridge, UK: Cambridge University Press.

Charteris, J., & Smardon, D. (2015). Teacher agency and dialogic feedback: Using classroom data for practitioner inquiry. *Teaching and Teacher Education, 50*, 114–123.

Cutri, R. M., & Whiting, E. F. (2015). The emotional work of discomfort and vulnerability in multicultural teacher education. *Teachers and Teaching, 21*(8), 1010–1025.

Dale, M., & Frye, E. M. (2009). Vulnerability and love of learning as necessities for wise teacher education. *Journal of Teacher Education, 60*(2), 123–130.

Erickson, E. H. (1968). *Identity, youth, and crisis*. New York: Norton.

Fischer-Rosenthal, W. (1995). The problem with identity: Biography as a solution to some (post) modernist dilemmas. *Comenius, 15*(3), 250–264.

Foucault, M. (1973). *The order of things: An archeology of the human sciences*. New York: Vintage.

Foucault, M. (1977). *Discipline and punish*. New York: Pantheon.

Foucault, M., & Nazzaro, A. M. (1972). History, discourse and discontinuity. *Salmagundi, 20*, 225–248.

Gee, J. P. (1999). *An introduction to discourse analysis: Theory and method*. London: Routledge.

Geertz, C. (1973). *The interpretation of cultures: Selected essays*. New York: Basic Books.

Gergen, K. (1994). *Realities and relationships: Soundings in social construction*. Cambridge, MA: Harvard University Press.

Hermans, H. J. M., Rijks, T. I., Harry, J. G., & Kempen, H. J. G. (1993). Imaginal dialogue in the self: Theory and method. *Journal of Personality, 61*(2), 207–236.

Holland, N. N. (1975). *5 Readers reading*. New Haven, CT: Yale University Press.

Izadinia, M. (2013). A review of research on student teachers' professional identity. *British Educational Research Journal, 39*(4), 694–713.

Kayi-Aydar, H. (2015). Teacher agency, positioning, and English language learners: Voices of pre-service classroom teachers. *Teaching and Teacher Education, 45*, 94–103.

Kegan, R. (1982). The evolving self: A process conception for ego psychology. *The Counseling Psychologist, 8*, 5–38.

Kelchtermans, G. (2005). Teachers' emotions in educational reforms: Self-understanding, vulnerable commitment and micropolitical literacy. *Teaching and Teacher Education, 21*(8), 995–1006.

Kohlberg, L. (1969). Stage and sequence: The cognitive-developmental approach to socialization. In D.A. Goslin (Ed.), *Handbook of socialization theory and research* (pp. N/A). Chicago: Rand McNally.

Kroger, J. (2004). *Identity in adolescence: The balance between self and other*. New York: Routledge.

Lasky, S. (2005). A sociocultural approach to understanding teacher identity, agency and professional vulnerability in a context of secondary school reform. *Teaching and Teacher Education, 21*(8), 899–916.

Loevinger, J. (1976). *Ego development: Conceptions and theories*. San Francisco: Jossey Bass.

Maclean, R., & White, S. (2007). Video reflection and the formation of teacher identity in a team of pre-service and experienced teachers. *Reflective Practice, 8*, 47–60.

McAdams, D. P. (1993). *The stories we live by: Personal myths and the making of the self*. New York: William Morrow.

Miller, C. R. (1984). Genre as social action. *Quarterly Journal of Speech, 70*(2), 151–167.

Polkinghorne, D. E. (1991). Narrative and self concept. *Journal of Narrative and Life History, 1*, 135–154.

Priestly, G. B., & Robinson, S. (2013). Teachers as 'agents of change': Teacher agency and emerging models of curriculum. In M. Priestley & G. J. J. Biesta (Eds.), *Reinventing the curriculum: New trends in curriculum policy and practice* (pp. 187–206). London: Bloomsbury Academic.

Trent, J. (2010). Teacher education as identity construction: Insights from action research. *Journal of Education for Teaching, 36*(2), 53–168.

Young, K. (1999). Narratives of indeterminacy: Breaking the medical body into its discourses; breaking the discursive body out of postmodernism. In D. Herman (Ed.), *Narratologies: New perspectives on narrative analysis* (pp. 197–217). Columbus, OH: Ohio State University Press.

Chapter 3
Identity-Agency in Progress: Teachers Authoring Their Identities

Maria Ruohotie-Lyhty

In this chapter I focus on a challenge that teachers all over the world face every day: how to negotiate between different roles, expectations, interests, and demands as professionals in the face of changing circumstances and changing relationships. I aim to provide a more thorough understanding of the ways in which teachers face these challenging situations and, in response, develop their identities, (i.e. the conceptualizations they have about themselves as professionals) (Vähäsantanen, 2015). The chapter is based on the results of three earlier studies, in which I examined pre- and in-service teachers' identity processes longitudinally.

Teacher identity has been a topic of intensive educational research in recent decades (Akkerman & Meijer, 2011; Beijaard, Meijer, & Verloop, 2004). Behind the rising interest can be seen a tendency in research towards a more holistic conceptualization of teacher development. As a concept, teacher identity implies a sensing, knowing, and purposeful subject that is self-involved in the development processes (Beijaard et al., 2004). Current professional identity theories, however, also recognize the fact that teachers are not independent of their environment: their identity development is closely linked to the affordances of their social and physical environment (Pappa, Moate, Ruohotie-Lyhty, & Eteläpelto, 2017; Ruohotie-Lyhty, 2011).

The research on teacher identities and identity development has shown that identities are central in understanding teacher socialization, the development of their expertise, and their relationships to pupils (Day, Kington, Stobart, & Sammons, 2006; Hong, 2010; Ruohotie-Lyhty, 2011). Although the centeredness of teachers' identity development is recognized and there is extensive empirical evidence of teachers' identities at different stages in their careers (Haniford, 2010; Hong, 2010; Thomas & Beauchamp, 2011; Timotštšuk & Ugaste, 2010), few longitudinal studies

M. Ruohotie-Lyhty (✉)
Department of Language and Communication Studies, University of Jyväskylä, Jyväskylä, Finland
e-mail: maria.ruohotie-lyhty@jyu.fi

have offered a longer-term view of individual teachers' identity development (see, however, Barkhuizen, 2016). There is therefore a need for sound, empirically based, models of teachers' identity development that could inform teacher education. To better understand the temporal dimension and changes over time in teacher identities, and how teachers author their identities in pre- and in-service conditions, I combine the results of three longitudinal studies (Ruohotie-Lyhty 2013, 2016; Ruohotie-Lyhty & Moate, 2016). The three primary studies are based on two different longitudinal data sets: a 10-year study following five in-service teachers and a 2-year study of six pre-service class teachers. I offer an advanced conceptualization of the ways in which the participants author their identity development processes.

Identity Development and Identity-Agency

To produce a comprehensive picture of teachers' identity development, I use a narrative approach (Barkhuizen, 2016; Bruner, 1990; Polkinghorne, 1988). This approach is compatible with socioculturally inspired identity theories in that it recognizes identity as a social, multiple, and discontinuous phenomenon (Akkerman & Meijer, 2011; Beijaard et al., 2004). This conceptualization holds that individuals can have various even contradictory conceptualizations of themselves and that these conceptualizations are socially constructed (Akkerman & Meijer, 2011). It also includes the idea of individuals as agentive in affecting the construction of their identities (Beijaard et al., 2004; Eteläpelto, Vähäsantanen, Hökkä, & Paloniemi, 2013). The special focus of the narrative approach is on this agentive activity of the individuals in making sense of their experiences. When conceptualized this way, identity also includes striving towards stability, continuity, and individuality (also Akkerman & Meijer, 2011). Consequently, the narrative approach, along with some other recent approaches, denies the idea of a completely decentralized identity (also Akkerman & Meijer, 2011; Eteläpelto et al., 2013) and concentrates on the ways in which identity is maintained and negotiated in the flux of sporadic, surprising, and even traumatic events (Crossley, 2000; Polkinghorne, 1996). With its focus on individual activity, a narrative framework is well suited for researching the individual side of teacher development. It also provides a methodological lens for exploring and understanding the contradictory forces of multiplicity and unity, discontinuity and continuity, and sociality and individuality.

Teachers' narrative identity as it is understood here is connected with professional agency, "individuals' socioculturally mediated capacity to act" (Ahearn, 2001, p. 112), in at least two important ways. First of all, an individual's agency in a particular environment is crucial to identity development (Eteläpelto et al., 2013; Vähäsantanen, 2015). In other words, professional identity is constructed as 'a history based constellation of teachers' perceptions as professional actors' (Vähäsantanen, 2015, p. 3). When individual student teachers or teachers act within a certain community, they draw upon their beliefs, ideas, and former experience when making decisions about ways to participate and to connect with others. This participation and the flux of relationships potentially challenge their former beliefs and identities and encourage a discussion of who they are and who they want to be as professional actors (Akkerman & Meijer, 2011). Secondly, agency is connected to the very nature of narrative identity development (Eteläpelto et al., 2013). Identity development is a process to which individuals actively invest in and which they themselves actively form (Beijaard et al., 2004; Eteläpelto, Vähäsantanen, & Hökkä, 2015). The narrative activity in which experiences are organized, drawn on and chosen as meaningful for teacher identity is therefore a process of human agency. This particular form of agency I call *identity-agency* (Eteläpelto et al., 2015; Ruohotie-Lyhty & Moate, 2016) and it is the activity of using personal experiences and participation in a community in developing professional identities (cf. Eteläpelto et al., 2015). As part of the identity development process, identity-agency is understood to play a mediatory role between environmental influences and individual identities. When facing an event, new information, theory or relationship that potentially challenges teachers' current understandings as professional actors, teachers can either reconsider their professional identities in light of this new experience or defend their original ideas of themselves against this influence (Vähäsantanen, 2015). Identity-agency is the mediator that helps to understand the relationship between social environment and individual identity.

Having now theoretically justified the capacity of individuals to author identity development, I will now further elaborate this concept by suggesting a theoretical model to understand the role of identity-agency in teachers' development and by using illustrative examples from my own three previous empirical studies to show identity-agency in practice.

Identity-Agency: A Model

The role of identity-agency in teachers' identity development can be described as mediatory, operating between the environment and teacher identity (Ruohotie-Lyhty, 2013, 2016; Ruohotie-Lyhty & Moate, 2016). In the conditions created by the particular environments in which teachers work, teachers excert their identity agency to organize and interpret their experiences and further to develop their professional identities (Eteläpelto et al., 2013; Ruohotie-Lyhty & Moate, 2016). Teachers are continually deciding either to renegotiate their identities or to defend their original conceptualizations (Ruohotie-Lyhty, 2013, 2016; Ruohotie-Lyhty & Moate, 2016). When opting for renegotiation, they adopt the expectations and tasks typical of their environment as part of their professional identities. When opting for defense, they refuse these environmental influences. These decisions vary in the effect they have on teachers' ability to feel agentic in the working community in which they find themselves. Studies on top-down pedagogic reforms show that teachers who do not align with new expectations often feel their agency in the workplace threatened (Vähäsantanen, 2015). This can lead to ambivalent agency in the community and teachers being forced to accept certain tasks against their will and

Fig. 3.1 Identity-agency
in authoring professional
identity

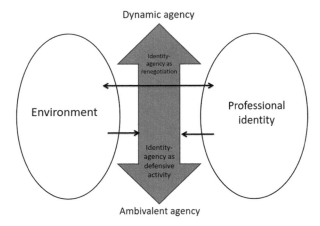

without personal investment (Vähäsantanen, 2015). In contrast, finding a satisfactory match between environment and identity allows teachers dynamic agency in the community (Ruohotie-Lyhty, 2016; Vähäsantanen, 2015). Although teachers can, in a conflict situation, seek solutions outside themselves by attempting to affect the specific environmental conditions they find problematic or by changing workplaces, identity-agency remains a central means for teachers to attenuate professional tensions and achieve the necessary conditions for professional development. I illustrate this role of identity-agency as a mediator in Fig. 3.1.

Having introduced the role of identity-agency in teachers' identity development, I will now present some empirical examples of this activity in practice. The illustrative examples provided are from my longitudinal studies into pre-service and in-service teachers' identity development (Ruohotie-Lyhty, 2013, 2016; Ruohotie-Lyhty & Moate, 2016). Two of the original studies (Ruohotie-Lyhty, 2013, 2016) utilized data from a 10-year longitudinal research project on newly qualified teachers' development. We followed a set of six language teachers (all female) during their first decade in the profession. The data of the third original study (Ruohotie-Lyhty & Moate, 2016) was generated as part of a project following the development of six pre-service teachers. Among their course assignments, the students (4 female and 2 male) wrote three essays reflecting on their experiences and identities over a 2-year period. Both of the studies have been conducted in the Finnish educational context, which emphasizes teacher autonomy and agency (Sahlberg, 2011).

Identity-Agency in Practice: Authoring Identities

In what follows, identity-agency as renegotiation and identity-agency as defense are illustrated with examples from the narratives of pre-service and in-service teachers. I first demonstrate the ways in which teachers author their identities by renegotiating them in order to add to them or to transform them. Second, I demonstrate how teachers can exert their identity-agency in defending their original identities. Along with each example I will give some examples of how teachers' identity-agency is connected with their agency in the community.

Renegotiatiating Identities: Additive Development

Identity renegotiation is here defined as a process in which teachers develop their identities to better match the environmental conditions and to develop professionally. Ideally, teachers exert their identity-agency as professionals in a working environment in which new challenges and changes match their expectations and values as teachers. This kind of identity development can include accepting new pedagogical convictions or new responsibilities as part of their professional self-understanding as well as developing their self-efficacy as a teacher. In such contexts, teachers do not feel they have to give up their original ideas about being a teacher, although they can report significant changes in the ways in which they perceive themselves as professionals (Ruohotie-Lyhty, 2013, 2016; Ruohotie-Lyhty & Moate, 2016). Teacher professionalism is in these cases enriched by contextual development opportunities.

My three studies all included several examples of situations where the teachers' original identities were sufficiently in line with the social environment to allow these kinds of developments to take place. In these cases, the teachers' identities can be characterized as a maturation process with additive elements: they developed their conceptualization of themselves as professionals as they took up their responsibilities in the work community and new pedagogical convictions.

A typical case that illustrates this kind of identity renegotiation is that of Marie who, at the end of her first year as a pre-service teacher, reported changes in her pedagogical beliefs as a result of getting to know the Jolly Phonics method of pronunciation teaching, and her determination to learn more about this method to be able to use it in her teaching:

> Jolly Phonics convinced me. I found them fascinating and practical – even for my own pronunciation and language learning. However, I will go through the book of Jolly Phonics I bought in order that I would know more about this learning method. Even though my knowledge of Jolly Phonics is very little and overall in Finnish schools it is still in its infancy, I really feel of being able to give something useful to my students-to-be with the help of Jolly Phonics. In fact, I am a bit shocked we never used them when I was in the school. What a great loss!

In this example, Marie excitedly and enthusiastically reports learning a new pedagogical approach that she feels gives her the possibility of being the kind of teacher she wants to be. This possibility also encourages her to be active in her studies. Her identity-agency takes the form of renegotiation as illustrated in Fig. 3.1, in which match between self and environment is maintained through accepting new conceptualizations of teaching as part of her teacher identity. In my study of pre-service-teachers, this kind of identity development was facilitated by the Finnish teacher education environment, which the student teachers experienced as allowing them to develop their teacher identity rather freely. Embracing some of the pedagogical models present in the teacher education environment and adding them to their pedagogical repertoire also increased the pre-service teachers' self-confidence.

Compared to pre-service teachers, in-service teachers produced fewer narratives in which developing a suitable professional identity was described as easy. In my studies, in-service teachers expressed conceptualizations of themselves as teachers that were less fluid and open to change. In-service teachers also reported that their immediate responsibilities and duties severely curtailed the possibilities they had of defining their identities themselves. Whether smooth additive developments were possible in the first place was dependent on how similar the teachers considered the expectations of the workplace to be to their professional self-conceptualizations. One example in my study (Ruohotie-Lyhty, 2013) was Suvi, a 25-year-old foreign language teacher, who initially felt that her expectations coincided well with what she encountered in the school. Before entering full time teaching, she had considered the teacher-pupil relationship to be the foundation for any kind of teacher activity. After 2 years of teaching she said that her starting point had been right and had made it possible for her to embrace more roles and duties inside the school:

> Another important thing (this year) was to realize in a pedagogical and educational sense that the work is getting increasingly smooth and easy and also that besides teaching I can see and understand more things inside school. By this I mean that I have learned more than just to take care of my own teaching: I have learned to concern myself with bullying, to educate the pupils, to communicate with them better and more effectively and to cooperate more closely with their parents. [...] During this year I feel I have found my place between teaching and education better.

Although Suvi did not consider herself to be the same teacher she had been when starting in the profession 2 years before, this identity renegotiation had taken place without any major crises. For Suvi, her initial identity had given her purposeful agency in the community, which had helped her to increase her professional self-efficacy and develop her repertoire. A prerequisite for this type of development was a perceived match between the teacher's own identity and their designated identity in the work place (see also Vähäsantanen, 2015).

Renegotiation Identities: Transformative Development

In cases where the teachers originally reported a considerable mismatch between their identity and what they felt was expected of them, the renegotiation of identity as illustrated in Fig. 3.1 was experienced as more demanding. Tension between the original identity and the environment caused teachers a significant emotional load and led to uncertainty about their professional competence. Taina, a newly qualified foreign language teacher, described these tensions and their consequences on two different occasions as follows:

> I would like to be more a language teacher, but somehow I feel that in secondary school I'm more, well I don't feel I'm an educator, but somehow I do something other than what a language teacher does. (The work) is sometimes so frustrating. You cannot really do anything else but nag; you cannot really do your own job. I mean the job you thought you got teacher education for.

For Taina, the wider educational responsibilities that every teacher must accept did not match her original idea of being a subject teacher. Feeling forced to accept a general educational role was frustrating and alienated her from her everyday professional practice.

Typically, teachers in my studies were not originally willing to change their conceptualizations of themselves as teachers even in cases were significant tensions were reported. However, in the course of the longitudinal studies (Ruohotie-Lyhty, 2013, 2016), several in-service teachers reported that although they had initially refused to renegotiate their identity, they had had significant emotional experiences that had pushed them into taking a new direction. In this process their professional mission was reformulated to allow more purposeful agency in their environment. In comparison with the additive development described above, this process was more demanding and had greater emotional intensity for the in-service teachers. The following two narratives from Saija, a teacher of Russian and Finnish as a second language, depicts a teacher who underwent a significant change as a teacher during her first 9 years in the profession. In her fourth year interview she still considered grammar-oriented teaching to be essential, although several times she also expressed a tension between her traditional idea of herself as a language teacher and the real life language skills her pupils wanted.

> But yes, it is in practice a necessity that if I'm going to teach the language, and especially if some of my students are going take the matriculation examination, like they do, that we have to go through (the grammar). It can't be avoided.

In an interview 5 years later, she said that she felt her identity as a traditional, grammar-focused teacher had completely changed after she started working with what she refered to as "illiterate" learners of Finnish. She narrated this encounter and its consequences as follows:

> When suddenly I had those illiterate students there, and I really couldn't go on in the same way as I'd been going before. I had to find something different, like move completely away from the old way of doing things. If I don't have any of these tools, then how can anyone learn? So then you have to go through quite a deep process at that point. And it was quite heavy and depressing in a way, but a lot of pretty fun things came out of it.

For Saija, the encounter with "illiterate" students forced her to find a resolution to the tensions that had been typical of her work. As a consequence, she made a conscious decision to find new ways of approaching her work and assumed a different pedagogical role. Although painful, this taking of a new direction was described in the teachers' stories as successful in that it defused professional tension, and it was felt to be a professionally significant way of developing as a teacher. As illustrated in Fig. 3.1, identity-agency mediated in these cases to restore a balance between teacher agency and professional demands to allow dynamic agency. For participants who reported these kinds of change, the process also offered the possibility of further additive identity development, with increasing responsibility and increasing professional confidence in their careers.

Defending Identities

Defending identities illustrated in Fig. 3.1 is defined here as the process in which teachers refuse to renegotiate their identities in situations where they experience a mismatch between themselves and the environment. Although identity renegotiation seemed to be essential to teachers' ability to dynamically respond to environmental challenges, my studies also included several examples of teachers practicing their identity-agency by refusing any changes to their identities. This kind of identity authoring was found in all of the three original studies.

As mentioned above, in my study the student teachers expressed a greater sense of freedom in developing their professional identities compared to the in-service teachers. They felt it was possible to determine which features of the designated identity (Billett, 2006) available in their environment they would accept and which they would reject. What they typically rejected, of the new ideas that were offered to them, were those features of identity that were in clear conflict with their individual experiences or preferences and those whose practical benefit was not made clear (Ruohotie-Lyhty & Moate, 2016). In their narratives they authenticated their original positions by recurring to former experiences and generalized these to apply to teachers' professional practice on a larger scale. This is evident in how Annie, a pre-service teacher, reasoned why it was unnecessary for her as a Finnish teacher to think about the role of the English language in her teaching:

> In my point of view and according to the discussions we have had during this course, the overall situation in Finland is very different compared to some other countries. Every Finn is capable of speaking and understanding English. In Finland there is no economic or social division. Every child has the right for proper education and the quality of education is roughly the same in every school.

Although rejecting new ideas or possible identities can be seen as partially limiting student teachers' professional identity development, it was also a necessary part of their development. To be able to invest in certain essential features of teaching, pre-service teachers had to choose a clear direction for their development. In these cases, they used their identity-agency to block environmental influence on themselves as illustrated in Fig. 3.1. They could make these choices rather freely, without their environment pushing them towards a predestined model of being a teacher. Therefore refusing to renegotiate their identity did not posit the same kind of threat to their satisfaction and professional confidence.

The in-service teachers' narratives in my studies also included several passages in which teachers authenticated their original position in order to defend their original subject teacher identities. They used their identity-agency to reject the ideas, tasks, and responsibilities that were suggested to them in their environment for inclusion in their professional identities. They also created boundaries for their professional identity by defining certain features of professional practice as irrelevant to their own identity, and they judged themselves incapable of some forms of professional practice that were typical of the designated identity in the work place. Especially difficult for the teachers was the contradiction between the innovative models of teacher education that they felt they were expected to apply and the resources available in the school community. Although willing to authenticate their original identity in the work community, the in-service teachers did not feel they had many opportunities to influence the content and direction of professional practice that were expected from them. Although they had the authority to decide their teaching methods, the educational role of the teacher in the school context put considerable demands on them. Maintaining their original professional identities therefore demanded more identity work from them than it demanded from the pre-service teachers. In-service teachers who wanted to protect their original professional identities reported that they were able to maintain their agency by keeping a distance from their pupils and colleagues and downplaying the importance of their professional identities in their life. Tuuli was an example of a teacher who did not report an identity change during the 10-year research period. In her fourth year interview she stated her identity clearly as follows:

Interviewer: What are you to your students?
Tuuli: Hopefully the teacher. And it's been like that all the time until now, although I'm maybe a little less formal than others, though they aren't looking for a friend or anything like that. I'm quite happy about that, I am, at least.

Typical of Tuuli was the ability to separate the personal from the professional, which allowed her to keep things in proportion and maintain a balance between her sense of herself and any setbacks she encountered at work. In the tenth year interview, Tuuli's conceptualization of herself as a subject teacher had not changed. In this interview, she also stated that her identity as a professional was not the identity she wanted to prioritize.

But what I've realized is that I don't take the work so seriously anymore, because, well, I have a family and if the teachers' meetings, for example, last longer than expected, I'll leave (laughing). I mean, my priorities are clear.

The pressure for change to the professional identity was connected not only to the beginning phase of professional careers; also changes in the place of work, in relationships and family situations gave rise to the need for professional renegotiation. Situations in which teachers did not have the resources or capacity to renegotiate their identities, but felt forced to assume new duties, severely threatened teachers' professional commitment, job satisfaction and the development of their professional capacities (cf. also Vähäsantanen & Eteläpelto, 2011).

Discussion

In this chapter I have sought to highlight the ways in which teachers are active in authoring their professional identities at different stages in their careers. To do this, I have used the results of my previous studies (Ruohotie-Lyhty, 2013, 2016; Ruohotie-Lyhty & Moate, 2016) to develop a model of the ways in which teachers author their identities through their identity-agency. The illustrative examples showed that the underlying dynamics of identity development were similar for pre-service and in-service teachers. However, the conditions and significance of the teachers' identity-agency differed to some extent in pre-service and in-service contexts.

The novel aspect of this chapter is that I highlight the role of identity-agency as both a renegotiating and a defensive capacity. I showed that pre- and in-service teachers used their identity-agency both in renegotiating the relationship between institutional demands and professional identity and in limiting interaction between the social and individual domains. For in-service teachers, the ability and willingness to renegotiate their identities, however, appeared to be a crucial way to develop professional competence, beliefs and job satisfaction. It was reported that resisting identity renegotiation demanded additional action from in-service teachers if they were going to be able to withstand the emotional and social pressure for change. These forms of agency could not, however, fully suppress the emotional and professional load caused by the mismatch between professional identity and the environment.

In this chapter I point to the significance of identity for understanding teachers' professional development, wellbeing, and professional agency (f. ex. Vähäsantanen, 2015). Rather than simply identity, I underline the role of identity-agency in negotiating a match between self and environment. This match does not mean assimilation into the social environment, but the ability to find a constructive balance between one's own aims and the needs of the workplace. In considering the significance of the results for the development of pre- and in-service teachers, identity-agency has an important role as a dynamic for either renegotiation or defense. Teacher education programs have been criticized for not supporting student teachers enough in the formation of their professional identities (Beauchamp & Thomas, 2009). However, the examples in this study show that pre-service teachers are able to author their identities at least in the culture that prevails in teacher education in Finland, where student teachers are allowed and indeed expected to develop their competences rather freely (Lanas & Kelchtermans, 2015). Nevertheless, these identity development processes might not fully prepare students for the development of their identities in the context of work life, where opting for renegotiation between self and environment was experienced as crucial for professional agency. Adequate focus on pre-service teachers' micro-political literacy and sociological understanding at large might offer a valuable medium for supporting the active identity work of pre-service and in-service teachers (Kelchtermans & Ballet, 2002).

References

Ahearn, L. M. (2001). Language and agency. *Annual Review of Anthropology, 30*(1), 109–137.

Akkerman, S. F., & Meijer, P. C. (2011). A dialogical approach to conceptualizing teacher identity. *Teaching and Teacher Education, 27*, 308–319.

Barkhuizen, G. (2016). A short story approach to analyzing teacher (imagined) identities over time. *TESOL Quarterly, 50*(3), 655–683.

Beauchamp, C., & Thomas, L. (2009). Understanding teacher identity: An overview of issues in the literature and implications for teacher education. *Cambridge Journal of Education, 39*(2), 175–189.

Beijaard, D., Meijer, P., & Verloop, N. (2004). Reconsidering research on teachers' professional identity. *Teaching and Teacher Education, 20*(2), 107–128.

Billett, S. (2006). *Work, change and workers*. Dordrecht, The Netherlands: Springer.

Bruner, J. (1990). *Acts of meaning*. Cambridge, MA: Harvard University Press.

Crossley, M. L. (2000). Narrative psychology, trauma and the study of self/identity. *Theory & Psychology, 10*(2), 527–546.

Day, C., Kington, A., Stobart, G., & Sammons, P. (2006). The personal and professional selves of teachers: Stable and unstable identities. *British Educational Research Journal, 32*(4), 601–616.

Eteläpelto, A., Vähäsantanen, K., & Hökkä, P. (2015). How do novice teachers in Finland perceive their professional agency? *Teachers and Teaching, 21*(6), 660–680.

Eteläpelto, A., Vähäsantanen, K., Hökkä, P., & Paloniemi, S. (2013). What is agency? Conceptualizing professional agency at work. *Educational Research Review, 10*, 45–65.

Haniford, L. C. (2010). Tracing one teacher candidate's discursive identity work. *Teaching and Teacher Education, 26*, 987–996.

Hong, J. Y. (2010). Pre-service and beginning teachers' professional identity and its relation to dropping out of the profession. *Teaching and Teacher Education, 26*, 1530–1543.

Kelchtermans, G., & Ballet, K. (2002). The micropolitics of teacher induction: A narrative-biographical study on teacher socialisation. *Teaching and Teacher Education, 18*(1), 105–120.

Lanas, M., & Kelchtermans, G. (2015). "This has more to do with who I am than with my skills": Student teacher subjectification in Finnish teacher education. *Teaching and Teacher Education, 47*, 22–29.

Pappa, S., Moate, J., Ruohotie-Lyhty, M., & Eteläpelto, A. (2017). Teachers' pedagogical and relational identity negotiation in the Finnish CLIL context. *Teaching and Teacher Education, 65*, 61–70.

Polkinghorne, D. E. (1988). *Narrative knowing and the human sciences*. Albany, NY: State University of New York Press.

Polkinghorne, D. E. (1996). Narrative knowing and the study of lives. In J. Birren (Ed.), *Aging and biography: Explorations in adult development* (pp. 77–99). New York: Springer.

Ruohotie-Lyhty, M. (2011). Constructing practical knowledge of teaching: Eleven newly qualified language teachers' discursive agency. *Language Learning Journal, 39*(3), 365–380.

Ruohotie-Lyhty, M. (2013). Struggling for a professional identity: Two newly qualified language teachers' identity narratives during the first years at work. *Teaching and Teacher Education, 30*(1), 120–129.

Ruohotie-Lyhty, M. (2016). Dependent or independent: The construction of the beliefs of newly qualified foreign language teachers. In P. Kalaja, A. M. F. Barcelos, M. Aro, & M. Ruohotie-Lyhty (Eds.), *Beliefs, agency and identity in foreign language learning and teaching* (pp. 149–171). London: Palgrave.

Ruohotie-Lyhty, M., & Moate, J. (2016). Who and how?: Preservice teachers as active agents developing professional identities. *Teaching and Teacher Education, 55*, 318–327.

Sahlberg, P. (2011). *Finnish lessons*. New York: Teachers College Press.

Thomas, L., & Beauchamp, C. (2011). Understanding new teachers' professional identities through metaphor. *Teaching and Teacher Education, 27*, 762–769.

Timotštšuk, I., & Ugaste, A. (2010). Student teachers' professional identity. *Teaching and Teacher Education, 26*, 1563–1570.

Vähäsantanen, K. (2015). Professional agency in the stream of change: Understanding educational change and teachers' professional identities. *Teaching and Teacher Education, 47*, 1–12.

Vähäsantanen, K., & Eteläpelto, A. (2011). Vocational teachers' pathways in the course of a curriculum reform. *Journal of Curriculum Studies, 43*(3), 291–312.

Chapter 4
Teacher Professional Identity and Career Motivation: A Lifespan Perspective

Paul W. Richardson and Helen M. G. Watt

The complex nature of teachers' work calls into play personal attributes, values, expectancies, and beliefs; task-related content and pedagogical knowledge, skills and abilities; as well as social relationships and the attendant emotional demands embedded in interactions with youth, colleagues, parents, and the wider society. A strength, but also a challenge to the study of the formation and development of teacher professional identity, is its multidimensional contextualised character, reflected in the diversity of conceptual and methodological perspectives drawn on to examine identity-related processes (e.g., Beauchamp & Thomas, 2009; Day, Sammons, Stobart, Kingston, & Gu, 2007).

Key studied constructs have included self-efficacy, expectancies, values, goals, attitudes, beliefs, and professional commitment. These derive from major motivational theoretical frameworks that emphasise the interplay among person, task, and context: expectancy-value theory (EVT; Eccles (Parsons) et al., 1983; Eccles, 2009), achievement goal theory (AGT; Ames, 1992; Nicholls, 1989), self-determination theory (SDT; Ryan & Deci, 2000), and self-efficacy theory (Bandura, 1997) each of which has been adapted to the exploration of teacher motivation (EVT: see Richardson & Watt, 2006; Watt & Richardson, 2007; AGT: see Butler, 2007, 2014; SDT: see Roth, 2014; self-efficacy: see Klassen, Durksen, & Tze, 2014; Tschannen-Moran & Woolfolk Hoy, 2001).

An observation made some time ago that "teachers are workers, teaching is work, and the school is a workplace" (Connell, 1985, p. 69), has important ramifications for understanding teachers' motivations and the formation and development of their professional identities in particular work contexts. It is in specific school

P. W. Richardson (✉)
Faculty of Education, Monash University, Melbourne, Australia
e-mail: paul.richardson@monash.edu

H. M. G. Watt
School of Education and Social Work, The University of Sydney, Camperdown, Australia
e-mail: helen.watt@sydney.edu.au

© Springer International Publishing AG, part of Springer Nature 2018
P. A. Schutz et al. (eds.), *Research on Teacher Identity*,
https://doi.org/10.1007/978-3-319-93836-3_4

cultures and workplace environments governed by local and global social and political forces, that teachers realise their career motivations and goals and configure their professional identities.

We begin this chapter by outlining how we see identity and how it has been researched from varying disciplinary perspectives, before reflecting on the development of teachers' professional identities. Next, we propose how major motivation theories provide windows into identity development at different points during teachers' career lifespan. We then propose Selection, Optimisation, and Compensation (SOC) theory as an integrative framework within which to systematically explore how teachers regulate their personal and workplace resources and how these are implicated in shaping their professional identities across the career lifespan.

Defining Identity

"Identity" is an elusive, dynamic, and multidimensional construct that changes shape dependent on the theoretical lens through which it is observed. Researchers from philosophy (Mead, 1934), psychology (Erickson, 1989; Vignoles, Schwartz, & Luyckx, 2011), anthropology (Holland, Lachicotte, Skinner, & Cain, 1998), neuroscience (Quartz & Sejnowski, 2002) and sociology (Côté & Levine, 2002; Goffman, 1956) have provided insights from different disciplinary perspectives. A rich literature demonstrates that identity is not a singular construct, and specific identity domains (e.g., occupation, spirituality, ethnicity, gender) are experienced and enacted by individuals in sociocultural contexts through the lifespan. Changing physiological, biological, and psychological needs, together with larger sociopolitical forces, activate identity shifts and development.

Some motivation researchers distinguish personal and social identities. Personal identities provide an expression of individuality and relate to traits, attributes, goals, values, competencies, and self-concepts. Social identities refer to relational or interpersonal roles and group memberships (Tice & Baumeister, 2001). These commitments can be "self-chosen or ascribed" (Vignoles et al., 2011, p. 4). The twin concepts of ascribed and achieved identities help distinguish dimensions of identity that derive from social positioning versus personal attributes (Linton, 1936). Ascribed identities are those assigned by virtue of an individual's sex, race, socioeconomic status or cultural group; whereas achieved identities arise from individuals' personal agency, choice, efforts, and persistence. Both are implicated in the formation, development, and maintenance of teacher identity, because choosing teaching as a career involves individual qualities, expectancies, values, beliefs and talents, as well as accommodating required social roles, responsibilities, and expectations.

Social identities associate with norms, behaviours, and values ascribed to group identities and constitute one's identification with and self-awareness of *belonging*. Group membership is contingent on congruence between personal identities and the roles and relationships required for group memberships – what Foote called *identification* (1951). These ties "help individuals define who they are both for themselves and for the people with whom they interact" (Eccles, 2009, p. 79). In this way, teacher identity includes "how teachers define themselves to themselves and to others" (Lasky, 2005, p. 901).

Teacher Professional Identity

In a review of the literature on teachers' professional identity, Beijaard, Meijer and Verloop (2004) identified a lack of definitional clarity, and considerable diversity in how it had been researched. Studies of teacher identity have ranged from the highly particular focused on a single construct, through to studies drawing on several constructs (e.g., Canrinus, Helms-Lorenz, Beijaard, Buitink, & Hofman, 2012). Taking into account what is known about identity formation and development, we propose that *teacher identity* is dynamic and shaped by career choice motivations and goals, reflecting the degree to which a person categorises her/himself personally and occupationally as someone who enacts the roles required of a teacher, engages with the social ties of the profession, and is committed to the career into the future. Rather than conceiving of teacher identity as static, such a description highlights the roles of personal and social identities in development over time, which involve drawing on personal and workplace resources to sustain goals, satisfy needs, and balance demands, within the relational and political context of the workplace and wider systemic influences on the profession.

Aspects of teachers' ascribed identity come with the territory of sociocultural models and roles assigned by the schema of "teacher". D'Andrade (1992), a cultural anthropologist, identified schema as "conceptual structure[s] which makes possible the identification of objects and events" (p. 28), that can "function as goals" (p. 29). Expectations of the "teacher" schema are embedded in social and cultural practices enacted in multiple micro-level interactions, with which personal goals and motivations intersect. For instance, what "teacher" means in Indonesia is not exactly the same as in Australia or the USA. Cultural expectations of teachers in Indonesia are reflected in the word "guru", Bahasa Indonesia for "teacher". Inscribed in this word are the professional and wider social roles teachers are expected to play by acting as a source of guidance and wisdom, with the important role of promoting social harmony.

The exercise of choosing teaching as a career path and exerting effort to achieve that goal is central to the process of achieving motivations, confirming self-conceptions, and being recognised and ratified by members of the social group who constitute the teaching profession. Occupational identity is central to a person's self-worth and a meaningful, healthy life (Ashforth, 2001). In contemporary society, much of our life is taken up by the work we do, which is related to our self-constructions and who we perceive ourselves to be at different points in time (Guichard, 2009). These are intimately interwoven with the pursuit of occupational goals and meaning (Cochran, 1991). Changing patterns of individualism, the renegotiation and reconstruction of social systems, and contingency of values on context, suggest an identity that is foreclosed and rigid and not open to evolution to be problematic, especially in times of rapid social and cultural change (Luyckx, Goossens, & Soenens, 2006). As Fouad and Bynner (2008) observed, personal goals, social affinities, and socioeconomic position are inscribed in our occupational work. Teachers who lack confidence in their abilities to meet the relational and knowledge demands of the job, or are avoidant and minimalist in their efforts, are unlikely to exhibit high levels of identification and commitment to the career.

What Insights Do Theories of Teacher Motivation Offer Teacher Identity?

Theories of motivation were developed to explain processes that energise individuals to attend to, engage in, and persist with tasks to achieve goals. There is an explicit link between the self, identity, and motivation such that the self and identity forecast "what people are motivated to do, how they think, and make sense of themselves and others, the actions they take, and their feelings and ability to control or regulate themselves" (Oyserman, Elmore, & Smith, 2012, p. 70). While in everyday parlance "motivation" can be characterised as a single attribute – a person is motivated or not – teachers' career motivations are multidimensional, complex, and responsive to contextual factors (Butler, 2007, 2014; Richardson & Watt, 2006; Roth, 2014; Watt & Richardson, 2007).

Diverse motivational theories offer insights at different points of a teacher's career lifespan to understand how identity influences what teachers are motivated to do and vice versa. How teachers prioritise, optimise their resources, and compensate for barriers to achieve their goals, offer insights into the motivational drivers that influence shifts in occupational identity. The major motivation theories investigated so far in relation to teachers and teaching have shed light on teachers' confidence (self-efficacy theory); why people choose the career (EVT); what teachers aim to achieve (AGT); and, what sustains or undermines their commitment (SDT). This burgeoning literature has collectively foregrounded the powerful influence of context (school, community, district, state and national policies, sociopolitical discourses) on teachers' engagement, behaviours, and wellbeing, that impact the lives of students. We outline the key tenets of each of these theories below, and empirical findings these lenses have afforded in the study of teachers' motivations, highlighting their relevance to teachers' identity development.

Teacher Self-Efficacy

Based in social cognitive theory (Bandura, 1997), the literature on teacher self-efficacy has grown rapidly over more than two decades. The dominant framework is that developed by Tschannen-Moran and Woolfolk Hoy (2001) who measure dimensions of efficacy for student engagement, instructional practice, and classroom management. Other motivational theories have examined conceptual cousins (such as success expectancies and perceived competence). Notwithstanding differences in measurement and conceptualisation, teachers' self-efficacy associates with their goals and aspirations (Muijs & Reynolds, 2002), responses to innovation and change (Guskey, 1988), use of effective teaching strategies (Woolfolk et al., 1990), likelihood to remain in the profession (Glickman & Tamashiro, 1982) and positive behaviours, and, as such, with teachers' identity development.

Why Teach?

There have been many studies investigating why people choose teaching as a career. Our interest in this question emerged with the publication of the Factors Influencing Teaching Choice (FIT-Choice; www.fitchoice.org) framework (Richardson & Watt, 2006; Watt & Richardson, 2007), which enabled comparisons across samples and settings (Watt, Richardson, & Smith, 2017). Grounded in Eccles' et al. EVT (1983; Eccles, 2009), it offers a multidimensional account of teachers' career choice motivations and the emergence of initial teacher identity. Collectively, the continuing FIT-Choice program has proven fruitful in measuring and understanding beginning teachers' motivations; established how they matter for later outcomes including professional engagement, behaviours, and wellbeing; for different types of beginning teachers across diverse contexts.

We have distinguished three "types" of beginning teachers according to their motivational profiles, highlighting different nascent teacher identities even at the outset of their careers (Watt & Richardson, 2008). The *highly engaged persisters* were most motivated by an inherent valuing of the career, perceiving they had the abilities to be a good teacher, desire to make a social contribution, and, were the least motivated by choosing teaching as a fallback career. *Highly engaged switchers* similarly wanted to make a social contribution, intrinsically valued the career, planned to exert high effort and energy, had leadership aspirations, but were not planning to stay long in teaching because of plans to pursue a different career. The third type, *lower engaged desisters,* exhibited a rather negative motivational profile. They did not identify with the profession and were less motivated to take on the role because of adverse practicum experiences, the demanding nature of teachers' work, lack of school structural supports for beginning teachers, and prospects of insecure employment.

By comparing changes in motivations over the first years of teaching, we found that *highly engaged persisters* who exhibited an apparently positive profile at the end of teacher education, appeared the most psychologically vulnerable to stressors during early career–experiencing reduced career satisfaction, planned persistence and self-efficacies, all of which signal less robust personal and social ties to the profession and a refashioning of their self perceptions, motivations, and identity. This appeared to be the price of continuing to hold idealistic motivations in environments where they may not be able to be attained (see Watt & Richardson, 2010). On the other hand, *highly engaged switchers* adjusted their motivations downwards to sustain levels of planned persistence, self-efficacies, and satisfaction with choice of career. The *lower engaged desisters* who did enter teaching appeared to find unexpected rewards from the career. Their motivations were adjusted upwards and satisfaction with choice, planned persistence, and self-efficacies remained stable, foregrounding motivational adjustments as an adaptive coping mechanism in response to contextual demands. Personal and social identities are responsive to different contextual factors and influence what teachers are motivated to do, the action they will take to achieve their goals, how well they will "fit" within the work culture of the school, their work satisfaction and whether the resources available to them support or undermine their commitment, persisitence and identity as a teacher.

What Do Teachers Aim to Achieve?

Butler and her colleagues' work makes important theoretical and practical contributions to understanding that teachers adopt different goals in relation to what they are trying to achieve, reflecting different types of professional identification, commitment, effort, and work satisfaction; with important ramifications for instruction and student outcomes. The recognition that school is an "achievement arena" for teachers and not only students, led Butler (2007) to develop AGT to study teachers already in their careers, in her Goal Orientation for Teaching (GOT) approach. She showed that teachers pursue *relational* goals (to create close, caring, personal interactions with students), *mastery* goals (reflecting a wish to learn more about teaching and develop skills and abilities), *ability-approach* goals (to exhibit superior teaching abilities), *ability-avoidance* goals (to avoid demonstrating poor teaching), and *work-avoidance* goals (to do as little as possible to get by).

The new class of relational goals was theorised through Butler's insight that students' and teachers' motivations are uniquely intertwined, in that teachers incorporate the motivation of their students as integral to their own motivations. In a recent TALIS survey (OECD, 2014), positive teacher-student relationships and collaborative work among teachers were found to boost their work satisfaction. It has been eloquently observed that, for many teachers "relationships make their curricula vital and real; the human connection gives visible meaning and tangible purpose to their work" (Bernstein-Yamashiro & Noam, 2013, p. 56).

Relational goals are central for teachers, and predictive of their providing positive socioemotional support, cognitively stimulating instruction and adaptive coping (Butler, 2014). Mastery goals are also positive, in terms of associations with teacher support and positive responses to students seeking help. In contrast, ability-avoidance goals linked to student cheating on school work, and teachers' suppression of student questions and help seeking (see Butler, 2014). Relational and mastery goals reflect aspects of the basic needs of autonomy, competence, and belonging as proposed by self-determination theory (Ryan & Deci, 2000). Teachers whose main motivation is to avoid work will not experience a high level of competence, are less likely to seek to establish positive relationships with their students, or exhibit a strong sense of belonging to the profession or their school.

What Contexts Promote or Undermine Teachers' Motivations and Thriving?

SDT is the final major motivation theory we highlight that has been fruitfully studied in relation to teachers during their professional trajectories. SDT (Ryan & Deci, 2000) proposes the satisfaction of three basic needs–for competence, autonomy, and relatedness/belonging–as conditions for human flourishing. Motivations are defined as self-determined and autonomous, versus externally controlled. When teachers experience autonomous motivation in their work they enjoy positive outcomes such as sense of personal accomplishment, engagement in autonomy-supportive teaching behaviours, promotion of students' autonomous motivation to learn, and reduced levels of burnout (Roth, Assor, Kanat-Maymon, & Kaplan, 2007). On the other hand, controlled motivations produce negative outcomes for teachers and their students. Relatedness, the third pillar of SDT (also discussed as fundamental to teachers' goals and initial motivations in AGT and EVT) sits at odds with management models that take teachers away from their work in the classroom and opportunities for interaction with students. Teachers who feel unable to attain valued goals are likely to experience reduced autonomy and competence, and consequently experience reduced professional engagement.

School principals who believed that teachers need to experience autonomy in relation to their teaching, promote teachers' autonomous motivation (Roth, 2014). Externally directed accountability measures may lead teachers to engage in instructional practices that do not sit well with their beliefs and values, or reduce their sense of competence and autonomy, undermining their positive and autonomous motivation and leading to increased emotional exhaustion (Roth, 2014) or burnout (Fernet, Guay, Senécal, & Austin, 2012). Empirical studies point to these undesirable consequences of externally controlled accountability measures, and systems based on competition and standardised testing ostensibly designed to improve teacher quality and student achievement.

A Lifespan Perspective on Teacher Motivation and Identity Development

The motivation theories discussed are being systematically studied in relation to teachers' career choice and development (EVT, within the FIT-Choice program of research), teachers' goals (AGT, within the GOT program) and thriving (SDT and self-efficacy theories) which forecast key outcomes including professional engagement and wellbeing, teaching behaviours, and student outcomes. These all can be considered—and we consider them—dimensions of teacher identity development. How teachers regulate and marshall their personal resources to accommodate challenges across the career lifespan and how teacher professional identity changes in response to these demands, is not a trivial question. Teachers experience higher work-related stress (Travers & Cooper, 1993) and burnout than other professionals. Work-related stress, reduced work motivation and engagement, and low job satisfaction are persistent reasons for why people leave the profession (OECD, 2005). Studies have identified the following as sources of strain and tension for teachers: work intensification, heavy workload, negative professional interactions with colleagues, inadequate salary, students with behavioural problems, assertive and demanding parents, poor school leadership and absence of autonomy (Pithers & Soden, 1998; Pyhältö, Pietarinen, & Salmela-Aro, 2011). These have potential to drain teachers' energies and wear out even those most committed. Yet, the majority of those who stay in the career find it rewarding and satisfying (Borg & Riding, 1991). How do we understand what sustains people throughout a life-time career as a teacher?

The SOC framework was developed as a model of successful ageing (Baltes & Baltes, 1990) and has been applied to successful occupational lifespan development (Abraham & Hansson, 1995; Yeung & Fung, 2009). SOC offers a framework to study motivation and identity development through the teaching career lifespan, capable of encompassing the existing motivational theories targeted to different points during the career (i.e., EVT for initial career choice; AGT during within-classroom teaching; SDT for future growth and flourishing). *Selection* involves setting and prioritising important goals or tasks: elective selection reflects personal determination of goals on which to focus resources; loss-based selection results from a threat to undermine functioning that forces a reorganisation of one's goals (e.g., a teacher might find her/himself in a school context where personally important goals of promoting social equity are not able to be realised). *Optimisation* means investment in additional resources to achieve selected goals, such as additional efforts or enhancing current skills. *Compensation* involves using alternative means to maintain a level of functioning when current means are thwarted or unavailable.

A recent study drew on the SOC framework to examine how German secondary teachers ($N = 1939$; aged 25–65 years) managed their workload to maintain wellbeing (Philipp & Kunter, 2013). Both beginning and older teachers engaged in fewer tasks (*selection*); older teachers *optimised* by saving time on demanding tasks that they invested in other valued tasks such as interacting with students; and older teachers had fewer career ambitions (a form of *compensation*). A lifespan approach is concerned with individuals' development within context, in which selection, optimisation, and compensation are key to coming to grips with demands.

A lifespan perspective on teachers' identity development foregrounds the significant learning, development, and refinement of teaching-related skills throughout the career. From this perspective development is not conceptualised as irreversible or end-state (e.g. Day et al., 2007; Huberman, 1989). How teachers avoid depletion of their energies, mobilise resources to avoid emotional exhaustion, and remain engaged with and committed to the career, may be accounted for by the coordinated deployment of the complementary strategies of selection, optimisation, and compensation.

Teachers' professional lives are intertwined with their school and community contexts and larger policy frameworks that impinge on their practice. We might expect teachers' identity and motivations to be significantly impacted by the appointment of a new principal or supervising head teacher, assignments to teach difficult classes, or new high-stakes testing procedures. While we recognise that individual resources such as time, cognitive capacity, and social support are limited, there is considerable plasticity in intellectual functioning, personality, attitudes and interests, as well as stability over the course of development. It is not known if and how these contextual influences diminish a person's indentification with and investment in the career. Contexts that create tensions, frustrations and confusion for an individual have the potential to challenge motivations, emasculate confidence, and reduce occupational commitment and career satisfaction.

Outlook and Future Directions

SOC offers a potential integrative, coherent organisational framework capable of bringing together a range of theories and constructs that have been drawn on in the examination of teacher motivation and identity development; it embraces the unfolding of developmental processes in particular contexts and helps us think beyond assumed age and stage models of teacher identity and work commitment. In many countries recently, there has been an intense focus on teacher quality, early career attrition, work intensification, and accountability measures that refashion teachers' daily working lives. Teachers' motivations are intimately connected with how they perceive themselves and the work they do. For instance, teachers whose goals are to avoid work or get through the day with little effort have less positive relationships with students and are unlikely to be highly identified with the profession. Ideally, longitudinal studies could flesh out how teachers regulate their energies in relation to demands over the career lifespan. Although such work is costly and methodologically challenging, we need to know more about how teachers sustain their motivations and professional identities, cope with work demands into mid-career and beyond, and strategically deploy personal and workplace resources to thrive and remain committed to the profession.

Acknowledgements The FIT-Choice project (www.fitchoice.org) is supported by sequential Australian Research Council grants DP140100402 (Richardson & Watt), DP0987614 (Watt & Richardson) and DP0666253 (Richardson, Watt, & Eccles).

References

Abraham, J. D., & Hansson, R. O. (1995). Successful aging at work: An applied study of selection, optimization, and compensation through impression management. *The Journals of Gerontology: Series B: Psychological Sciences and Social Sciences, 50B*, 94–103. https://doi.org/10.1093/geronb/50B.2.P94

Ames, C. (1992). Goals, structures, and student motivation. *Journal of Educational Psychology, 84*, 261–271.

Ashforth, B. E. (2001). *Role transition in organizational life: An identity-based perspective.* Mahwah, NJ: Erlbaum.

Baltes, P. B., & Baltes, M. M. (1990). Psychological perspectives on successful aging: The model of selective optimization with compensation. In P. B. Baltes & M. M. Baltes (Eds.), *Successful aging: Perspectives from the behavioral sciences* (pp. 1–34). New York: Cambridge University Press. https://doi.org/10.1017/CBO9780511665684.003

Bandura, A. (1997). *Self-efficacy: The exercise of control.* New York: Freeman.

Beauchamp, C., & Thomas, L. (2009). Understanding teacher identity: An overview of issues in the literature and implications for teacher education. *Cambridge Journal of Education, 39*(2), 175–189.

Beijaard, D., Meijer, P., & Verloop, N. (2004). Reconsidering research on teachers' professional identity. *Teaching and Teacher Education, 20*, 107–128.

Bernstein-Yamashiro, B., & Noam, G. G. (2013). *Teacher-student relationships: Toward personalized education* (New Directions for Youth Development, 137). Wiley Periodicals, NJ: Hoboken.

Borg, M. G., & Riding, R. J. (1991). Towards a model for the determinants of occupational stress among schoolteachers. *European Journal of Psychology of Education, 6*(4), 355–373.

Butler, R. (2007). Teachers' achievement goal orientations and associations with teachers' help seeking: Examination of a novel approach to teacher motivation. *Journal of Educational Psychology, 99*, 241–252.

Butler, R. (2014). What teachers want to achieve and why it matters: An achievement goal approach to teacher motivation. In P. W. Richardson, S. A. Karabenick, & H. M. G. Watt (Eds.), *Teacher motivation: Theory and practice* (pp. 20–35). New York: Routledge.

Canrinus, E. T., Helms-Lorenz, M., Beijaard, D., Buitink, J., & Hofman, A. (2012). Self-efficacy, job satisfaction, motivation and commitment: Exploring the relationships between indicators of teachers' professional identity. *European Journal of Psychology of Education, 27*, 115–132. https://doi.org/10.1007/s10212-011-0069-2

Cochran, L. (1991). *Life-shaping decisions.* New York: Peter Lang.

Connell, R. W. (1985). *Teachers' work.* Sydney, Australia: Allen & Unwin.

Côté, J. E., & Levine, C. G. (2002). *Identity formation, agency, and culture: A social psychological synthesis.* Mahwah, NJ: Lawrence Erlbaum.

D'Andrade, R. (1992). Schemas and motivation. In R. D'Andrade & C. Strauss (Eds.), *Human motives and cultural models* (pp. 23–44). New York: Cambridge University Press.

Day, C., Sammons, P., Stobart, G., Kingston, A., & Gu, Q. (2007). *Teachers matter: Connecting work, lives and effectiveness.* Maidenhead, UK: McGraw Hill/Open University Press.

Eccles (Parsons), J., Adler, T. F., Futterman, R., Goff, S. B., Kaczala, C. M., Meece, J. L., & Midgley, C. (1983). Expectancies, values, and academic behaviors. In J. T. Spence (Ed.), *Achievement and achievement motives* (pp. 75–146). San Francisco, CA: W.H. Freeman & Co.

Eccles, J. (2009). Who am I and what am I going to do with my life? Personal and collective identities as motivators of action. *Educational Psychologist, 44*, 78–89.

Erickson, E. (1989). *Identity and the life cycle.* New York: International University Press.

Fernet, C., Guay, F., Senécal, C., & Austin, S. (2012). Predicting intraindividual changes in teacher burnout: The role of perceived school environment and motivational factors. *Teaching and Teacher Education, 28*, 514–525.

Foote, N. N. (1951). Identification as the basis for a theory of motivation. *American Sociological Review, 16*(1), 14–21.

Fouad, N. A., & Bynner, J. (2008). Work transitions. *American Psychologist, 63*(4), 241–251. https://doi.org/10.1037/0003-066X.63.4.241

Glickman, C. D., & Tamashiro, R. T. (1982). A comparison of first-year, fifth-year, and former teachers on efficacy, ego-development, and problem-solving. *Psychology in the Schools, 19*, 558–562.

Goffman, E. (1956). *The presentation of self in everyday life.* New York: Doubleday.

Guichard, J. (2009). Self-constructing. *Journal of Vocational Behavior, 75*, 251–258. https://doi.org/10.1016/j.jvb.2009.03.004

Guskey, T. R. (1988). Teacher efficacy, self-concept, and attitudes toward the implementation of instructional innovation. *Teaching and Teacher Education, 4*, 63–69.

Holland, D., Lachicotte, W., Skinner, D., & Cain, C. (1998). *Identity and agency in cultural worlds.* Cambridge, MA: Harvard University Press.

Huberman, M. (1989). On teachers' careers: Once over lightly, with a broad brush. *International Journal of Educational Research, 13*(4), 347–362.

Klassen, R. M., Durksen, T. L., & Tze, V. M. C. (2014). Teachers' self-efficacy beliefs: Ready to move from theory to practice. In P. W. Richardson, S. A. Karabenick, & H. M. G. Watt (Eds.), *Teacher motivation: Theory and practice* (pp. 100–115). New York: Routledge.

Lasky, S. (2005). A sociocultural approach to understanding teacher identity, agency and professional vulnerability in a context of secondary school reform. *Teaching and Teacher Education, 21*, 899–916.

Linton, R. (1936). *The study of man.* New York: Appleton-Century-Crofts, Inc.

Luyckx, K., Goossens, L., & Soenens, B. (2006). A developmental contextual perspective on identity construction in emerging adulthood: Change dynamics in commitment formation and commitment evaluation. *Developmental Psychology, 42*, 366–380.

Mead, G. (1934). *Mind, self and society.* Chicago, IL: The University of Chicago Press.

Muijs, D., & Reynolds, D. (2002). Teachers' beliefs and behaviours: What really matters. *Journal of Classroom Interaction, 37*, 3–15.

Nicholls, J. G. (1989). *The competitive ethos and democratic education.* Cambridge, MA: Harvard University Press.

OECD. (2005). *Teachers matter: Attracting, developing and retaining effective teachers.* Paris: OECD.

OECD. (2014). *New insights from TALIS 2013: Teaching and learning in primary and upper secondary education.* Paris: TALIS, OECD Publishing. https://doi.org/10.1787/9789264226319-en

Oyserman, D., Elmore, K., & Smith, G. (2012). Self, self-concept, and identity. In M. R. Leary & J. P. Tangney (Eds.), *Handbook of self and identity* (pp. 60–104). New York: The Guilford Press.

Philipp, A., & Kunter, M. (2013). How do teachers spend their time? A study of teachers' strategies of selection, optimisation, and compensation over the career cycle. *Teaching and Teacher Education, 35*, 1–12.

Pithers, R. T., & Soden, R. (1998). Scottish and Australian teacher stress and strain: A comparative analysis. *British Journal of Educational Psychology, 68*, 269–279.

Pyhältö, K., Pietarinen, J., & Salmela-Aro, K. (2011). Teacher–working-environment fit as a framework for burnout experienced by Finnish teachers. *Teaching and Teacher Education, 27*(7), 1101–1110.

Quartz, S. R., & Sejnowski, T. J. (2002). *Liars, lovers, and heroes: What the new brain science reveals about how we become who we are.* New York: Harper Collins.

Richardson, P. W., & Watt, H. M. G. (2006). Who chooses teaching and why? Profiling characteristics and motivations across three Australian Universities. *Asia-Pacific Journal of Teacher Education, 34*(1), 27–56.

Roth, G. (2014). Antecedents and outcomes of teachers' autonomous motivation: A self-determination theory analysis. In P. W. Richardson, S. A. Karabenick, & H. M. G. Watt (Eds.), *Teacher motivation: Theory and practice* (pp. 36–51). New York: Routledge.

Roth, G., Assor, A., Kanat-Maymon, Y., & Kaplan, H. (2007). Autonomous motivation for teaching: How self-determined teaching may lead to self-determined learning. *Journal of Educational Psychology, 99*, 761–774.

Ryan, R. M., & Deci, E. L. (2000). Self-determination theory and the facilitation of intrinsic motivation, social development, and well-being. *American Psychologist, 55*, 68–78.

Tice, D. M., & Baumeister, R. F. (2001). The primacy of the interpersonal self. In C. Sedikides & M. B. Brewer (Eds.), *Individual self, relational self, collective self* (pp. 71–88). Philadelphia, PA: Psychology Press.

Travers, C. J., & Cooper, C. L. (1993). Mental health, job satisfaction and occupational stress among UK teachers. *Work & Stress, 7*(3), 203–219. https://doi.org/10.1080/02678379308257062

Tschannen-Moran, M., & Woolfolk Hoy, A. (2001). Teacher efficacy: Capturing an elusive construct. *Teaching and Teacher Education, 17*(7), 783–805.

Vignoles, V. L., Schwartz, S. J., & Luyckx, K. (2011). Introduction: Toward an integrated view of identity. In S. J. Schwartz, K. Luychx, & V. L. Vignoles (Eds.), *Handbook of identity theory and research* (pp. 1–28). New York: Springer.

Watt, H. M. G., & Richardson, P. W. (2007). Motivational factors influencing teaching as a career choice: Development and validation of the FIT-Choice scale. *Journal of Experimental Education, 75*(3), 167–202.

Watt, H. M. G., & Richardson, P. W. (2008). Motivations, perceptions, and aspirations concerning teaching as a career for different types of beginning teachers. *Learning and Instruction, 18*(5), 408–428.

Watt, H. M. G., & Richardson, P. W. (2010, April). *'When the rubber hits the road': Changing motivations for teacher subtypes in the first 5 years of teaching*. Paper presented at the AERA Annual Conference, Denver, CO, April 30 – May 4, 2010.

Watt, H. M. G., Richardson, P. W., & Smith, K. (2017). *Global perspectives on teacher motivation*. New York: Cambridge University Press.

Woolfolk, A. E., Rosoff, B., & Hoy, W. K. (1990). Teachers' sense of efficacy and their beliefs about managing students. *Teaching and Teacher Education, 6*, 137–148.

Yeung, D. Y., & Fung, H. H. (2009). Aging and work: How do SOC strategies contribute to job performance across adulthood? *Psychology & Aging, 24*, 927–940. https://doi.org/10.1037/a0017531

Chapter 5
Critical Events, Emotional Episodes, and Teacher Attributions in the Development of Teacher Identities

Paul A. Schutz, Sharon L. Nichols, and Samantha Schwenke

Identity has become an increasingly useful construct for educational researchers. Scholars have explored how identities intersects with motivation (e.g., Flum & Kaplan, 2012; Kaplan & Flum, 2009), how identities relates to the development of learner dispositions (McCaslin, 2009; William & Wertsch, 1995), and how identities informs teachers' beliefs and practices (Fives & Gill, 2015). Despite this growing literature, it remains inconsistently defined, framed, and utilized. This is especially the case in research on teachers' professional identity (e.g., Akkerman & Meijer, 2011; Beijaard, Meijer, & Verloop, 2004; Hong, 2010; Izadinia, 2013; McAdams 2001; Nichols, Schutz, Rodgers, & Bilica, 2017; Stets & Burke, 2014). Scholars' conceptualizations of teacher identities vary in scope, theoretical framework, and purpose (e.g., Zembylas & Chubbuck, 2015, Chap. 16 this volume).

Despite this vast and varied literature, some common features have emerged regarding the development of a beginning teachers' professional identity (Nichols et al., 2017; Rodgers & Scott, 2008). First, teachers' identity development is fluid—it involves a continual process of becoming (Schutz, Cross, Hong, & Osbon, 2007; Sutherland, Howard, & Markauskaite, 2010). For example, Clarke (2009) discusses how teacher identities emerge through ongoing social negotiation (and reflection). Elsewhere, Akkerman and Meijer (2011) and others (e.g., Beauchamp & Thomas, 2009) contend teacher identities evolve through dialogical experiences and emerge through participation in "different discourse communities" (p. 309). This process of *becoming* involves transactions among teachers' goals, beliefs, and standards about

P. A. Schutz (✉) · S. L. Nichols
Department of Educational Psychology, University of Texas at San Antonio, San Antonio, TX, USA
e-mail: sharon.nichols@utsa.edu; paul.schutz@utsa.edu

S. Schwenke
Department of Educational Leadership and Policy Studies, University of Texas at San Antonio, San Antonio, TX, USA
e-mail: robyn.schwenke@utsa.edu

© Springer International Publishing AG, part of Springer Nature 2018
P. A. Schutz et al. (eds.), *Research on Teacher Identity*,
https://doi.org/10.1007/978-3-319-93836-3_5

who they are and what they want to be as a teacher, their broader conceptions of how they see themselves as a person, and their developing understanding of the perceived constraints and affordances related to their current social and/or historical contexts (Akkerman & Meijer, 2011; Beauchamp & Thomas, 2009; Hsieh, 2015; Schutz, 2014; Smagorinsky, Cook, Moore, Jackson, & Fry, 2004; Zembylas & Chubbuck, 2015).

Second, an emerging teacher identity involves the extent to which teachers' autonomy (i.e., having a sense of control over one's teaching context), competency (i.e., believing in ones' skills and strategies as a teacher), and relatedness (i.e., having feelings of belonging with others) needs are met (Deci & Ryan, 2000; Ryan, Huta, & Deci, 2008). In the teacher identity literature, agency (i.e., a sence of control) has become a key construct with useful implications for thinking about identity processes (McAdams & McLean, 2013; Nichols et al., 2017; Rodgers & Scott, 2008; Zembylas & Chubbuck, 2015, Chap. 16 this volume).[1] For example, Beauchamp and Thomas (2009) argue that one of the key activities of a new teacher is the "search for agency" and that "developing a strong identity has to do with the emergence of agency as a way to externalize identity, as the outward expression of one's identity and an influence on the ongoing shaping of an identity" (p. 7). Elsewhere, Beijaard, Meijer, and Verloop (2004) conclude from their review of the literature that the formation of a teacher identity involves agency and an active pursuit of one's goals. As teachers navigate the constraints and affordances of their classroom experiences, the extent to which their sense of agency is understood and fulfilled gives rise to emergent identity beliefs.

Third, a teacher's developing identity involves a process of integrating our naturally existing sub-identities that may or may not conflict with one another (Akkerman & Meijer, 2011; Stets & Burke, 2014). For new teachers, these processes are especially salient. For example, a new teacher may enter the classroom with the identity of "being a good teacher" as well as that of "teacher as savior." For these teachers, the reality that not all students can be saved inherently raises questions about these incoming identity processes, forcing new teachers to renegotiate and redefine what it means to be a "good" teacher and what it means to "save" students (Chen, Horn, & Nolen, Chap. 8, this volume; Flores & Day, 2006; Nichols et al., 2017). Faced by students who consistently challenge and resist teachers' efforts, the belief that I am a teacher "who saves" students is questioned. How teachers handle this conflict determines how identities get resolved—whether they shift and become unified and cohesive or remain disjointed and unsteady. Does the teacher maintain a "savior" identity, thereby continuing a way of engaging with students that may be counterproductive, or does the teacher rectify their incoming identity with these experiences, making an identity adjustment that leads to a more realistic way of engaging with students? For most teachers, these conflicts present an opportunity for identity shifts that may or may not lead to a more cohesive and unified sense of self in the classroom (e.g., Alsup, 2006; Beijaard et al., 2004).

---

[1] Although we believe all three bacic needs from SDT are involved in teacher identity development, in this chapter we focus on the need for autonomy.

According to McAdams (1985, 2001), an identity integration process emerges through the narratives or stories we tell ourselves about who we are (Alsup, Chap. 2, this volume). McAdams (2001) discussed two types of identity integration processes. The first is a synchronic process that involves making sense of differing (and sometimes conflicting) identities. For example, we might struggle with the dual identities being a son in some situations, and a friends in others [e.g., "when I am with my father, I feel sullen and depressed, but when I talk with my friends I feel a great surge of optimism and love for human kind." (McAdams, 2001, p. 102)]. For teachers, a synchronic process may involve how we rectify the identities of being an innovator in the classroom, but someone who is traditional/rulebound at home. Thus, integration towards unity involves the development of a narrative (story) where teachers make sense of all aspects of ones' current, sometimes conflicting collection of identities.

A second type of identity integration process involves integrating one's identity story over time, or diachronically (McAdams, 2001). For example, how one might integrate the idea that "I used to loathe the idea of working with kids, but now I love it." Akkerman and Meijer (2011) argue that ongoing self-dialogue regarding the continuity of the many, sometimes conflicting, experiences one has during their lives prompts a diachronic integration process. For example, "I never thought about becoming a teacher in high school. I started college as a business major, but then I did some tutoring for a service learning project and I fell in love with teaching." New teachers, confronted by new experiences that challenge pre-existing identity structures engage in self-narratives (story telling) that help to shape a new more unified sense of self.

Akkerman and Meijer (2011) also discuss a third feature of the process of identity integration they refer to as "social-individual." In this view, identity development occurs within relationships while transacting among social historical contexts (e.g., need for relatedness). Thus, teachers transact with other teachers, administrators, students, etc. while developing understandings of how they see themselves within social historical contexts. This means that teachers tend to engage in self-dialogue regarding how they see themselves individually as a teacher (e.g., I enjoy my students; the diversity in my students bring a challenge I thrive on; I want to use more student-centered activities), while also engaging in, transactional relationships with others who may have differing views (e.g., The students in this school don't want to learn; the students have no respect for authority; we need to use more discipline in our classrooms). Again, these self-dialogues (or stories) occur during transactions with the social historical dimensions of being a teacher at a point in time (e.g., societal undervaluing of teachers and systemic sexism and racism related to schooling).

These ongoing identity development narratives revolve around teachers' goals, standards, and beliefs, the perceived constraints and affordances within their current activity setting, and influences that emerge within their social historical contexts. Next, we propose a model for understanding how these processes might relate and unfold for new teachers.[2] Our model incorporates the main themes described above (and throughout the extant literature) by proposing how beginning teachers' reflections on critical classroom incidents and their associated emotional interpretations and attributions may inspire an identity-generative processes.

Teacher Identity Development Processes

Our goal here is to describe a *process* of identity development that emerged from recent investigations (Nichols et al., 2017). Our approach is informed by three common features identified in the literature and offers a way to think more specifically about the identity development process. Our approach includes four transactional processes that occur in social historically constructed spaces (Nichols et al., 2017; Schutz, 2014). To explicate these processes, we begin with a discussion of "critical events" as key to emergent identities. We theorize that teachers' identities develop incrementally in the first few years in the classroom. These developments are sometimes triggered by critical events that serve as focal points for identity-based reflection and exploration (i.e., identity work). We then move to explain four transactional processes of: (1) incoming identity goals, standards, and beliefs; (2) emotional episodes; (3) teacher attributions, and (4) identity adjustments. From our perspective, one of the key impetuses for those identity adjustments are the critical events, the emotions associated with those events, and the attributions we make about those events occurring during transactions with social historical contexts.

Identity Work and the Critical Event

Scholars have used a variety of terms to describe important or identity changing events: critical incident (Miles & Huberman, 1984; Tripp, 1994), peek/nadir experience (Maslow & Arieti, 1961; Thorne, 1963), or nuclear episodes (McAdams, 1985). Although these critical incidents occur infrequently, they have the potential to signal a significant turning point or change in one's life and more specifically for our discussion in this chapter, one's identity development (McAdams, 1985; Miles & Huberman, 1984; Tripp, 1994). These critical incidents tend to be significant and important high points (i.e., Peak experience – associate with things going well and pleasant emotions) or low points (i.e., Nadir experience – associate with things not going well and unpleasant emotions) in ones' life (Maslow & Arieti, 1961; Thorne, 1963). However, it is important to keep in mind that what makes these events "critical" are the meanings assigned to those experience by the individual, the

---

[2]Although we focus on beginning teachers in this chapters – we believe that similar identity development processes have the potential to occur throughout a teacher career as different social-historical events occur (e.g., approaching retirement).

emotional episodes (pleasant or unpleasant) that are associated with those events, and the identity stories that are told and retold related to those events.

In a recent study, we asked beginning teachers to reflect on their critical events and to explore their thoughts, emotions, and reactions to those events (Nichols et al., 2017). Our analysis of the data yielded four key processes that were suggestive of how these teachers grappled with and negotiated their emergent identities as teachers.

Teachers' Goals, Standards, and Beliefs

From our data, we learned that when teachers are asked to reflect upon salient and/ or emotionally charged classroom experiences, they often frame their reflection with some incoming belief system we refer to as "Incoming Goals, Standards, and Beliefs" (Chen, Horn, & Nolen, (Chap. 8, this volume; Nichols et al., 2017; Schutz et al., 2006). These incoming goals, standards, and beliefs are reference points teachers used to judge where they are as compared to where they want to be. They are the expectations for how things in the classroom could and should go. They emerge during transactions as part of social historical contextual ways teachers think their classrooms should and could be, as well as the ways they would not like their classrooms to be (Ford, 1992; Markus & Nurius, 1986; Schutz, 1991, 1994; Schutz et al., 2001). For example, new teachers may believe they will have no problem handling classroom disruptions, only to discover when disruptions occur, they were ill-equipped to deal with them and experience unexpected frustration and anger. Incoming goals, standards, and beliefs become more relevant when incoming expectations are met by experiences that conflict with them. A first-year teacher experiences a series of ongoing matches and mismatches related to incoming expectations and the lived experiences of teaching that result in the emotional episodes (e.g., frustration, anger, joy, pride) we associate with our teachers' identity work and the emotional labor associated with that work.

As explained by Akkerman and Meijer (2011), one key feature of the teacher identity development process involves the tendency to integrate sub-identities when engaged in transactions that reveal contradictory information about our self (e.g., synchronic identity integration process). Thus, when teachers' incoming goals, standards and beliefs, are met with contradictory evidence, it may force them to make sense of (or integrate) those conflicting beliefs with their experiences – an important first step in understanding how they may (or may not) change or evolve.

Teacher Identity Emotional Episodes

Teacher Identity Emotional Episodes are experiences that have the potential to "signal" and/or influence teacher identity "work" (Schutz, 2014; Zembylas & Chubbuck, 2015). These emotional episodes emerge during social transactions or experiences with students, teachers, or administration. Although not all emotional episodes have the potential to influence a teacher's emerging identities, there are critical emotional events that are tied to some ongoing identity negotiation.

A key component of emotional episodes is that they involve conscious and/or unconscious judgments regarding perceived successes at attaining goals or maintaining standards or beliefs (Schutz, 2014; Schutz et al., 2006). From our perspective, teachers' goals, standards, and beliefs represent the reference points used by teachers to judge where they are in relation to where they want to be (Carver & Scheier, 2000; Cross & Hong, 2009; Frenzel, Goetz, Stephens, & Jacob, 2009; Powers, 1973; Schutz, 2014). As reference points, they provide directionality to teachers' thoughts and activities and tend to be what teachers use to judge how successful they see themselves during those activities, and evoke emotional responses. From our data, several teachers explained how judgments of experiences related to their incoming beliefs, goals, and standards triggered emotionally-suggestive reactions that would either call into question, or affirm their perceptions of themselves as teachers. For example, one new teacher struggled with what it meant to be a "mean" teacher. For her, "giving" students autonomy (believed by her to be a sign of respect) backfired and created classroom management problems. These frustrating experiences caused her to rethink her role as a disciplinarian (and what it means to respect students). For another teacher, having a positive or negative day often served to either confirm or undermine his sense of self-worth as a teacher. Thus, the type and intensity of emotions (e.g., frustration, anger, joy, happiness) emerge based on the teachers' appraisals of how successful their goal pursuits are within a classroom context. These judgments about success of classroom events also involve attributions about the reasons for those successes or failures (Nichols et al., 2017).

Teachers' Attributions

Attributions are the reasons teachers use to describe, understand, and make sense of their experiences and the pleasant and unpleasant emotional episodes associated with those experiences (Weiner, 1994, 2007, 2010). Researchers interested in identity development have suggested that agency and the attributions associated with agency beliefs tend to be key to the identity development process (Nichols et al., 2017; Rodgers & Scott, 2008; Zembylas & Chubbuck, 2015; Chap. 16 this volume). For example, teachers at times report that emotionally challenging/satisfying episodes were either due to reasons under their personal control (e.g., they are a bad/good teacher), or not under their control (e.g., I have no power over these students). One key area where teachers tend to make important attributions is while they are talking about their struggles related to their perceived control in the classroom (Aultman, Williams-Johnson, & Schutz, 2009). For example, teachers might use internal or external agency attributions to navigate a heightened sense of frustration when students are not behaving (or performing academically) in expected or desired ways. In these cases, those attributions tend to be the perceived reasons for success or a lack of success and, as such have the potential to influence future identity perceptions.

The Adjustment

We are suggesting that critical emotional episodes and the attributions associated with those episodes provide opportunities for potential adjustments teachers make in the ways they approach and think about teaching (Akkerman & Meijer, 2011). In other words, these critical events have the potential to challenge (e.g., nadir, unpleasant emotional experience) or support (e.g., peek, pleasant emotional experience) teachers' goals, values, and beliefs and depending on the attributions and emotional responses, may result in important identity work. From our work, we found that teachers may "adjust" their identity-related beliefs following some critical event or emotional episode. Although the stability of that adjustment was not clear from our data, what was evident was that many of our new teachers "learned" from these emotional episodes and would consciously make an identity-related "shift." For example, one of our teachers was especially emotional about his desire to help his students, with whom he identified significantly. However, through the year, his goals, standards, and beliefs, challenged by ongoing emotional experiences led to a subtle shift. Whereas at the beginning of the year he saw himself more as his students' friend and savior—thus employing internal attributions for explaining his role and impact with students—by the end he had adopted more of an authoritarian role—acting on changing attributions that viewed his power and control over students as waning. His agency attributions regarding his efficacy to control students shifted. He began believing he would have a great deal of power and control to change students' lives only to be confronted with emotionally charged interactions with students that caused a shift towards more external orientation of control. We saw his transformation as the result of emotions and attributions assigned to transactional experiences wherein incoming beliefs, goals, and standards were challenged and exposed.

Identity Work as a Process

To illustrate how these processes may play out, we use the reflections of Ms. Miller, who shared with us her experiences as a (second career) first year science teacher. Her words demonstrate her identity work and highlighted possible theoretical connections among these four processes (Nichols et al., 2017).

> "This is a very high stress job [Teachers Identity Emotional Episode]. I never expected it to be so high stressed [Incoming Identity Belief]. Because I want so much to be that teacher that inspires a child, and I guess my lofty goal was "I'm just going make all of these kids love science." [Incoming Identity Beliefs] And it's just not happening. It's not very relevant to them [Teacher Attribution] and I'm learning to deal with that on my own. And now when I have a bad day, I'm just like "It was a bad day. It's not the end of the world." [Teacher Identity Adjustment] I have kids that will come visit me during lunch. I have kids that come visit me in the morning. I have kids that I've made a connection with. And those are the kids that I'm trying to focus on. Those are the kids that may just need a role model, may just need someone to talk to. And if I make a difference in one of their lives, then it doesn't matter if I've taught them chemistry or balancing equations. I'm not there just to teach science. I'm there to make a difference in somebody's life. [Teacher Identity Adjustment]" (Nichols et al., 2017, pp. 415–416).

As a way of suggesting the critical nature of Ms. Miller's identity work during her first year of teaching, it is important to note that over the course of this 1 h interview she used the words 'stress,' 'stressful,' or 'stressed' 17 times (Nichols et al., 2017). With that in mind, we see Ms. Miller's incoming identity beliefs when she suggests that her goal is to make her kids love science. Yet the reality of her actual classroom experience challenged that belief: 'I never expected it [teaching] to be so high stressed.' This mismatch between her incoming beliefs and her experience led to an ongoing examination of the degree to which she could control students' ability to "love science." Her actual teaching experiences confronted this internal belief resulting in an adjustment of attributions regarding students' behavior and achievement. Whereas at the beginning of the year she went into the classroom believing she had agency over students' love and interest for the subject, as time progressed, the emotional challenges confronting students who resisted causing her to adjust her beliefs about how much control she did and did not have. This episode does not reveal the long-term effects of these experiences but provides insight into the way in which beliefs, emotions, and attribution systems may interact as beginning teachers grapple with their new profession.

We have also seen this adjustment during pleasant or peek emotional experiences as with Ms. Ann, a preservice teacher who got a chance to view her old third grade teacher in action:

> "I knew I wanted to deal with people and I liked kids a lot and—but I didn't want to go into teaching because I thought, 'Well, they don't get paid enough' and this and that [Teachers' goals, standards, and beliefs.] And then I took a career exploration class and I went to my old third grade teacher and I got chills [Teacher Identity Emotional Episodes] when I walked in the school because I was just like 'This is what I want.'" [Teachers' Attributions, and Adjustment] (Schutz, Crowder, & White, 2001, p. 303)

Again, in this example, incoming goals, standards, beliefs were challenged in a critical emotional event that resulted in Ms. Ann changing attributions regarding her agency about being the teacher she eventually became (Schutz et al., 2001).

Discussion and Implications for Practice and Policy

A teacher's professional identity has become a useful construct for understanding development throughout the professional life of teachers. Over time scholars have begun to coalesce around several key aspects of professional identity. The model we describe here, based on data from beginning teachers, provides further evidence of this idea. From our model, we see that teachers' incoming beliefs about what they think teaching will be like is confronted by ongoing classroom experiences that often challenge those beliefs. From our data, the emotions associated with those experiences (frustration, helplessness, stress, surprise, joy) offer key feedback for teachers upon which to reflect and react. Change is not immediate, but the result of ongoing experiences through which teachers must reflect, analyze, and make sense of for a cohesive teacher identity to emerge.

Teachers leave the profession as disproportionately high rates during the first few years of their career (Achinstein, 2006; Darling-Hammond, 1999). One of the reason for this exodus has to do with the emotional labor required to manage complex classroom environments (see Schutz & Zembylas, 2009). Classrooms are challenging spaces that require teachers to manage a complex array of social, cognitive, academic, and emotional demands. Given that it takes years to understand this complexity, it is not surprising new teachers are especially burdened as they learn how to navigate these demands.

One aspect of a new teacher's life has to do with how they come to understand their identity as a teacher. A vast literature suggests that beginning teachers go through a process of "becoming" that emerges through social historical transactions involving ongoing identity-related negotiations, conflicts, and exploration. Teachers who struggle to understand their role and place in the classroom are more likely to burn out and leave; whereas teachers who are more successful in understanding and adjusting their identities as teachers might be more willing to persevere. Understanding how teachers' identities develop within sociohistorical contexts could provide some insight into ways we might help beginning teachers manage the first few years of their professional lives.

In this chapter, we presented one model that frames how reflections of critical incidents and the associated emotional and attributional responses may contribute to identity-generative processes. One implication from this model is the importance of reflection for laying bare the role of goals, standards, and beliefs surrounding emotionally-salient critical events. New teachers are not often aware of these processes, nor do they have time to be reflective about them. Teacher preparation programs could purposefully create opportunities for teacher candidates to reflect upon critical events to help thwart maladaptive attributional adjustments and emotional regulation. These kinds of experiences could be embedded in coursework through case study experiences and throughout the student teacher experience.

Being a new teacher is difficult. In spite of the preparation new teachers might receive through accredited university programs, there remain vast chasms between content and practice. Teacher candidates are exposed to a wealth of information regarding the philosophy, history, theory, and techniques of teaching, but too often this content is disconnected from teachers' actual teaching experience. Therefore, upon entering the classroom, teachers often feel unprepared. Teacher preparation programs must consider innovative ways to help their candidates meet certification requirements (learning about content) while at the same time providing complementary and ongoing teaching experiences. Teaching is not a technical skill that can be memorized, but a craft that requires sophisticated decision making capabilities by professionals who must navigate a complex and unpredictable array of demands (comply with policies, please parents, address individual learner needs and so forth). Much like the medical model of education where new doctors spend a great deal of time shadowing expert doctors and practicing their craft through internship models, teachers must be given the same type of learning opportunities to practice their professional craft under the supervision, support, and guidance of expert teachers. Through intensive internship-like experiences teachers can learn about what it is actually like to apply the methods they learn in school and subsequently discover how it makes them feel and how it might inform their emergent identity. Informed by our model, teacher education programs can strategically facilitate new teachers' reflections on their classroom-based experiences, helping them to be mindful about how their incoming beliefs, emotions, and attributions impact their emergent identity and developing instructional practices.

References

Achinstein, B. (2006). New teacher and mentor political literacy: Reading, navigating and transforming induction contexts. *Teachers and Teaching: Theory and Practice, 12*(2), 123–138.

Akkerman, S. F., & Meijer, P. C. (2011). A dialogical approach to conceptualizing teacher identity. *Teaching and Teacher Education, 27*(2), 308–319.

Alsup, J. (2006). *Teacher identity discourses. Negotiating personal and professional spaces.* Mahwah, NJ: Lawrence Erlbaum Associates, Inc.

Aultman, L. P., Williams-Johnson, M. R., & Schutz, P. A. (2009). Boundary dilemmas in teacher-student relationships: Struggling with "the line". *Teaching and Teacher Education, 25*, 636–646.

Beauchamp, C., & Thomas, L. (2009). Understanding teacher identity: An overview of issues in the literature and implications for teacher education. *Cambridge Journal of Education, 39*(2), 175–189.

Beijaard, D., Meijer, P. C., & Verloop, N. (2004). Reconsidering research on teachers' professional identity. *Teaching and Teacher Education, 20*, 107–128.

Carver, S. C., & Scheier, M. F. (2000). On the structure of behavioral self-regulation. In M. Boekaerts, P. R. Pintrich, & M. Zeidner (Eds.), *Handbook of self-regulation* (pp. 41–84). San Diego, CA: Academic.

Clarke, M. (2009). The ethico-politics of teacher identity. *Educational Philosophy and Theory, 41*(2), 185–200.

Cross, D. I., & Hong, J. Y. (2009). Beliefs and professional identity: Critical constructs in examining the impact of reform on the emotional experiences of teachers. In P. A. Schutz & M. Zembylas (Eds.), *Advances in teacher emotion research: The impact on teachers' lives* (pp. 273–296). New York: Springer Publishing.

Darling-Hammond, L. (1999). *Solving the dilemmas of teacher supply, demand, and standards: How we can ensure a competent, caring, and qualified teacher for every child*. New York: National Commission on Teaching and America's Future.

Deci, E. L., & Ryan, R. M. (2000). The 'what' and 'why' of goal pursuits: Human needs and the self-determination of behavior. *Psychological Inquiry, 11*, 227–268.

Fives, H., & Gill, M. G. (Eds.). (2015). *International handbook of research on teacher beliefs*. New York: Routledge.

Flores, M. A., & Day, C. (2006). Contexts which shape and reshape new teachers' identities: A multi-perspective study. *Teaching and Teacher Education, 22*, 219–232.

Flum, H., & Kaplan, A. (2012). Identity formation in educational settings: A contextualized view of theory and research in practice. *Contemporary Educational Psychology, 37*, 240–245.

Ford, M. E. (1992). *Motivating humans: Goals, emotions, and personal agency beliefs*. Newbury Park, CA: Sage.

Frenzel, A. C., Goetz, T., Lüdtke, O., Pekrun, R., & Sutton, R. E. (2009). Emotional transmission in the classroom: Exploring the relationship between teacher and student enjoyment. *Journal of Educational Psychology, 101*(3), 705–716.

Hong, J. Y. (2010). Pre-service and beginning teachers' professional identity and its relation to dropping out of the profession. *Teaching and Teacher Education, 26*, 1530–1543.

Hsieh, B. (2015). The importance of orientation: Implications of professional identity on classroom practice for professional learning. *Teachers and Teaching: Theory and Practice, 21*, 178. https://doi.org/10.1080/13540602.2014.928133

Izadinia, M. (2013). A review of research on student teachers' professional identity. *British Educational Research Journal, 39*(4), 694–713.

Kaplan, A., & Flum, H. (2009). Motivation and identity: The relations of action and development in educational contexts—An introduction to the special issue. *Educational Psychologist, 44*(2), 73–77.

Markus, H., & Nurius, P. (1986). Possible selves: The interface between motivation and the self-concept. In *Self and Identity: Psychosocial Perspectives* (pp. 157–172). Oxford, UK: Wiley.

Maslow, A., & Arieti, S. (1961). Peak experiences as acute identity experiences. *American Journal of Psychoanalysis, 21*(2), 254.

McAdams, D. P. (1985). *Power, intimacy, and the life story: Personological inquiries into identity*. Homewood, IL: Dorsey Press.

McAdams, D. P. (2001). The psychology of life stories. *Review of General Psychology, 5*, 100–122.

McAdams, D. P., & McLean, K. C. (2013). Narrative identity. *Current Directions in Psychological Science, 22*(3), 233–238.

McCaslin, M. (2009). Co-regulation of student motivation and emergent identity. *Educational Psychologist, 44*(2), 137–146.

Miles, M. B., & Huberman, A. M. (1984). *Qualitative data analysis: A sourcebook of new methods*. Beverly Hills, CA: Sage.

Nichols, S. L., Schutz, P. A., Rodgers, K., & Bilica, K. (2017). Early career teachers' emotion and emerging teacher identities. *Teachers and Teaching, 23*(4), 406–421.

Powers, W. T. (1973). *Behavior: The control of perception*. Chicago, IL: Aldine.

Rodgers, C., & Scott, C. (2008). The development of the personal self and professional identity in learning to teach. In M. Cochran-Smith, S. Feiman-Nemser, D. J. McIntyre, & K. E. Demers (Eds.), *Handbook of research on teacher education* (pp. 732–755). New York: Routledge.

Ryan, R. M., Huta, V., & Deci, E. L. (2008). Living well: A self-determination theory perspective on eudaimonia. *Journal of Happiness Studies, 9*, 139–170.

Schutz, P. A. (1991). Goals in self-directed behavior. *Educational Psychologist, 26*, 55–67.

Schutz, P. A. (1994). Goals as the transactive point between motivation and cognition. In P. R. Pintrich, D. Brown, & C. E. Weinstein (Eds.), *Perspectives on student motivation, cognition and learning: Essays in honor of Wilbert J. McKeachie* (pp. 135–157). Hillsdale, NJ: Erlbaum.

Schutz, P. A. (2014). Inquiry on teachers' emotion. *Educational Psychologist, 49*(1), 1–12.

Schutz, P. A., & Zembylas, M. (Eds.). (2009). *Advances in teacher emotion research: The impact on teachers' lives*. New York, NY: Springer Publishing.

Schutz, P. A., Crowder, K. C., & White, V. E. (2001). The development of a goal to become a teacher. *Journal of Educational Psychology, 93*, 299–308.

Schutz, P. A., Cross, D. I., Hong, J. Y., & Osbon, J. N. (2007). Teacher identities, beliefs and goals related to emotions in the classroom. In P. A. Schutz & R. Pekrun (Eds.), *Emotion in education* (pp. 223–241). San Diego, CA: Elsevier Inc.

Schutz, P. A., Hong, J. Y., Cross, D. I., & Osbon, J. N. (2006). Reflections on investigating emotion in educational activity settings. *Educational Psychology Review, 18*(4), 343–360.

Smagorinsky, P., Cook, L. S., Moore, C., Jackson, A. Y., & Fry, P. G. (2004). Tensions in learning to teach: Accommodations and the development of a teaching identity. *Journal of Teacher Education, 55*(1), 8–24.

Stets, J. E., & Burke, P. J. (2014). The development of identity theory. In *Advances in group processes* (pp. 57–97). Bingley, UK: Emerald Group Publishing Limited.

Sutherland, L., Howard, S., & Markauskaite, L. (2010). Professional identity creation: Examining the development of beginning perservice teachers' understanding of their work as teachers. *Teaching and Teacher Education, 26*, 455–465.

Thorne, F. C. (1963). The clinical use of peak and nadir experience reports. *Journal of Clinical Psychology, 19*(2), 248–250.

Tripp, D. (1994). Teachers' lives, critical incidents, and professional practice. *Qualitative Studies in Education, 7*(1), 65–76.

Weiner, B. (1994). Integrating social and personal theories of achievement striving. *Review of Educational Research, 64*, 557–573.

Weiner, B. (2007). Examining emotional diversity in the classroom: An attribution theorist considers the moral emotions. In P. A. Schutz & R. Pekrun (Eds.), *Emotions in education* (pp. 75–88). San Diego, CA: Elsevier Inc.

Weiner, B. (2010). The development of an attribution-based theory of motivation: A history of ideas. *Educational Psychologist, 45*(1), 28–36.

William, P. R., & Wertsch, J. V. (1995). Vygotsky and identity formation: A sociocultural approach. *Educational Psychologist, 30*(2), 83–93.

Zembylas, M., & Chubbuck, S. (2015). The intersection of identity, beliefs, and politics to conceptualizing 'teacher identity. In H. Fives & M. Gill (Eds.), *International handbook of research on teachers' beliefs* (pp. 173–190). New York: Routledge.

Chapter 6
Professional Identity Matters: Agency, Emotions, and Resilience

Christopher Day

I will take as given that: (1) a core defining feature of teacher professionalism is a positive sense of professional identity; (2) identity is an amalgam of the personal and professional selves, and is represented through the dynamic interplay between efficacy, agency, emotions in the context of personal biographies, workplace structures and cultures, and policy influences; (3) teachers' professional identity is inherently unstable, subject to fluctuation. Its formation and management are not entirely rational processes; (4) preserving a strong, positive sense of professional identity requires on-going emotional as well as intellectual energy. Both a continuing sense of agency and emotional wellbeing are 'factors that have a bearing on the expression of identity and the shaping of it' (Beauchamp & Thomas, 2009 p. 180), and (5) whilst resilience is essential for these to be sustained, by itself it is an insufficient condition for building and sustaining a sense of a positive professional identity through which teachers remain committed and able to teach to their best and well. These three strands: (1) identity, efficacy, and agency, (2) identity and emotions; and (3) identity and resilience are often reported in isolation, separated by the different ontological, epistemological, and ideological positions of teacher educators, critical theorists, and school improvement researchers.

I argue in this chapter, that it is their collective influence that contributes to understandings of teacher identity in contexts of continuing reform. It is important not only to understand how professional identities influence/fluctuate positively or negatively among and between teachers in different phases of their lives, careers, and changing work contexts, but also what is required in managing, as distinct from coping with them. 'Coping' implies survival, whereas 'managing' implies being able to meet challenges in such a way that success is achieved i.e., the individual progresses beyond the use of coping strategies (Day & Hong, 2016). Taken together, the three strands provide powerful evidence of the complex construction of

C. Day (✉)
Faculty of Social Science, School of Education, University of Nottingham, Nottingham, UK
e-mail: christopher.day@nottingham.ac.uk

© Springer International Publishing AG, part of Springer Nature 2018
P. A. Schutz et al. (eds.), *Research on Teacher Identity*,
https://doi.org/10.1007/978-3-319-93836-3_6

'professional identity' itself, the dynamic interrelationships among its constituent parts. Their key influences upon teachers' professional identities point to the need for individual teachers, teacher educators, school principals, and policy makers who are concerned with recruiting and sustaining a high quality teaching force, to take each of these and the interaction among them into account in pre-service education and training, recruitment and selection, in-service programmes and school led support and challenge opportunities.

I will take a socio-cultural, life course perspective (Zittoun, 2012) in order to understand how identities are able to be managed in the contexts of personal, policy, and systemic changes and challenges and, within this, what are the workplace conditions that enhance or constrain their willingness, wellbeing, and capacities to teach to their best. As Etelapelto and her colleagues assert:

> ... if our aim is to understand how individual subjects renegotiate their work identities when they move from one working context to another, or when they navigate their pathways across workplace reforms, we need a developmental and life-course perspective (Vähäsantanen & Eteläpelto, 2011). In the absence of conceptual and analytical tools to address developmental perspectives, we leave subjects at the mercy of temporary and precarious working life conditions. Without such tools we cannot conceptualize how subjects re-negotiate their work identities in continuously changing professional contexts, or how they creatively transform their work practices, cultures, and discourses in their work organizations and communities... (Etelapelto et al., 2013: 61)

Identity, Efficacy, and Agency

> The key to grasping the dynamic possibilities of human agency is to view it as composed of variable and changing orientations within the flow of time (Emirbayer & Mische, 1998: 964).

Efficacy has been defined as: "Judgements about how well one can organise and execute courses of action required to deal with prospective situations that contain many ambiguous, unpredictable, and often stress, elements" (Bandura, 1982:122). Bandura has claimed that sustained effort and perseverance in the face of difficulty is likely to strengthen teachers' sense of efficacy and result in a stronger sense of agency and positive professional identiy; and that *personal efficacy* beliefs are capabilities or capacities, not a fixed state, but subject to social influence. This is important because, 'When faced with obstacles, setbacks, and failures, those who doubt their capabilities slacken their efforts, give up, or settle for mediocre solutions. Those who have a strong belief in their capabilities redouble their effort to master the challenges'(Bandura, 2000, p. 120). He emphasised, also, the power of *collective efficacy*, claiming, that:

> The strength of schools lies in teachers' sense of collective efficacy that they can solve their problems and improve their lives through collective effort...[and that]...Effective action for social change requires merging diverse self-interests in support of common goals... People who have a sense of collective efficacy will mobilise their efforts and resources to cope with external obstacles to the changes they seek. But those convinced of their inefficacy will cease trying even though changes are attainable through concerted effort (Bandura, 1982:143–4).

> There seems to be little doubt that collective efficacy beliefs are an important aspect of an organization's operative culture … Indeed, research … suggests that a strong sense of collective efficacy enhances teachers' self-efficacy beliefs while weak collective efficacy beliefs undermine teachers' sense of efficacy, and vice versa. This mutual influence relationship helps explain the consistent finding that perceived collective efficacy is a significant factor in the attainment of organizational goals. (Goddard et al., 2004, p. 10)

Teachers' individual and collective efficacy are closely associated with their individual and collective sense of agency (Eteläpelto, Vähäsantanen, Hökkä, & Paloniemi, 2013). Thus, any discussions of the nature of teacher identity must include a consideration of the extent to which individual teachers – and whole schools – may exercise efficacy and agency within changing economic, cultural, and social structures. (Hitlin & Elder, 2007).

The research community is divided over the extent to which teachers' professional identities are or are not determined by these changes. Eteläpelto et al. (2013) observe a divide between these 'critical theory' sociologists (e.g. Fuchs, 2001; Braverman, 1974) who see power as; (i) embedded in discourses as well as structures (McNay, 2003) that have 'a degrading effect on human work, with complete subjugation of agency for the individual worker' (Eteläpelto et al., 2013: 48) and (ii) the findings from mixed methods and qualitative empirical studies (e.g. Day, Sammons, & Stobart, 2007, 2011) that agency continues to be practised by individual teachers and schools, despite current political and social circumstances and ideologies (Apple, 2013; Giddens, 1984). In these schools, 'learning has further been seen not merely as the individuals' active construction and generation of knowledge, but also as social participation involving the construction of identities in socio-culturally determined knowledge communities' (Eteläpelto et al., 2013, p. 46).

> As actors move [in terms of their orientation] within and among these different unfolding contexts [i.e., the past, the future and the present], they switch between (or "recompose") their temporal orientations—as constructed within and by means of those contexts—and thus are capable of changing their relationship to structure. (Emirbayer & Mische, 1998: 964)

Whilst the power exerted by structures and discourses which inform these are undeniable influences, nevertheless, they need not *determine* how individuals feel or act. It is not that oppressive structures and discourses do not exist, and that these do not affect teacher professionalism and identity. Rather, it is not necessarily the case that their existence, by definition, must always result in negative effects on all teachers. There is a wide range of international research on improving, effective, and successful schools which demonstrates how teachers mediate, resist, and find productive room to manoeuvre, asserting their individual and collective sense of agency within a sense of positive identity.

> … in examining changes in agentic orientation, we can gain crucial analytical leverage for charting varying degrees of maneuverability, inventiveness, and reflective choice shown by social actors in relation to the constraining and enabling contexts of action. (Emirbayer & Mische, 1998: 964)

Whilst a sense of efficacy and agency are integral parts of teachers' professional identities, located in their past histories and present circumstances and actions as they engage in the daily uncertainties and vulnerabilities of teaching and learning, they will 'never be *completely* determined or structured' (Emirbayer & Mische, 1998:1004). They are part of an on-going, complex interactional dynamic between individual strength of (moral) purpose and the emotional dynamic of workplace and external social and policy environments. Their presence and expression are a reflection of teachers' identities, their projected views of themselves as professionals (their professionalism) and their future willingness and capacities to respond (positively or negatively) as they manage externally imposed changes in their work and working conditions, whether through their individual management of external reforms or surrogate, school – led responses to these.

Many qualitative studies direct attention to the influence of work contexts, and the ways in which the individual experiences, interactions with colleagues and students directly (as well as the demands from outside the school) play a key role in the ways they see themselves. In short, the culture of the school, defined as 'who we are and the way we do things around here' (Bower, 1966 cited in Morrison & Wilhelm, 2005), is an important mediating force in influencing teachers' capacities for efficacy and agency, and thus, their professional identities. The social (school) context is perceived by them to play an important role in supporting (or constraining) both; and it is suffused with emotion.

Identity and Emotion

Emotion, or the 'affective' dimension, is integral to the work of teachers and their teaching. It may be understood as a form of psychic energy... 'the strength of the investment people have in their experiences, practices, identities, meanings' (Grossberg, 1992, p. 82). Emotion 'determines or constitutes what matters to individuals' (Harding & Pribram, 2004: 873). Numerous studies have found that emotions play a key part in shaping professional identity (e.g. Schutz & Zembylas, 2009; van Veen & Sleegers, 2006). It is self-evident that being able to understand and manage their own and others' emotions is a key part of teachers' professional identity as they navigate the complex, sometimes conflictual, worlds of classroom and staffroom, learning and teaching, and external expectations and demands.

> Nowadays it seems obvious that emotions play an important role in the workplace. This can be true especially in the case of teachers whose role is not only to teach, but also to establish and maintain a learning-friendly environment. In practice, it may mean showing enthusiasm while conducting classes, reacting with empathy to pupils' worries and needs, hiding fatigue and annoyance or displaying positive emotions even when pupils are being difficult and rude. Teachers have to educate and, at the same time, manage their own emotions to meet the expectations associated with their profession.... In other words, they perform emotional labor. (Wróbel, 2013:581.)

Wrobel's claim that teaching is 'emotional labor' is based upon the work of Hochschild (1983). Her research, which was not conducted with teachers, identified 'emotional labor' as "the management of feeling to create a publicly observable facial and bodily display; emotional labor is sold for a wage and therefore has *exchange value"* (Hochschild, 1983; p.7). Sub-titled 'The commercialization of human feeling', she found that work in certain organisations requires the presentation of a particular emotional self on the part of the employees. When employees, for example flight stewards or bill collectors, must, as part of their work, empathise with customers and always exhibit positive emotions on a regular basis which they themselves do not feel, they are said to engage in 'emotional labor'. They do so, it has been claimed, by means of the use of 'surface' or 'deep' acting (Grandey & Gabriel, 2015). 'Surface' acting is defined as ' pretending, suppressing, and faking expressions' (op cit:326). It is associated with low levels of job satisfaction, emotional exhaustion, and burnout, and may create dissonance between expression and feelings both in and outside the workplace. Citing Chau, Dahling, Levy, and Diefendorff (2009) and Goodwin, Groth, and Frenkel (2011), Grandey and Gabriel (2015: 335) claim that there are associations between surface acting and 'the desire to withdraw from work and actual turnover'. In contrast, they claim that 'deep acting' attempts to bring moods and attitudes in line with emotional requirements' (Grandey & Gabriel, 2015: 335). It marks an internally accommodated shift in values, so that apparent congruence between teachers' own educational values and beliefs and the challenges of externally initiated changes that challenge and, in these cases, seek to replace previously held educational values, is achieved (Harding & Pribram, 2004). However, despite Harding and Prigram'a (2004) claim, that 'deep' acting may result in less emotional exhaustion and even lead to increased satisfaction, where this continues, it is likely to have longer term negative consequences on the passion, motivation, and energy with which they entered teaching. These essential parts of their professional identities may become diminished. Teaching may become less associated with 'care'. It may become 'just a job' (Day et al., 2007).

Teaching is not by definition emotional labour, but it is undoubtedly emotional work, because it requires teachers 'to invest their authentic selves in understanding others, to feel their feelings as part of their own'(England & Farkas, 1986:91), and in doing so to build and sustain authentic relations of care. To teach to their best and well requires that teachers are willing and able to draw upon continuing reserves of emotional energy on a daily basis (Furu, 2007; Hargreaves & Fullan, 1992; Pyhalto, Pietarinen, & Salmela-Aro, 2011). Moreover, teachers' work has a different and distinct set of conditions and characteristics from those that apply to the bill collectors and airline stewards in Hochschild's research. In business, 'customers' or 'clients' choose to visit; whereas in schools, students must attend by law. Whereas most other workers have relatively short and occasional interactions over limited periods of time with single or at most small groups of individuals, teachers must, perforce, engage in intense, sustained interactions with larger groups of students who do not necessarily choose to be in school and some of whom are likely to have special learning and behavior management needs. Moreover, because teacher-student interactions are sustained over at least 1 year and usually more, and because the teaching-learning relationship demands a level of trust between teacher and learner, both'surface' and 'deep' acting are unlikely to be possible on a continuing basis, since both involve levels of self-deception.

There will inevitably be occasions when teachers need to present a 'professional' face to their students, despite perhaps feeling exhausted, disenchanted, or unwell. At these times, they will likely be engaged in teaching as emotional labor. However, these periods are likely to be relatively short. Where they persist, they are likely to result in diminished commitment to work for the 'betterment' of their students (Fullan, 1992), and erosion of the ethics of care and moral purpose (Goodlad, 1992; Hansen, 1993). If emotional work is replaced by emotional labor, and results, for example, in authentic 'care' being replaced by inauthentic 'care', then it is likely that their credibility in the eyes of their students will diminished.

Whether *emotional work* becomes emotional labor, and whether teachers will necessarily engage in 'surface' or even 'deep' acting, then, depends on a number of mediating factors. The first is the internal strength of the individual teacher's moral purposes and commitment; the second is their capacity for resilience; the third is their 'academic optimism' (Hoy, Tarter, & Hoy, 2006). However, these may be more, or less strong, depending on the values, qualities, relationships and actions of school leadership, colleagues, and personal influences. School environments in which working conditions and cultures serve to suppress professional beliefs, values, and identities are likely to result in teaching as 'emotional labor,' rather than 'emotional work'. In a small scale study of the positive and negative effects of the emotional labour of caring in enacting teaching in an inclusive classroom, Isenbarger and Zembylas (2006) found that, whilst care was multi-faceted, mediated by the strength of teachers' vocation and moral purposes, caring relationships could also become, 'a source of emotional strain, anxiety, disappointment,' and have an impact on teachers' commitment, satisfaction and self-efficacy.

Teaching as Emotional Work

For teachers who strive to teach to their best, teaching is more than a series of cognitive, pedagogical, and content-based knowledge transactions. To teach well requires that teachers are able to draw upon continuing reserves of emotional energy on a daily basis (Furu, 2007; Hargreaves & Fullan, 1992; Pyhalto et al., 2011). The best teaching is emotional work which requires teachers to teach to their best and well, to sustain a capacity for *professional empathy*. I use the term 'professional empathy' in order to distinguish it from 'empathy'. Whereas the latter is usually defined as an ability or pre-disposition to understand and share the feelings of another (OECD, 2017), the former indicates that this is followed up by appropriate interventions by the teacher that provide enhanced learning opportunities for the student. Below is an extract from an interview with a secondary school principal that illustrates the importance of empathy in teaching, associating this with teacher effectiveness.

> Where I see teachers not doing well with children, there's often no empathy, and the ability to have empathy is massive in teaching. You have to be able to understand, have compassion for the children you are working with. Where I see teachers not working very

well, they don't really like young people, and I question why they are in teaching. Understanding and compassion are the first steps, before knowledge about how to teach. Young people are very adept at knowing whether you like them. It's very clear when you sit in a classroom whether the teacher has a presence and trust and they know you are there for them, and that you will do everything that you can to support them and get them qualifications.....Often people who haven't got that empathy and compassion can't understand that if you are behaving like this or not marking work, then students are going to misbehave, that's going to cause lack of progress, then students aren't going to achieve qualifications, can't get into College...I mean being a good, effective professional. You can be a professional but still be ineffective....with no empathy or compassion, if you haven't got moral purpose, you cannot be a good professional (Secondary School Headteacher)

It is important to acknowledge, as Zembylas (2003 p. 122) did, that how teachers experience emotions in different school, classroom, and staffroom settings is likely to 'expand or limit possibilities' in the opportunities to teach well. The consequences may be negative or positive. Thus, they may experience their job as 'emotional work' or 'emotional labour' and this may affect their willingness and ability to build (in their early years) and 'sustain' (as they progress through their careers) their self-efficacy, agency, commitment, and capacity for resilience (i.e. a positive sense of professional identity).

Identity and Resilience

It is clear, then, that there are associations between teachers' efficacy, agency, professional empathy and their willingness and ability to manage the emotional arenas of teaching. Yet managing their own and others' emotions demands considerable energy and requires that they have an on-going capacity for resilience. Resilience has been traditionally associated with 'bouncing back' from the trauma of adverse physical and psychologically threatening experiences, actions or events. However, this image has been challenged by Bronfenbrenner's (1979, 1995) socio-ecological perspective, and the later work of Ungar (2005, 2015). Research on resilient teachers and resilient schools (Day & Gu, 2014) also identified resilience as a capacity rather than a fixed trait. It found that this capacity fluctuated according to the willingness, commitment and ability of the individual to manage successfully a number of potentially conflicting forces of different magnitudes; and that they were helped or hindered in this partly by the strength of their inner commitment to teaching, often referred to as 'moral purpose' (Goodlad, 1992), and partly by the interactions within the workplace. According to these research-informed perspectives, then, teachers' capacity for resilience is associated both with individuals' internally driven strength of purpose and relationships within the workplace. Drawing on this, and the work of the anthropologist, Levi-Strauss (1962), Downes (2017) conceptualises resilience, not in terms of 'bouncing back', with the implication that the original 'shape' may be regained, but in terms of dynamic 'transition points in space' between individuals and their environments in which they are able to exercise 'spatial-relational agency' as they 'co-exist in mutual tension':

> Key goals of this spatial interrogation are twofold. Firstly, there is a need to identify struc-tural features of blockage in systems hindering resilience and to develop structural features of inclusive systems for fostering resilience in the face of adversity and vulnerability. Secondly, resilience rests on assumptions of agency, of the active experience of the indi-vidual in the face of causal influences by environmental and/or genetic factors… (Downes, 2017:100)

These researchers identify and problematize a number of influences which are in 'functional relation' with one or more continually competing for attention (Lévi-Strauss, 1973:73). The assumption is that, although the strength of competition between any single one or combinations of influences may vary at any given time, they nevertheless pose constant challenges to the nature and relative stability of teachers' sense of identity, and that identity itself is closely associated with teach-ers' sense of professionalism. Unless they are able to manage these, it is likely that teachers will struggle to form and sustain a positive, stable sense of identity. Moreover, to do so, they are likely to require a capacity for 'everyday resilience' (Day and Gu, 2014); and such capacity will need to be developed and sustained.

Conclusions

In this chapter I have argued that to succeed over time as professionals, teachers need to have and sustain a positive sense of professional identity. Key components of professional identity are individual and collective efficacy, agency, emotional management professional empathy, and a capacity for resilience. These do not exist independently of each other, but are in a dynamic relationship. They are influenced by individuals' inner strength of purpose but mediated by their workplace contexts and cultures and unanticipated personal experiences. It is important, therefore, that they are understood and managed. In the predominant systemic view of 'organisa-tional professionalism,' teachers' work and worth have become defined by the extent to which they succeed in implementing the overwhelmingly functionalist focuses of external policies to raise academic standards of student attainment. The risk is that, without active mediation, this may diminish teachers' broader sense of positive professional identity and, as we have seen, lead to frustration, disengage-ment, and alienation and erode teachers' willingness and ability to teach to their best and well.

References

Apple, M. W. (2013). *Education and power*. New York: Routledge.
Bandura, A. (1982). Self-efficacy mechanism in human agency. *American Psychologist, 37*(2), 122.

Bandura, A. (2000). Cultivate self-efficacy for personal and organizational effectiveness. *Handbook of Principles of Organization Behavior, 2*, 0011–0021.

Bower, M. (1966). *The will to manage*. New York: McGraw-Hill.

Braverman, H. (1974). *Labour and monopoly capital: The organisation of work in the twentieth century*. New York: Monthly Review Press.

Bronfenbrenner, U. (1979). *The ecology of human development*. Cambridge: Harvard University Press.

Bronfenbrenner, U. (1995). Developmental ecology through space and time: A future perspective. In P. Moen, G. Elder, K. Luscher, & U. Bronfenbrenner (Eds.), *Examining lives in context: Perspectives on the ecology of human development* (pp. 619–647). Washington, DC: American Psychological Association.

Beauchamp, C., & Thomas, L. (2009). Understanding teacher identity: An overview of issues in the literature and implications for teacher education. *Cambridge Journal of Education, 39*(2), 175–189.

Chau, S. L., Dahling, J. J., Levy, P. E., & Diefendorff, J. M. (2009). A predictive study of emotional labor and turnover. *Journal of Organizational Behavior, 30*(8), 1151–1163.

Day, C., & Gu, Q. (2014). *Resilient teachers, resilient schools: Building and sustaining quality in testing times*. New York: Routledge.

Day, C., & Hong, J. (2016). Influences on the capacities for emotional resilience of teachers in schools serving disadvantaged urban communities: Challenges of living on the edge. *Teaching and Teacher Education, 59*, 115–125.

Day, C., Sammons, P., & Stobart, G. (2007). *Teachers matter: Connecting work, lives and effectiveness*. London: McGraw-Hill Education.

Day, C., Sammons, P., Leithwood, K., Hopkins, D., Gu, G., Brown, E., & Ahtaridou, E. (2011). *Successful school leadership: Linking with learning*. Maidenhead, UK: Open University Press.

Downes, P. (2017). Reconceptualising foundational assumptions of resilience: A cross-cultural, spatial systems domain of relevance for agency and phenomenology in resilience. *International Journal of Emotional Education, 9*(1), 99–120.

Emirbayer, M., & Mische, A. (1998). What is agency? *American Journal of Sociology, 103*(4), 962–1023.

England, P., & Farkas, G. (1986). *Households, employment, and gender: A social, economic, and demographic view*. New York: Aldine.

Eteläpelto, A. Vähäsantanen, K., Hökkä, P. and Paloniemi, S. (2013, December). What is agency? Conceptualizing professional agency at work. *Educational Research Review, 10*, 45–65.

Fuchs, S. (2001). What makes sciences "Scientific?". In *Handbook of sociological theory* (pp. 21–35). New York: Kluwer Academic/Plenum Publishers.

Fullan, M. (1992). *Successful school improvement: The implementation perspective and beyond*. London: McGraw-Hill Education.

Furu, E. M. (2007). Emotional aspects of action learning. In E. M. Furu, T. Lund, & T. Tiller (Eds.), *Action research. A Nordic perspective* (pp. 185–202). Kristiansand, Norway: Høyskoleforlaget: Norwegian Academic Press.

Giddens, A. (1984). *The constitution of society: Outline of the theory of structuration*. Berkeley, CA: Univ of California Press.

Goddard, R., Hoy, W. K., & Woolfolk Hoy, A. (2004, April). Collective Efficacy Beliefs: Theoretical Developments, Empirical Evidence, and Future Directions. *Educational Researcher, 33*(3), 3–13.

Goodlad, J. I. (1992). The moral dimensions of schooling and teacher education. *Journal of Moral Education, 21*(2), 87–97.

Goodwin, R. E., Groth, M., & Frenkel, S. J. (2011). Relationships between emotional labor, job performance, and turnover. *Journal of Vocational Behavior, 79*(2), 538–548.

Grandey, A. A., & Gabriel, A. S. (2015). Emotional labor at a crossroads: Where do we go from here? *Annual Review of Organizational Psychology and Organizational Behavior, 2*(1), 323–349.

Grossberg, L. (1992). *Is there a fan in the house? The affective sensibility of fandom* (Vol. 59). London: Routledge.

Hansen, D. T. (1993). From role to person: The moral layeredness of classroom teaching. *American Educational Research Journal, 30*(4), 651–674.

Harding, J., & Pribram, E. D. (2004). Losing our cool? Following Williams and Grossberg on emotions. *Cultural Studies, 18*(6), 863–883.

Hargreaves, A., & Fullan, M. G. (1992). *Understanding teacher development.* New York: Teachers College Press.

Hitlin, S., & Elder, G. H. (2007). Time, self, and the curiously abstract concept of agency. *Sociological Theory, 25*(2), 170–191.

Hochschild, A. (1983). *The managed heart.* Berkeley: University of California Press.

Hoy, W. K., Tarter, C. J., & Hoy, A. W. (2006). Academic optimism of schools: A force for student achievement. *American Educational Research Journal., 43*(3), 425–446.

Isenbarger, L., & Zembylas, M. (2006). The emotional labour of caring in teaching. *Teaching and Teacher Education, 22*(1), 120–134.

Lévi-Strauss, C. (1962). *The savage mind.* London: Weidenfeld & Nicolson, 1966.

Lévi-Strauss, C. (1973). *Structural anthropology: Vol. 2* (M. Layton, 1977, Trans.). Allen Lane: Penguin Books.

McNay, L. (2003). Agency, anticipation and indeterminacy in feminist theory. *Feminist Theory, 4*(2), 139–148.

Morrison, A. D., & Wilhelm, W. J. (2005, February). *Culture, competence, and the corporation.* Available at SSRN: https://ssrn.com/abstract=700041 or https://doi.org/10.2139/ssrn.700041

OECD. (2017). *Global competency for an inclusive world.* Paris: OECD.

Pyhalto, K., Pietarinen, J., & Salmela-Aro, K. (2011). Teacher-working-environment fit as a framework for burnout experienced by Finnish teachers. *Teaching and Teacher Education, 27*(7), 1101–1110.

Schutz, P. A., & Zembylas, M. (Eds.). (2009). *Advances in teacher emotion research: The impact on teachers' lives.* New York: Springer.

Ungar, M. (Ed.). (2005). *Handbook for working with children & youth: Pathways to resilience across cultures and contexts.* Thousand Oaks, CA/London: Sage.

Ungar, M. (2015, July 1–4). *Diagnosing – Resilience across cultures and contexts: Seeing the positive in young people even when there are serious problems. Keynote presentation,* 5th ENSEC (The European ISSN 2073-7629 Network for Social and Emotional Competence) Conference, Social Emotional Learning and Culture, University of Lisbon.

Vähäsantanen, K., & Eteläpelto, A. (2011). Vocational teachers' pathways in the course of a curriculum reform. *Journal of Curriculum Studies, 43*(3), 291–312.

van Veen, K., & Sleegers, P. (2006). How does it feel? Teachers' emotions in a context of change. *Journal of Curriculum Studies, 38*(1), 85e111.

Wróbel, M. (2013). Can empathy lead to emotional exhaustion in teachers? The mediating role of emotional labor. *International Journal of Occupational Medicine and Environmental Health, 26*(4), 581–592.

Zembylas, M. (2003). Interrogating "teacher identity": Emotion, resistance, and self-formation. *Educational theory, 53*(1), 107–127.

Zittoun, T. (2012). Life-course: A socio-cultural perspective. In *Handbook of culture and psychology* (Vol. 60, No. 23, pp. 513–535). Oxford: Oxford University Press.

Chapter 7
Teacher Identity and Motivation: The Dynamic Systems Model of Role Identity

Avi Kaplan and Joanna K. Garner

Teacher identity is thought to relate to central aspects of teachers' professional lives: their conception of the teacher role, motivation for teaching, choice of teaching methods, willingness to change, and the trajectory of their professional learning and development (Beijaard, Meijer, & Verloop, 2004; Beauchamp & Thomas, 2009; Olsen, 2014). It is no wonder, then, that over the past two decades, scholars have found the concept of teacher identity attractive for research on pre-service and in-service teachers' motivation for entering the profession, learning to teach, adopting pedagogical practices, and coping with policy changes (Avraamidou, 2014; Izadinia, 2013; Lutovac & Kaasila, 2018; Sachs, 2005). Correspondingly, there is growing recognition that teacher education and professional development (PD) programs must address not only subject-matter content and pedagogy, but also the complex processes involved in teachers' professional identity that drive them to learn, develop, and sustain commitments to educational practice and to the profession (Horn, Nolen, Ward, & Campbell, 2008; Jenlink, 2014).

However, the contribution of the growing literature on teacher identity is hindered by the very diverse and often vague treatment of the teacher identity concept (Beijaard et al., 2004; Olsen, 2016). Alongside other recent advances in integrative perspectives on teacher identity (Beauchamp & Thomas, 2009; Cross & Hong, 2010; Henry, 2016; Olsen, 2008; Schutz, Cross, Hong, & Osbon, 2007), in this chapter, we present a model of teacher identity and motivation that synthesizes understandings across perspectives and holds potential to guide integrative

A. Kaplan (✉)
Department of Psychological Studies in Education, Temple University,
Philadelphia, PA, USA
e-mail: akaplan@temple.edu

J. K. Garner
Center for Educational Partnerships, Old Dominion University, Norfolk, VA, USA
e-mail: jkgarner@odu.edu

© Springer International Publishing AG, part of Springer Nature 2018   71
P. A. Schutz et al. (eds.), *Research on Teacher Identity*,
https://doi.org/10.1007/978-3-319-93836-3_7

theory-building, research, and design of educational and PD programs: The Dynamic Systems Model of Role Identity (DSMRI; Kaplan & Garner, 2017).

The Dynamic Systems Model of Role Identity

The Dynamic Systems Model of Role Identity (DSMRI) reflects the intuitive under-standing that a teacher acts in order to achieve goals on the basis of his or her beliefs about the situation and about him- or her-self as a teacher in that situation. In the DSMRI, these beliefs, goals, self-perceptions, and actions are conceptualized as continuously emerging and integrating to reflect who the person is and how he or she acts as a teacher—the teacher's role identity. The development of the DSMRI has been informed by social psychological and social-cultural conceptions of iden-tity (Burke & Stets, 2009; Holland, Lachicotte Jr., Skinner, & Caine, 1998) that define the primary unit-of-analysis of teacher identity as *the personal meaning of occupying the teacher role in a particular social-cultural situation.* In the DSMRI, this meaning is the manifestation of a complex dynamic system (Henry, 2016; Opfer & Pedder, 2011)—an ever emergent interconnected network of role-specific assumptions and beliefs, self-perceptions and self-definitions, values, goals, emo-tions, and actions that are held by the person to be central to who he or she is as a teacher in the situation (Kaplan & Garner, 2017).

One central dimension of the DSMRI is the extent to which the person considers being a teacher an important aspect of who he or she is. But, beyond the *level of commitment* to the teaching role, the DSMRI emphasizes three facets of the teacher identity: *content*, *structure*, and *process*. Two teachers may have similar levels of commitment to being a teacher, but hold quite different assumptions, goals, values, emotions, and perceptions about teaching (content), which may be more or less aligned with each other (structure), and that emerge through different processes (process). Differences in content, structure, and process would result in different interpretation of situations and response to events, consideration and enactment of instructional strategies, and trajectories of professional growth (Bullough, 1997; Horn et al., 2008).

Components of the Teacher Role Identity System

The DSMRI draws on Maehr's (1984) Personal Investment Theory to specify four contextually constructed, interdependent, and partially overlapping components of the teacher identity system: (1) ontological and epistemological beliefs relevant to teaching; (2) purpose and goals in teaching; (3) self-perceptions and self-definitions in teaching; and (4) perceived action possibilities in teaching. Each of these compo-nents involves teacher-related knowledge (e.g., knowledge about teaching and learning, knowledge about the context, knowledge about oneself, knowledge of possible instructional strategies) and emotion (e.g., emotions tied to certain assumptions about teaching and learning, teaching goals, teaching-related self-perceptions, and teaching-related strategies).

Ontological beliefs concern the knowledge and related emotion that the teacher constructs from formal learning and from personal and vicarious experiences and holds as true regarding teaching (Richardson, 1996). These beliefs may include knowledge, assumptions, and related emotions about how students learn, causal attributions about students' success and failure (Weiner, 2011), implicit and explicit beliefs about students' ability in different domains (Dweck, 1999), assumptions regarding the instructional strategies that would be effective in certain domains and for certain students (Cross & Hong, 2010), and also perceptions about the particular teaching context and people with who the teacher works. *Epistemological beliefs* concern the teacher's sense of certainty, complexity, and the credibility of sources of their ontological beliefs, and the emotions tied to this sense of knowledge (Hofer & Pintrich, 2004). For example, a pre-service teacher may perceive knowledge of classroom management to be complex, have little confidence in the credibility of his classroom management instructor, and feel highly frustrated about his knowledge in this area. In comparison, an experienced teacher may perceive her knowledge about classroom management to be complex and conditional, but also certain, and may feel satisfaction about the certainty and sophistication of her knowledge.

Purpose and goals refer to the teacher's knowledge and emotions about his or her personal purpose for teaching and the more concrete personal goals and objectives in teaching (Schutz et al., 2007). These purpose and goals can vary on dimensions such as intrinsic-extrinsic, personal-interpersonal-collective, proximal-distal, specific-global, self-oriented-other-oriented, and mastery-performance orientations, with consequences to motivation and emotions (Butler, 2007; Locke & Latham, 2002; Roth, 2014).

Self-perceptions and self-definitions concern the teacher's knowledge and emotions regarding his or her own personal and social attributes and characteristics that are relevant to teaching. Overall self-concept of ability in teaching, self-efficacy to pursue various teaching goals successfully, and the emotions tied to these perceptions are likely to be central to this component (Woolfolk Hoy, Hoy, & Davis, 2009). In addition, this component involves the teacher's self-perceived worldview and values, interests, personality attributes, physical characteristics, and other self-descriptors that he or she consider relevant for being a teacher in the context. Self-perceptions and self-definitions also involve the teacher's social group memberships that are salient in the teaching context, and the meanings and emotions associated with these social categorizations. Depending on the context, these may include membership in demographic collectives such as gender, ethnicity, and religion, but also formal and informal teaching-related social groups such as subject-matter certification, grade-level assignment, and seniority group in the school.

Finally, *perceived action possibilities* concern the teacher's perceptions and emotions regarding behaviors and strategies as available and unavailable for him or her to enact in the teaching role, particularly as they pertain to advancing achievement of teaching purpose and goals. Whereas two teachers may have ontological beliefs about certain instructional strategies, one may perceive them to be appropriate

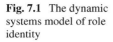

Fig. 7.1 The dynamic systems model of role identity

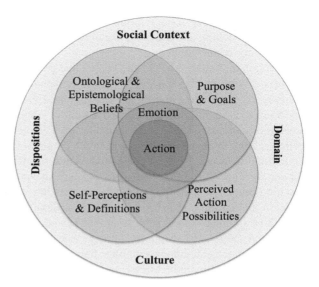

for her to apply in her teaching context while another may perceive them as inappropriate, ineffective, or impossible for him to practice in light of incompatible ontological beliefs about the context or the students, self-perceptions, or goals. This component includes declarative knowledge and behavioral intentions (Fishbein & Ajzen, 2011) regarding instructional strategies and classroom management strategies and their regulation, but also other actions in the teaching role such as regarding interactions with colleagues, superiors, parents, and mentees.

The visual representation of the DSMRI in Fig. 7.1 reflects the central location of action as the "anchor" of the teacher role identity system. It also reflects the reciprocal interrelations and partial overlap among the four role identity components. The interdependence of the components conveys the complex dynamic systems assumption that understanding teacher identity and action cannot be reduced to one component, but needs to be considered together across system components. Furthermore, the continuous emergence of the teacher role identity is mediated by social interactions that are framed by the socio-cultural context, subject domain (e.g., science, humanities), as well as the teacher's implicit dispositions (e.g., temperament, unconscious motives, conditioned emotions).

Content, Structure, and Process in the Teacher Role Identity System

The DSMRI highlights three facets of the teacher role identity system that vary within a teacher across contexts and time, as well as characterize different teachers: content, structure, and process of formation. The *content* of the teacher's identity concerns the person's teaching-related ontological and epistemological beliefs, purpose and goals, self-perceptions and self-definitions, and perceived action possibilities and their associated emotions. Each component in the DSMRI harbors multiple constructs and dimensions. Variation in this content can refer to difference or change in amount, kind, and complexity of knowledge and beliefs, goals, self-perceptions, action possibilities, and emotions. Variability in content can also refer to difference or change in salience of constructs. Both the content and its salience may change within the same teacher's identity across time and situations (e.g., decrease in salience of perceived self-efficacy and increase in salience of perceived personal interest), and be different between teachers.

The *structure* of the teacher identity system concerns the level of harmony between elements within the system's components, the extent of alignment between the four components, and the degree of integration between the teacher role identity and other central role identities of the person, and the emotions associated with these structural features. *Within* components, for example, a teacher's multiple goals for students and for the self may be in harmony, or be in tension and elicit negative emotions and dilemmas about actions. *Between* components, high alignment in the teacher role identity system would manifest in sense of coherence in the role, and commonly with positive feelings of satisfaction. Teachers with an aligned role identity would engage in actions that they perceive as available, appropriate, and effective for them to enact in the pursuit of their purpose and goals in light of their beliefs about the situation and about themselves within that situation. In comparison, misalignment between components is likely to manifest in tensions and negative emotions. *Across* role identities (e.g., teacher and parent), integration would be experienced as overall personal coherence and positive emotions, and tensions would be experienced as a personal dilemma or even an internal conflict (e.g., when goals of being successful as a teacher and as a parent are perceived to be strongly competing).

The *process* facet of the DSMRI reflects the assumptions of a complex dynamic system approach regarding system change, and depicts teacher role identity as continuously emerging in non-linear and non-deterministic ways that are highly sensitive to the system's history, characteristics, and context. Processes of teacher identity formation can involve change in content of the role identity components, change in the nature of the structural interrelations within and across components, and change in the relations of the teacher role identity with other central role identities. These processes can vary along time in breadth (number and type of elements within components), depth (magnitude of deliberation within components), affective intensity, and psychological mechanism of the identity construction process (e.g., personal exploration, norm-oriented construction, avoidance of identity issues; Berzonsky, 2011).

The process of teacher role identity formation occurs within a cultural landscape of prevalent configurations of relatively aligned teaching-related beliefs, goals, self-perceptions, and perceived action possibilities (e.g., a teacher-centered configuration, a student-centered configuration). A teacher role identity that reflects a coherent cultural configuration is more likely to manifest stability—a system state that is called an attractor (Koopmans & Stamovlasis, 2016). These cultural configurations provide positive and negative guides for the teacher's role identity formation, with the activation of one component in a configuration triggering the others and promoting change towards that configuration or attractor. From this perspective, differences in teacher role identity and its formation across socio-cultural contexts reflect, to a large degree, the relative prevalence of different attractors in the cultural landscape (Zusho & Clayton, 2011). But, in addition to the role of cultural configurations as framing the teacher role identity formation, teachers can also assume agency in initiating and guiding identity construction (Flum & Kaplan, 2006). Particularly following events that trigger tensions within the system (e.g., contextual change, personal transitions, PD programs), identity formation may involve the teacher in active and volitional exploration of teaching-related beliefs, goals, self-perceptions and definitions, perceived action possibilities and their relations. These processes may be cognitively and emotionally intense or be conducted in a more cursory or superficial manner, and they may employ different exploratory and construction strategies (e.g., personal reflection through writing or meditation, social conversations, or experimentation).

These features of the DSMRI can capture different patterns of teachers' identity, motivation, and learning. For example, in PD programs that aim to promote adoption of new student-centered pedagogical practices, the DSMRI would guide definition of teachers' learning and motivation as developing knowledge about the student-centered practices, and trying to align them with their ontological and epistemological beliefs, purpose and goals, and self-perceptions and self-definitions in a way that renders these practices viable action possibilities. Teachers would be more likely to perceive newly learned student-centered strategies as action possibilities and enact them in their classroom practice when these practices align with already existing student-centered elements in the teacher identity (e.g., student-centered ontological beliefs, student-centtered purpose and goals). In comparison, participating teachers with an aligned teacher-centered role identity system are likely to experience tension with newly learned student-centered practices. Such teachers would be less likely to readily align the new practices with their existing identity content and to perceive them as action possibilities; and, hence, they would be less motivated to learn about them and enact them in their classroom. PD experiences that perturb the teacher identity system and trigger structural identity tensions could lead to re-evaluation of existing teacher-centered content, and scaffold consideration of alternative, student-centered content and its alignment. Such system perturbation would be needed for promoting change in initially teacher-centered particiapnts's motivation to learn and enact new student-centered practices.

One feature of the DSMRI that is important especially for conceptualizing teacher identity formation in teacher education and PD is the temporal dimension of the identity system. In addition to the role identities that the person presently occupies, the identity system includes role identities for past roles that are no longer occupied, and role identities for future-imagined roles (Markus & Nurius, 1986). Past role identities provide content and structural bases for the construction of present and future-imagined role identities. Future-imagined role identities constitute a central feature in professional training; for example, when pre-service teachers who are occupying a current "Student-Teacher" role identity are tasked with constructing a future-imagined "Teacher" role identity (Nolen et al., 2011). The inherent task of professional training is to encourage participants to transfer from experiences in current training role identities (e.g., "Student-Teacher," "PD Participant) to future role identities (e.g., "Teacher").

Our Use of the DSMRI Framework in Research on Teacher Identity

In the past several years, we and our colleagues have used the DSMRI to investigate the content, structure, and process of teacher identity among individuals or groups of teachers of different characteristics and in different contexts. For example, Gunersel, Kaplan, Barnett, Etienne & Ponnock (2016) used the DSMRI for investigating the change in the emerging teacher role identities of graduate student instructors who went through a semester-long Teaching in Higher Education certificate program. As part of the program, participants wrote a teaching philosophy statement at the beginning of the semester and revised it at the end of the semester. The philosophy statement assignment asked participants to describe who they are as teachers, what they believe, value, aim for, and do when teaching. The researchers used aspects of the DSMRI framework to code and characterize the content and structure of the teacher role identity at each time point, and its change when comparing the pre- and post-certificate philosophy statements. Table 7.1 presents a truncated example of a teaching philosophy statement of a chemistry instructor coded for the DSMRI role identity components.

Gunersel et al. (2016) identified different types of change in the different DSMRI components of participants' teacher role identity, including dramatic change, moderate change, no change, and even some cases of reversal (e.g., removing content) in quan-

Table 7.1 Truncated example of teaching philosophy coded according to DSMRI components

Text	Code
"The most effective teachers are those that are able to impart not only knowledge about their own subject to their students, but also some exemplary trait such as diligence or enthusiasm.	Ontological beliefs
I became an instructor because I have passion for my area of expertise and for steering students through their educational development.	Self-perceptions
The chief goals for all my courses incorporate students grasping the foundational aspects of the respective coursework and becoming passionate about chemistry.	Goals
My general strategies to accomplish this	Action possibilities
include: first, creating an atmosphere that fosters learning; second, challenging the students through hard work; and third, being a mentor to students in and out of class."	Alignment goals-action possibilities

tity and type of beliefs, goals, self-perceptions, and action possibilities when comparing philosophy statements at the beginning and at the end of the program. The analysis also pointed to three different overall types of teacher identity change in content and structure, which the authors labeled "transformation," "elaboration," and "stagnation," which could be considered to reflect different movements between the teacher-centered and student-centered cultural configurations or attractors. These different types of cange also manifested the sensitivity of the role identity change to the participant's initial identity system and the contextual features of the certificate program.

Researchers have used the DSMRI framework to analyze other kinds of qualitative data such as open-ended longitudinal interviews, longitudinal diaries and reflective journals, and conversation transcripts in order to understand teacher identity change of participants in PD programs (Hathcock, Garner, & Kaplan, 2014), teacher mentors (St. Pierre & D'Antonio, 2016), and teachers during the first year of teaching (Vedder-Weiss, Biran, Kaplan, & Garner, in-Press). For example, in a case study of a veteran science teacher who participated in a PD summer institute about inquiry instructional strategies (Garner & Kaplan, 2017), we used the DSMRI framework to analyze the teacher's pre-PD, mid-PD, and post-PD open-ended interviews. The analysis began by identifying the participant's salient role identities, coding each role identity's content, structure, and process of formation, and characterizing the overall identity system of the participant in each interview. Then, the analysis focused on changes in the participant's identity as reflected both in comparing the analyses of the three interviews and in the participant's own reflective statements about such change.

The analysis of the pre-PD interview depicted a role identity of an experienced teacher with a very strong commitment to teaching (perceiving teaching as his "destiny"). The teacher formed his teacher role identity on the basis of past role identities—those of a passionate and curious child interested in figuring out how mechanical objects work, and a high school student and college student for who physics did not come easy, but who persevered through hard work and persistence. The content of these past role identities were incorporated into the teacher role identity. It manifested in ontological beliefs that physics is all around in everyday life and that every student can learn it if they persist, goals of promoting students' meaningful understanding of physics, self-perceptions as a teacher who continues to learn by investing time and effort, and in tensions between ontological beliefs about student learning and the curriculum and actions imposed by the district. This tension manifested in frustration but also in very limited flexibility in perceived instructional action possibilities. Table 7.2 presents examples of the teacher's statements that were coded according to the DSMRI components.

The analysis of the two later interviews highlighted the role of the PD context and social interactions with the PD facilitators and peers in the teacher's role identity processes. The PD context triggered an initial salience of the PD-participant (rather than science teacher) role identity. This was followed by triggered reflection on and reconsideration of ontological beliefs regarding students' experiences and the role of students' background knowledge. This in turn prompted generating and considering new action possibilities of pedagogical activities and pre-assessments.

Table 7.2 Examples of teacher statements from interviews and their DSMRI codes

	Example statement	DSMRI code
Pre-PD interview	*"I believe anybody can learn anything if they want to, if they're interested and they stick with it…"*	Ontological beliefs
	"Physics fascinates me…sometimes I'll see things and I'll think, 'Wow, that's cool'…"	Self-perceptions (emotion: fascination)
	"I just want my kids to be prepared for the next step, no matter what direction it's in…"	Purpose
	"I've tried to work with my students. Every year I throw out this invitation 'does anybody want to do research?'… but nobody takes it…"	Action possibilities (emotion: frustration)
Mid-PD interview	*"The first two days, I wasn't thinking about me as a teacher at all. I wasn't even thinking about how it related to the classroom…"*	PD-participant role identity salience
	"When we would go out in the field, and [Facilitator] would ask us questions and…I just, I did not know how to answer them because, you know, I just don't know anything about Geology…I don't see the big picture the way they do…"	Context (interdisciplinary field inquiry); social interaction (facilitator); self-perceptions
	"And, um, while all this was going on, I'm asking myself, how often does this happen to my students?…"	Integration (transfer) between PD-participant and teacher role identities
	"How often is it that I may give them a data table and it does not work for them because it's not their data table?… I need to let them do it all from the ground up, maybe."	Epistemological beliefs (uncertainty); action Possibiliites (reconsidered and new)
Post-PD interview	*"…it's kind of like my attitude was, 'OK you're a clean slate'… [But, I realized that] they need to build on what experiences they have… using their experiences, background knowledge…"*	Ontological beliefs (change)
	"I'm asking myself, what kind of preassessments do I want to do?"	Epistemological beliefs (uncertainty); action possibilities (reconsidered)
	"I think my pre-assessments need to be real world questions. I think, you know, describe, or try to explain what's happening here, and see how they respond to those types of questions…I haven't normally thought that way"	Ontological beliefs (change); action possibilities (new); epistemological beliefs (uncertainty); alignment of new action possibilities with new ontological beliefs

These new action possibilities were aligned with the changes to the ontological beliefs, but reflected epistemological uncertainty. Similar to other findings, the analysis pointed to the sensitivity of the teacher's role identity change to its initial configuration, as well as to the role of the social-cultural context within which the teacher role identity was emerging.

Conclusion

Teacher identity scholars grapple with reconciling apparent dichotomies in conceptualizing teacher identity. Teachers are, simultaneously, "sociocultural products shaped by history, formal learning and social practice; and…phenomenological agents, constructing themselves inside the daily work of teacher preparation and classroom teaching" (Olsen, 2014, p. 79). The DSMRI framework allows us to integrate seemingly diverging characteristics of teacher identity in a single coherent conceptual framework that is congruent with a dynamic systems perspectives on identity, teacher identity, and teacher learning (Henry, 2016; Opfer & Pedder, 2011). It provides a conceptual tool that can guide investigating teacher identity and its change as contextualized and dynamic phenomena while employing concepts that afford comparison and integration of understandings across contexts and groups of teachers. It also presents an established epistemological foundation for interventions in teacher education and teacher professional development that are dynamic, participant-centered, and poised to embrace formative evaluation.

References

Avraamidou, L. (2014). Studying science teacher identity: Current insights and future research directions. *Studies in Science Education*. https://doi.org/10.1080/03057267.2014.937171

Beauchamp, C., & Thomas, L. (2009). Understanding teacher identity: An overview of issues in the literature and implications for teacher education. *Cambridge Journal of Education, 39*(2), 175–189.

Beijaard, D., Meijer, P. C., & Verloop, N. (2004). Reconsidering research on teachers' professional identity. *Teaching and Teacher Education, 20*, 107–128.

Berzonsky, M. D. (2011). A social-cognitive perspective on identity construction. In S. J. Schwartz, K. Luyckx, & V. L. Vignoles (Eds.), *Handbook of identity theory and research* (pp. 55–76). New York: Springer.

Bullough, R. V. (1997). Practicing theory and theorizing practice. In J. Loughran & T. Russell (Eds.), *Purpose, passion and pedagogy in teacher education* (pp. 13–31). London: Falmer Press.

Burke, P. J., & Stets, J. E. (2009). *Identity theory*. Oxford, UK: Oxford University Press.

Butler, R. (2007). Teachers' achievement goal orientations and associations with teachers' help seeking: Examination of a novel approach to teacher motivation. *Journal of Educational Psychology, 99*(2), 241.

Cross, D. I., & Hong, J. Y. (2010). Beliefs and professional identity: Critical constructs in examining the impact of reform on the emotional experiences of teachers. In P. A. Schutz & M. Zembylas (Eds.), *Advances in teacher emotion research: The impact on teachers' lives* (pp. 273–296). New York: Springer.

Dweck, C. S. (1999). *Self-theories: Their role in motivation, personality, and development*. Philadelphia: Psychology Press.

Fishbein, M., & Ajzen, I. (2011). *Predicting and changing behavior: The reasoned action approach*. Taylor & Francis.

Flum, H., & Kaplan, A. (2006). Exploratory orientation as an educational goal. *Educational Psychologist, 41*, 99–110.

Garner, J. K., & Kaplan, A. (2017). *A complex dynamic systems perspective on teacher learning and identity formation: A case study.* Manuscript submitted for publication.

Gunersel, A. B., Kaplan, A., Barnett, P., Etienne, M., & Ponnock, A. R. (2016). Profiles of change in motivation for teaching in higher education at an American research university. *Teaching in Higher Education, 21*(6), 628–643.

Hathcock, S. J., Garner, J. K., Kaplan, A., (2014, January). *Using professional identity to examine impacts of professional development.* Paper presented at Association of Science Teacher Education (ASTE) International Conference, San Antonio, TX, USA.

Henry, A. (2016). Conceptualizing teacher identity as a complex dynamic system: The inner dynamics of transformations during a practicum. *Journal of Teacher Education, 67*(4), 291–305.

Hofer, B. K., & Pintrich, P. R. (2004). *Personal epistemology: The psychology of beliefs about knowledge and knowing.* Mahwah, NJ: Erlbaum.

Holland, D., Lachicotte Jr., W., Skinner, D., & Caine, C. (1998). *Identity and agency in cultural worlds.* Cambridge, MA: Harvard University Press.

Horn, I. S., Nolen, S. B., Ward, C., & Campbell, S. S. (2008). Developing practices in multiple worlds: The role of identity in learning to teach. *Teacher Education Quarterly, 35*(3), 61–72.

Izadinia, M. (2013). A review of research on student teachers' professional identity. *British Educational Research Journal, 39*(4), 694–713.

Jenlink, P. M. (2014). *Teacher identity and the struggle for recognition: Meeting the challenges of a diverse society.* Lanham, MD: Rowman & Litlefield Education.

Kaplan, A., & Garner, J. K. (2017). A complex dynamic systems perspective on identity and its development: The dynamic systems model of role identity. *Developmental Psychology, 53*(11), 2036–2051.

Koopmans, M., & Stamovlasis, D. (Eds.). (2016). *Complex dynamical systems in education: Concepts, methods and applications.* New York: Springer.

Locke, E. A., & Latham, G. P. (2002). Building a practically useful theory of goal setting and task motivation: A 35-year odyssey. *American Psychologist, 57*(9), 705.

Lutovac, S., & Kaasila, R. (2018). Future directions in research on mathematics-related teacher identity. *International Journal of Science and Mathematics Education, 16*(4), 759–776.

Maehr, M. L. (1984). Meaning and motivation: Toward a theory of personal investment. In C. Ames & R. Ames (Eds.), *Research on motivation in education: The classroom milieu* (Vol. 1, pp. 115–144). Cambridge, MA: Academic Press.

Markus, H., & Nurius, P. (1986). Possible selves. *American Psychologist, 41*, 954–969.

Nolen, S. B., Horn, I. S., Ward, C. J., & Childers, S. A. (2011). Novice teacher learning and motivation across contexts: Assessment tools as boundary objects. *Cognition and Instruction, 29*, 88–122.

Olsen, B. (2008). Introducing teacher identity and this volume. *Teacher Education Quarterly, 35*(3), 3–6.

Olsen, B. (2014). Learning from experience: A teacher-identity perspective. In V. Ellis & J. Orchard (Eds.), *Learning teaching from experience: Multiple perspectives and international contexts* (pp. 79–94). London: Bloomsbury.

Olsen, B. (2016, April). Discussion in a symposium titled *The Value of teacher identity as a conceptual tool for understanding teacher development and educational equity*, presented at the annual meeting of the American Educational Research Association, Washington, DC.

Opfer, V. D., & Pedder, D. (2011). Conceptualizing teacher professional learning. *Review of Educational Research, 81*(3), 376–407.

Richardson, V. (1996). The role of attitudes and beliefs in learning to teach. In J. Sikula, T. J. Buttery, & E. Guyton (Eds.), *Handbook of research on teacher education.* New York: Simon & Schuster Macmillan.

Roth, G. (2014). Antecedents and outcomes of teachers' autonomous motivation: A self-determination theory perspective. In P. W. Richardson, S. Karabenick, & H. M. G. Watt (Eds.), *Teacher motivation: Theory and practice* (pp. 36–51). New York: Routledge.

Sachs, J. (2005). Teacher education and the development of professional identity: Learning to be a teacher. In P. Denicolo & M. Kompf (Eds.), *Connecting policy and practice: Challenges for teaching and learning in schools and universities* (pp. 5–21). Oxford, UK: Routledge.

Schutz, P. A., Cross, D. I., Hong, J. Y., & Osbon, J. N. (2007). Teacher identities, beliefs, and goals related to emotions in the classroom. In P. A. Schutz & R. Pekrun (Eds.), *Emotion in education* (pp. 223–241). San Diego, CA: Elsevier.

St. Pierre, M., & D'Antonio, M. (2016, April). Professional identity of science faculty serving as mentors in teacher professional development: An interview study. *Poster presented at the annual convention of the American Educational Research Association*, Washington, DC.

Vedder-Weiss, D., Biran, L., Kaplan, A., & Garner, J. K. (in press). Reflexive inquiry as a scaffold for teacher identity exploration during the first year of teaching. In E. Lyle (Ed.), *The negotiated self: Employing reflexive inquiry to explore teacher identity*. Rotterdam, The Netherlands: Sense Publishers.

Weiner, B. (2011). An attribution theory of motivation. In P. A. M. Van Lange, A. W. Kruglanski, & E. T. Higgins (Eds.), *Handbook of theories of social psychology* (pp. 135–155). Thousand Oaks: Sage.

Woolfolk Hoy, A., Hoy, W. K., & Davis, H. (2009). Teachers' self-efficacy beliefs. In K. Wentzel & A. Wigfield (Eds.), *Handbook of motivation in school* (pp. 627–654). Mahwah, NJ: Lawrence Erlbaum.

Zusho, A., & Clayton, K. (2011). Culturalizing achievement goal theory and research. *Educational Psychologist, 46*, 239–260.

Part III
Teacher Identity Development in Various Learning Contexts

Chapter 8
Engaging Teacher Identities in Teacher Education: Shifting Notions of the "Good Teacher" to Broaden Teachers' Learning

Grace A. Chen, Ilana S. Horn, and Susan Bobbitt Nolen

What precisely is the connection between *who* teachers are and *how* they think about their work? Teachers' personal histories, school experiences, and social identities significantly shape their pedagogical decisions, yet the processes by which teacher identities influence practice have been undertheorized. In this chapter, we explore how teachers' identities affect their choices. First, we consider how teachers' identities motivate what they want to learn. Then, we describe a pedagogy for expanding teachers' identity-rooted motivations that engages who they see themselves becoming.

Conceptions of Teacher Identity and Learning to Teach

Scholars have examined identity as beliefs (Spillane, 2000), stories people tell themselves (Sfard & Prusak, 2005), determined by social group membership (Wenger, 1998), and through numerous other lenses. In this chapter, we take a sociocultural approach that acknowledges teachers' *narrative identities*, or the characteristics ascribed to them, their *positional identities*, or their relative status in the context of other people, and their *agency* in navigating these identities (Holland et al., 1998). Narrative identity includes the stories told about a group of presumably similar people. A refugee mother, for example, might be seen as unfamiliar with local United States customs, valuing family strongly, not fluent in English, or a hard worker. Positional identity, on the other hand, foregrounds a person's power and

G. A. Chen (✉) · I. S. Horn
Department of Teaching and Learning, Vanderbilt University, Nashville, TN, USA
e-mail: grace.a.chen@vanderbilt.edu; ilana.horn@vanderbilt.edu

S. B. Nolen
Learning Sciences & Human Development, University of Washington, Seattle, WA, USA
e-mail: sunolen@uw.edu

© Springer International Publishing AG, part of Springer Nature 2018   85
P. A. Schutz et al. (eds.), *Research on Teacher Identity*,
https://doi.org/10.1007/978-3-319-93836-3_8

status relative to other people in a social world. As a woman, this refugee mother may be perceived to be "lesser than" a man; as a refugee, she may be considered "lesser than" native-born citizens; as a mother, she may be viewed as having power over her child. This refugee mother may adopt, reject, or redefine these possible identities as she interacts with others around her.

Drawing on related theories, Battey and Franke (2008) suggest that teaching is participation in a practice that forms and re-forms teachers' identities as they take up (or not) opportunities to enact particular ways of being in the world. In other words, teachers' previous experiences navigating multiple identities shape how they engage in the work of teaching. Indeed, the influence of teachers' histories-in-action on their practice has been well-documented. Lortie's (1975) classic work documents the far-reaching impact of teachers' "apprenticeship[s] of observation," which lead them to re-enact what they experienced as students. Lawrence-Lightfoot (2003) extends this idea by discussing "ghosts in the classroom," where both teachers and parents repeat what "made them feel strong and worthy, or they want to do exactly the opposite" (p. 22).

Identity in Practice: A Focus on Parent-Teacher Relationships

Like Lawrence-Lightfoot, we explore the connection between teachers' identity and practice by rooting our theory-building in parent-teacher relationships.[1] Teacher education programs seldom explicitly prepare pre-service teachers (PSTs) for parent-teacher relationships; most programs recognize that parent-teacher relationships matter, but offer few experiences designed to support PSTs' related learning (Epstein & Sanders, 2006). Since teachers are largely unguided in communicating with students' families, their relationship-building practices become fertile ground for exploring the influence of PSTs' identities and prior experiences. Second, parent-teacher relationships are a common site for the reproduction of stereotypes and deficit assumptions that lead to the inequitable treatment of parents from non-dominant communities; this is especially likely when teachers' backgrounds greatly differ from that of their students' parents (Baquedano-López, Alexander, & Hernandez, 2013; Ishimaru, 2014).

The remainder of the chapter is organized as follows. First, we introduce motivational filters and their relationship to narrative identity. To do so, we examine how PSTs' conceptualizations of parent-teacher relationships shape their motivational filters in interactions with an actor playing a Kurdish refugee mother, and in their subsequent reflections on that interaction. Next, we consider how simulation cycles foreground the positional identities of the teacher and actor, drawing attention to the relationship between two people. Then, we turn to how motivational filters and

---

[1] We recognize that children's primary caregivers are not always their parents. We use the term "parent-teacher relationships" for continuity with existing literature, and because the focal caregiver in our data is a parent.

simulation cycles together can help us understand teacher learning as conceptual change rooted in teacher identity. Finally, we conclude by discussing implications of this theoretical perspective for broader conversations about equity, power, and education.

Motivational Filters

PSTs are unlikely to take up every practice, strategy, or theory they are exposed to during their teacher education programs and field experiences; in fact, their sense-making around learning opportunities varies considerably. After a multi-year case-based ethnography of beginning teachers, Nolen et al. (2009) argued that, rather than indicating varying competence or general motivation, these differences in teachers' learning reflect, in part, differences in motivational filters. The researchers collected extensive data from eight focal teachers, including numerous observations and interviews during teacher education coursework, student teaching, and the first year of professional teaching. They then used interpretive methods and discourse analysis to understand what teachers were seeking to learn and why.

The focal teachers reported actively making decisions about which practices to take up. Nolen and colleagues referred to these agentic decisions as *motivational filters*. These filters reflect teachers' perceptions of how *useful* the practices seemed (*utility filters*), how *feasible* the practices seemed (*feasibility filters*), and how trusted the promoter of a particular practice was as a conveyer of good teaching (*relational filters*). For instance, a teacher may minimally engage in an assignment on rubric construction because "teachers would never do this much work in the real world." This teacher's conclusion relies on her conception of what it takes to construct a rubric, as well as her perception of the utility and feasibility of this practice in school contexts. Together, these filters shape a teacher's engagement in and, ultimately, her learning of teaching practices around rubric development and use. If her ideas about the utility and feasibility of rubrics shift, however, her filters may evolve as well. Thus, motivational filters serve as agentic tools that help teachers decide what to learn as they negotiate who they are becoming as teachers.

Teachers' invocation of motivational filters frequently entails ideas about "good teaching" that are rooted in teachers' notions of students, of the conditions of teaching, and their own sense of teacher identity. These ideas are formed by teachers' personal and professional histories-in-action, and may or may not align to others' conceptions of "good teaching." For example, a teacher accustomed to the intense rivalries and public evaluation of being an athlete might believe that a "good teacher" is one who cultivates competitive classroom environments, whereas a teacher who thrives under conditions of anonymity and groupwork might define "good teaching" very differently. "Good teaching," therefore, connects strongly with teachers' narrative identities, and shapes the teaching practices they find useful or feasible and worth learning.

If teachers are guided by a narrative identity of "good teachers" as people who participate in parent-teacher conferences by reporting student progress, eliciting parent reactions, sharing responsibility with parents to achieve mutual goals, and earning parental approval, then teachers will be motivated to learn these practices. This particular set of parent-teacher conference practices represents what many teachers describe as "good teaching," yet it also assumes that parents are eager to participate exactly as teachers believe they ought. Furthermore, it reflects a limited view of what parent-teacher relationships often are and what they could be, constrained by the White, middle-class conceptions of schooling and parenting that are most familiar to the majority of U.S. teachers (Lareau, 2011). Strong parent-teacher relationships, however, require teachers to account for the particularities of students, parents, and contexts rather than adhering to idealized views. This need to develop nonideal reasoning (Jaggar, 2015) becomes evident in a simulation cycle.

Simulation Cycles

Self (2016) designed simulation cycles to support PSTs' understanding of culturally responsive teaching practices. A simulation cycle (see Fig. 8.1) typically unfolds over 1–2 weeks within a university course. First, PSTs read a scenario and write a "pre-reading" reflection about the interaction they anticipate based on the scenario. During the simulation interaction, which is video- and audio-recorded, they engage with an actor portraying a student, parent, or colleague. The actor has been trained to follow a protocol that includes body language, verbal triggers, and information to share or withhold, so that PSTs have an experience that is consistent without being robotic. Immediately afterwards, PSTs independently video-record reflections using an iPad. Later, they submit a written "re-reading" reflection, responding to questions that the instructor designs after watching PSTs' actor interactions and immediate debrief videos. Finally, the instructor facilitates a video-recorded whole-group debrief during the next class session.

Here, we draw on data from a larger study located in a selective secondary licensure program located in a mid-Southern U.S. city where many resettled refugees enroll children in the public school district. In our focal simulation cycle, 24 PSTs met with an actor portraying Maryam, a Kurdish refugee, to discuss her 12-year old

Fig. 8.1 The simulation cycle

son Aran's struggles with reading. Horn, Self, and Chen (2016) collected a variety of data, including fieldnotes from the simulation cycle, PSTs' written assignments including reflections from optional group conversations about the simulation cycle, and videos from the interactions and debriefs. Then, they conducted a grounded theory analysis of what PSTs expected from meeting with Maryam prior to their interaction and how they made sense of the interaction afterwards.

We built on this analysis by looking for PSTs' conceptions of "good teaching," as evidenced by what they aspired to and how they assessed their own performances. Statements like "I will" or "I should" or "I want to" suggested that, prior to meeting Maryam, PSTs intended to engage in "good teacher" practices that reflected the idealized White middle-class schooling practices described above. The following quote is representative:

> I will begin by asking Maryam how Aran generally behaves at home and how involved she and her husband are in Aran's schoolwork... By the end of the conference, I want to have laid out a plan for how exactly I as a homeroom teacher can support Aran in the classroom, how other teachers can help him best to improve his readings skills, and how Maryam and her husband can support Aran at home. (Adrienne; White, middle-class)[2]

Although PSTs used words like "collaborative" and "partner" in describing their goals for the interaction, their perceptions of "collaboration" and "partnership" assumed that Maryam would engage on their terms.

When PSTs actually met Maryam, they found that she spoke limited English and appeared to defer to everything they said. Depending on how PSTs reacted, Maryam may have revealed that she had previously been offered a translator that spoke a different dialect, that she herself only has an eighth grade education, or that Aran's father had been a physics professor in Iraq—information that could have been useful for supporting Aran and for building a strong parent-teacher relationship. Most PSTs, however, did not ask Maryam about her or her family's schooling history, instead speaking *at* Maryam for extended periods of time. In their immediate debriefs, these PSTs reported feeling uncertain that Maryam understood them and also, dissatisfied with their inability to enact the "good teacher" identity they had hoped to perform.

After the interaction, PSTs reviewed their own videos and reflected on, among other things, how other people—such as Aran's father, the school principal, or the author of a course reading—might interpret their interaction with Maryam. For many PSTs, these questions obliged them to reconsider what it means to be a "good teacher" for Aran and his family, disrupting their reliance on their own experiences. Although they had tried to engage in "good teacher" practices with Maryam, PSTs now suspected that people other than themselves may not have perceived what they did as characteristic of a "good teacher." These suspicions supported some PSTs in

---

[2]All teachers' names in this chapter are pseudonyms; social identity markers are included as descriptors only if teachers self-reported during the simulation cycle that these identities influenced their perspectives (e.g. "as a White woman..." or "I went to public schools in a middle-class neighborhood..."). In contrast to Maryam, all but two of the PSTs in this study spoke English as their primary language and completed most or all of their K-12 schooling in the United States.

recognizing both the partiality of their perspective (Self, 2016) and their positionality (Horn et al., 2016).

Partiality describes PSTs' realization that their initial ideas of Aran's needs and of what would constitute a successful parent-teacher relationship reflected a particular set of values that may differ from Maryam's perspective:

> I am actually thinking much more critically about why I want to be a teacher, and which experiences in my education I want to duplicate as ideal, and which ones I want to completely overturn... Do parents [in my home country] also value obedience more? Am I overriding their goals if I teach their children critical thinking skills? Whose goal is more important? Is there a middle ground? (Kaleb, multilingual, international student)

After interacting with Maryam, Kaleb thought more deeply about the relationality of parent-teacher interactions. His reflection suggested that he now saw engaging constructively with a parent as potentially requiring nonideal reasoning—negotiating the give-and-take of his interests and parents' interests—instead of simply following an idealized script.

Unlike Kaleb, however, other PSTs conceded the partiality of their perspective without recognizing the value of Maryam's perspective. Why this happened is beyond the scope of this analysis, but it suggests that simply acknowledging partiality does not guarantee PSTs' responsiveness. For example, although Jennifer accepted that she and Maryam may have viewed school differently, she interpreted Maryam's notions as demonstrating a lack of investment and involvement, and seemed to be primarily concerned with persuading Maryam to change:

> How do you get parents to be more invested and involved in their child's education when their culture has a different perspective on the designated role teachers and parents should play? (Jennifer, White)

Jennifer recognized her partiality, and that her ideal about parent-teacher relationships may not be shared, but she adhered to the White middle-class norm and maintained a deficit view of Maryam's position.

For this reason, we consider PSTs' learning about positionality to be separate from their learning about partiality. PSTs like Kaleb, who honored Maryam's views as equally valid, appreciated that they inhabited positions of greater status and power than Maryam in this context due to their language proficiency, familiarity with U.S. schooling customs, education, authority as a teacher, and in some cases, their race, gender, or class. As they moved through the simulation cycle, these PSTs became aware that not only were they in a position to impose—and that many of them *did* attempt to impose—their assumptions about a good parent-teacher relationship on Maryam without considering her perspective, but also, that such assumptions were grounded in their own upbringings:

> Maryam mentioned a couple of times making Aran work harder at home and asked about his behavior in school. In my experience, the "normal" [sic] American[3] parent does the

---

[3] Peggy, like other PSTs, drew contrasts between "American" parents and parents like Maryam, suggesting that such parents are not American. This contrast suggests that the predominantly White, predominantly U.S.-born PSTs in our study ascribe a narrative identity of "not American" to Maryam, most likely as a result of her limited English proficiency.

opposite, worrying about grades but reluctant to remedy the issues at home and expecting the teacher to take care of it. To what extent can or should we draw upon the fact that culture and language go together in education without stereotyping? (Peggy, White)

Interacting with Maryam led to insights about partiality and positionality that shifted how PSTs' took up the narrative and positional identities available to them, and consequently, revised PSTs' motivational filters. In their re-reading reflections, PSTs reported a range of practices that they now considered useful and feasible, such as learning to speak Kurdish (although they noted the impossibility of learning every student's home language, especially in a diverse school district), understanding how translators are assigned, and speaking more accessible English. Each of these possibilities for learning offer opportunities for PSTs to refine their conception of the "good teachers" they aspire to be in light of new discoveries about their narrative and positional identities. To predict and understand how PSTs might navigate these potential routes, we return to motivational filters as agentic tools that teachers use to negotiate who they want to become.

Exercising Agency Over Learning

For many PSTs, the simulation cycle refined their narrative identities of "good teacher" and their understanding of "good teacher" practices for interacting with parents. This happened when they recognized the partiality of their perspective and their positionality in relation to Maryam, and developed more nuanced ideas about communicating with parents and about what mutually beneficial parent-teacher relationships might look like. One PST explained:

> We are taught to view teaching and learning from a very collaborative focus. However, many cultures do not have the same mindset when it comes to education, evident in Maryam's repetition of phrases like, "If that is what you think is best." Additionally, some cultures have such a high regard for teachers that parents may not feel comfortable expressing discontent or seeking ways to advocate for their children. I would like to discuss how to make these relationships mutual and collaborative within these cultural differences. (Melanie, White, middle-class, female)

We posit that PSTs take up or reject the pedagogical practices they encounter by employing motivational filters based on utility and feasibility, and that these filters are determined by their shifting notions of what it means to be a "good teacher." As a result of the simulation cycle, PSTs may find practices useful that they previously did not see as important, or resist practices that they think would not have been useful in interacting with Maryam. For example, a mentor teacher might advise that a PST engage in self-disclosure to build trust with parents. Christina, on the one hand, may dismiss such practices because she suspects they will not be useful:

> I thought that I would be able to seem more relatable to Maryam by bringing up my experiences with a bilingual household, and that it would make her feel more comfortable… However, Maryam's lack of response persisted and I was not able to elicit any increased conversation with her, which made me feel like my personal anecdote might have been better not shared at all. (Christina, bilingual)

Cindy, on the other hand, reported a motivation to equalize power relations within the parent-teacher relationship after meeting with Maryam:

> I would like to focus on how we can break down the power structure/hierarchy that exists between parents and teachers, especially with regards to parents of a nondominant race/culture/SES [socioeconomic status].

Therefore, Cindy may perceive sharing her personal history—rather than remaining aloof, official, and detached—to be a practice that is useful and feasible for mitigating her positional identity and breaking down power structures, which are important to her in enacting her evolving conception of a "good teacher."

Of course, PSTs' evaluation of the utility and feasibility of teaching practices may not align with what their instructors and mentors would like them to learn. For example, some PSTs indicated that they would find it useful to learn practices that essentially amounted to pressing their perspective on Maryam. Instead of recognizing the limitations of their idealized vision of parent-teacher relationships and shifting to nonideal reasoning, these PSTs wanted to do a better job of what they originally set out to do:

> I would like to focus on how I can… communicate with parents who speak little English. I would also like to focus on ways to explain concepts to these parents without sounding condescending. How do I ensure that these parents [are] well informed on what is going on with their child in the classroom. (Ashley)

Ashley's takeaway was not about building strong parent-teacher relationships, or about understanding or even adopting elements of the parent-teacher relationship that Maryam imagines, but rather, about guaranteeing that Maryam would understand and accept her (Ashley's) ideal. Ashley's aspirational "good teacher" ensures that parents inhabit the narrative identity of a "good parent" that she is offering rather than one they might themselves author, and so Ashley might be motivated to learn practices that reproduce dominance: repeating oneself more loudly, only communicating when a translator is available, or appealing to a higher authority such as a principal for reinforcement.

Leigh did not have specific practices in mind, but she did maintain a strong conception of a "good teacher" as someone who knows which practices to deploy in which situations:

> I will be honest, I still don't know exactly what the outcome of that parent teacher conference should've been. My idea of reading in English at home got shot down in class, so obviously I didn't do it right. I guess hopefully I'll know what to do [by] the time I get to a situation like that. (Leigh, White, middle-class, woman)

The narrative identity that Leigh aspires to assumes that "good teachers" always know what to do, and that there is a "correct" outcome for every situation. This identity relies on an idealized version of parent-teacher relationships wherein ideas of what's "right" are obvious. A different "good teacher" narrative identity might instead expect teaching to be complex, uncertain, and contextual, and if this identity were more salient to Leigh, she might seek out adaptive and responsive practices as being more useful and feasible than "right answers."

Finally, Jamie wrote in her post-interaction reflection that she wanted to learn "how to derive the most from an otherwise seemingly-dead [sic] end scenario such as a language barrier that inhibits comprehension." If she sees a difference in primary language as an insurmountable obstacle to building a parent-teacher relationship, she may be reluctant to take up practices that focus on communication and mutual understanding, instead finding it more feasible to seek out practices that circumvent parent involvement. Alternately, if Jamie sees practices connected to cross-cultural or nonverbal communication as being useful for "deriv[ing] the most" from a conversation with Maryam, she might be eager to learn them. How Jamie appraises her pedagogical options through her aspirational "good teacher" lens and through her motivational filters could lead to very different choices: either a form of benign neglect that relegates parents—particularly parents of color and parents from historically marginalized backgrounds—to passive roles in their children's education, or a form of allyship that positions these same parents as agentic advocates for their children.

Implications and Conclusion

In this chapter, we offer another way of understanding the connection between who teachers are and how they think about their work. Teachers, as learners, make choices about which practices they seek to develop. These choices are informed by their identity-rooted motivational filters. This insight leads to a conundrum for teacher educators: if who teachers are shapes so much of what they want to know, as informed by their extant notions of good teaching, can teacher educators ensure that what PSTs want to know includes the development of responsive teaching practices?

This is an especially urgent question in U.S. public schools, where White, middle-class women, inhabiting the authoritative role of teacher, reproduce long-standing patterns of oppression by imposing culturally-biased expectations on students and parents in less privileged positions (Leonardo & Boas, 2013). If teachers are to work with students and their families in what Valenzuela (1999) calls authentically caring ways, accounting for the impacts of culture and power in education, they must recognize the partiality of their perspectives and their positionality in relation to others. First, doing so supports teachers' ability to access multiple and complex narrative identities for others—especially people with significantly different social experiences from their own—instead of resorting to simple stereotypes. For example, teachers might learn to see a refugee mother as being unfamiliar with the U.S. schooling system *and* as a powerful advocate for her child, or as someone who trusts teachers *and* has her own goals for her child.

Second, recognizing partiality and positionality enables teachers to interrogate "good teacher" narrative identities that, when unexamined, may replicate existing forms of dominance. Analyzing the sources of their conceptions of "good teaching," and the conditions under which these ideas may be productive or limiting, could expand teachers' understanding of "good teaching" and their skill at nonideal reasoning. Rather than simply seeking to replicate aspirational "good teacher" practices, teachers could then focus on the relationship between who they are and who a parent is, and co-construct with parents a set of "good teacher" practices that accommodate both their conceptions. From the stories of PSTs like Kaleb, Peggy, and Melanie, it appears that carefully designed simulation cycles have the potential to foreground PSTs' consciousness of the partiality and positionality behind their conceptions of a "good teacher" identity, thus availing PSTs of a range of "good teacher" practices.

However, our study also suggests that simply attending to PSTs' motivational filters and engaging them in simulation cycles does not guarantee that PSTs develop practices related to building strong parent-teacher relationships. In this simulation cycle, many PSTs' initial plans assumed that teachers hold unilateral power to shape parent-teacher relationships. Furthermore, when it became clear that Maryam had a different understanding of the ideal parent-teacher relationship, several PSTs shifted what they wanted to learn in ways that were not necessarily less oppressive. Ashley's new learning goal, for example, centered on compelling Maryam to engage in the practices that she expects, in line with what Leonardo and Boas (2013) call the White woman teacher's "civilizing" and "domesticating" role in society. Similar learning goals emerged even for some PSTs who were not White, middle-class women, testifying to the pervasiveness of an idealized vision of "good teachers" grounded in White, middle-class norms.

Since PSTs ultimately retain the agency to determine which "good teacher" identities underlie the practices they are motivated to take up, more research is needed to better understand the possibilities and conditions for designing and facilitating simulation cycles that incline PSTs to adopt conceptions of "good teaching" that disrupt (rather than perpetuate) the marginalization of parents from non-dominant backgrounds. We recommend that teacher educators consider simulation cycles as a promising pedagogy for supporting PSTs' development of teacher identities and teaching practices, but also remain aware that simulation cycles in and of themselves do not direct how PSTs' identities develop.

In Maryam's case, we would hope that teachers enact parent-teacher relationship practices that mitigate rather than exacerbate power imbalances; that reject Maryam's positional identity as "lesser than;" and that represent possibilities for what it means to be a "good teacher" beyond the White, middle-class ideal. We also know, however, that teachers exercise agency over their learning by deploying motivational filters, taking up practices they find to be useful and feasible and ignoring those they do not. We propose that pairing motivational filters and simulation cycles can offer a productive set of tools for researchers examining why teachers learn what they learn and how they become who they become. As a construct, motivational filters illuminate which practices teachers are more likely to take up as they refine their narrative identities of "good teacher." As a pedagogy, simulation cycles can offer opportunities for disrupting narrative identities of "good teacher" and accounting for teachers' positional identities in relation to other people. Together, motivational filters and simulation cycles extend our understanding of how teachers' identities, as evidenced by the practices they enact and take up, are agentically formed.

References

Baquedano-López, P., Alexander, R. A., & Hernandez, S. J. (2013). Equity issues in parental and community involvement in schools: What teacher educators need to know. *Review of Research in Education, 37*(1), 149–182.

Battey, D., & Franke, M. L. (2008). Transforming identities: Understanding teachers across professional development and classroom practice. *Teacher Education Quarterly, 106*(Summer), 127–149.

Epstein, J. L., & Sanders, M. G. (2006). Prospects for change: Preparing educators for school, family, and community partnerships. *Peabody Journal of Education, 81*(2), 81–120.

Holland, D. C., Skinner, D., Lachicotte, W., & Cain, C. (1998). In D. C. Holland (Ed.), *Identity and agency in cultural worlds*. Cambridge, MA: Harvard University Press.

Horn, I.S., Self, E., & Chen, G.A. (2016, June). *Cultural responsiveness for teaching: The development of pre-service teachers' sensemaking in clinical simulations.* Paper session presented at the European Association for Research on Learning and Instruction SIG 11 conference in Zurich, Switzerland.

Ishimaru, A. M. (2014). When new relationships meet old narratives: The journey towards improving parent-school relations in a district-community organizing collaboration. *Teachers College Record, 116*(2), 1–49.

Jaggar, A. M. (2015). Ideal and nonideal reasoning in educational theory. *Educational Theory, 65*(2), 111–126.

Lareau, A. (2011). *Unequal childhoods: Class, race, and family life*. Berkeley, CA: University of California Press.

Lawrence-Lightfoot, S. (2003). Ghosts in the classroom. In *The essential conversation: What parents and teachers can learn from each other* (pp. 3–41). New York: Ballantine Books.

Leonardo, Z., & Boas, E. (2013). Other kids' teachers: What children of color learn from White women and what this says about race, whiteness, and gender. In M. Lynn & A. D. Dixson (Eds.), *Handbook of critical race theory in education* (pp. 313–324). New York: Routledge.

Lortie, D. (1975). *Schoolteacher: A sociological study*. Chicago: University of Chicago Press.

Nolen, S. B., Ward, C. J., Horn, I. S., Childers, S., Campbell, S. S., & Mahna, K. (2009). Motivation development in novice teachers: The development of utility filters. In M. Wosnitza, S. A. Karabenick, A. Efklides, & P. Nenniger (Eds.), *Contemporary motivation research: From global to local perspectives* (pp. 265–278). Ashland, OH: Hogrefe & Huber.

Self, E. (2016). *Designing and using clinical simulations to prepare teachers for culturally responsive teaching*. Unpublished dissertation, Vanderbilt University.

Sfard, A., & Prusak, A. (2005). Telling identities: In search of an analytic tool for investigating learning as a culturally shaped activity. *Educational Researcher, 34*(4), 14–22.

Spillane, J. P. (2000). A fifth-grade teacher's reconstruction of mathematics and literacy teaching: Exploring interactions among identity, learning, and subject matter. *The Elementary School Journal, 100*(4), 307–330.

Valenzuela, A. (1999). *Subtractive schooling: U.S.-Mexican youth and the politics of caring*. Albany, NY: State University of New York Press.

Wenger, E. (1998). *Communities of practice: Learning, meaning, and identity*. Cambridge, UK: Cambridge University Press.

Chapter 9
Supervision Dialogues in Teacher Education: Balancing Dis/continuities of the Vocational Self-Concept

Martine M. van Rijswijk, Larike H. Bronkhorst, Sanne F. Akkerman, and Jan van Tartwijk

Dear Ms. X,

During my internship, especially last week, I was confronted with the fact that my classroom management problems for a large part are connected to the way I am as a person. By nature, I am very conflict avoidant. I do not like arguments (I cannot remember the last time I had an argument, even with my girlfriend), I always search for the positive and try to keep things peaceful. I know this about myself.

What I have noticed is that I find it very difficult to adjust my behavior when I am in front of the class. I must not be myself at that moment, but have to act according to my role as a teacher.

I can implement small corrections, but what I really have to learn is to correct in a big way, as a part of my role as a teacher. Every time when I have to act like that I notice something in me revolts.

The question you could ask of course is: Why is something in me revolting? Is it being afraid of being disliked? Maybe, but I also think it has to do with the question that always rises whether my correction/(played out) anger is justified at the moment.

Do you recognize the problem of conflict management (it wouldn't surprise me if it did) and do you have suggestions for me how to deal with it?

Regards, John

For John, a student teacher in a 1-year, post-master, teacher education program at a Dutch research university, development as a teacher is hard. He encounters problems in his teaching practice that he relates to perceived personal characteristics. He notices that how he sees himself does not correspond with what he thinks being a teacher means or should mean. He reflects on what he needs to learn and wonders why he finds showing particular behavior difficult.

This original email illustrates a student teacher's thinking about his *teacher identity*, that is his "image-of-self-as-teacher" (Beijaard & Meijer, 2017), which generally

M. M. van Rijswijk (✉) · L. H. Bronkhorst · S. F. Akkerman · J. van Tartwijk
Department of Education, Utrecht University, Utrecht, The Netherlands
e-mail: M.M.vanRijswijk@uu.nl; L.H.Bronkhorst@uu.nl; S.F.Akkerman@uu.nl;
J.vanTartwijk@uu.nl

is understood to be dynamic, shifting over time, because of internal and external factors such as emotions and life experiences (Beauchamp & Thomas, 2009) and definable for teachers' professional behavior. Accordingly, researchers argue that student teacher development should involve making sense of oneself based on teaching experiences and observed characteristics next to acquiring skills and knowledge (e.g., Rodgers & Scott, 2008; van Rijswijk, Akkerman, Bronkhorst & van Tartwijk, 2018).

Teaching experiences are known to elicit reflections aimed at answering identity questions such as: Who am I? How do I tend to act in practice? Is there a match between my actions and the demands of the profession? (Alsup, 2006). Differences among these reflections have been referred to as professional identity tensions, that is, conflicts between personal desires and beliefs and what is considered relevant to the teaching profession (Pillen, Beijaard, & den Brok, 2013). Professional identity tensions are related to a sense of discontinuity in student teachers: a lack of temporal coherence in the understanding of one's self. Sensed discontinuity has been known to lead to anxiety and research shows that people try to re-establish continuity for reasons of general well-being and self-confidence (Akkerman & Meijer, 2011; Caspi & Moffitt, 1991). Because teacher education characteristically includes experiences that are confronting and challenging for student teachers, it is likely that sensed discontinuity is a normal part of student teacher development (Ahonen, Pyhältö, Pietarinen, & Soini, 2015; Akkerman & Meijer, 2011).

John, in his email to his supervising teacher educator, shares his concerns about a tension typical to the profession: having to act as a classroom manager while feeling this does not match his desire to avoid conflicts. He asks his teacher educator to reflect on his predicament and to help him deal with it. His request resonates appeals emerging from research: Teacher educators increasingly are called upon to support student teachers in how they make sense of themselves as teachers (Meijer, 2011).

Teacher educators are expected to engage student teachers in a reflective discourse that includes analyzing past experiences and exploring future expectations (Conway, 2001) and to help them resolve tensions (Hammerness et al., 2005). Yet, research up to now provides limited clues as to how student teachers and teacher educators could deal with tensions in supervision dialogues. In this chapter, we first conceptualize student teachers' personal sense making processes and the tensions therein and subsequently explore how tensions are addressed in supervision of teacher education practice.

Past Perceptions and Future Expectations of Student Teachers

Previous research has shown how general beliefs about the teaching profession and/ or convictions about what it takes to be a good teacher influence student teacher development (e.g., Alsup, 2006). Important, in light of teacher identity, is what student teachers believe about themselves in relation to the profession. To conceptualize these beliefs, we use the *vocational self-concept:* "[t]he constellation of

Table 9.1 Past perceptions and future expectations in the vocational self-concept of student teachers

	Type	Definition
Past perceptions	Consistency related to characteristics	Perception of the past that reflects certainty and confidence about specific characteristics and abilities
	Consistency related to experiences	Perception of a specific experience with teaching, with other professional experiences, and/or as a student.
	Lack of experience	Perception of the past that indicates no sufficient or no relevant experience with teaching.
	Problems of the past	Perception of negative characteristics and problems that reflect weak teacher conduct.
Future expectations	Confidence	Expectation indicating clarity and certainty of future characteristics and professional conduct as a teacher and indicating confidence in a continuous development.
	Development	Expectation indicating probability of anticipated characteristics and professional conduct as a teacher and indicating a phased nature of the developmental trajectory.
	Goals	Expectation indicating pursued characteristics and professional conduct, without specific information about what it will take to reach these goals
	Challenges	Expectation problematizing the feasibility of acquiring required characteristics and carrying out professional conduct, and the developmental trajectory toward this.

self-attributes considered by the individual to be vocationally relevant" (Super, Starishevsky, Matlin, & Jordaan, 1963, p. 20). To illustrate: John, in his email, explicates that he has started to doubt the value of his conflict-avoidant nature because he has noticed that he needs to correct unwanted behavior while teaching. He is triggered to reconsider the relevance of his self-attributes and engages in sense making about himself as a teacher, an ongoing internal and reflective narrative about teaching experiences and the consequent relevance of personal characteristics for the profession (Ezzy, 1998; Hermans, 2002).

Sense making is temporal in nature: past perceptions, an individual's selection of appropriate past events, and future expectations determine its course (Polkinghorne, 1996; Zittoun et al., 2013). In previous empirical research on 35 profiles of student teachers, we identified four types of past perceptions and four types of future expectations included in the vocational self-concept of student teachers (van Rijswijk, Akkerman, Schaap, & Tartwijk, 2016). These are detailed in Table 9.1.

Past perceptions that reflect *consistency related to characteristics* or *consistency related to experiences* and future expectations that reflect *confidence* and *development* contribute to a sense of temporal coherence within student teachers. For instance, a student teacher might say: "I always knew I wanted to be a teacher. I played school with my younger sister at an early age, and I feel my enthusiasm for instruction will benefit my development as a teacher." These past and future references point to what has been theorized as *sensed continuity*, that is coherence in the sense of one's self over time which is identified as an important drive in development for humans (Sani, 2008; Zittoun et al., 2013).

Past perceptions that reflect a *lack of experience* or *problems* in the past and future expectations that reflect *goals* or *challenges* include perceived problems and attest to a lack of temporal coherence within student teachers. For instance, the quote "I know I can be very impatient, and I will have to change that in order to be a teacher. I feel this will be a struggle, and I do not know if I will like it" indicates perceived challenges regarding development as a teacher. A match with the profession is not evident, and expectations emphasize uncertainty about if and how one will succeed in development as a teacher. Caspi and Moffit (Caspi & Moffitt, 1991) showed that people try to re-establish continuity if they experience discontinuity to avoid feelings of anxiety and insecurity.

Student teachers also have been found to combine references reflecting discontinuity with references reflecting continuity, thus expressing an ambiguous sense of dis/continuity toward development as a teacher (van Rijswijk et al., 2016). Consider this statement, for example: "Because of my work as a travel guide, I know I can explain things quite well; but doing this in a group of 30 15-year-olds will be tricky for me." In this example, the student teacher combines a past perception reflecting consistency related to experiences (former employment as a travel guide that helps her to act in a certain way) with a future expectation reflecting a challenge (expected difficulties when doing this as a teacher in a class setting). Likewise is this statement: "I have had some problems communicating with others because of my bluntness, but I'm sure this will not be a problem when I deal with students in the second grade because I will make sure to think before I speak." In this example, the student teacher combines a past perception reflecting problems in the past (problems with communicating because of bluntness) with a future expectation reflecting confidence (this will not be a problem when teaching).

Continuity and Discontinuity in Supervision Dialogues

Teacher education programs increasingly include instruments that provoke intrapersonal dialogues about teaching experiences within student teachers; for instance journals (e.g., Korthagen, 2001) and portfolios (e.g., van Tartwijk, van Rijswijk, Tuithof, & Driessen, 2008). Moreover, teacher educators engage with student teachers in supervision dialogues, using strategies to evoke reflection on development as a teacher and discussing teacher performance and professional demands (cf. Beijaard & Meijer, 2017) as well as self-attributes and their vocational relevance (cf. Alsup, 2006). Consequently, teacher educators become partners in student teachers' sense making. Student teacher and teacher educator participation and contribution in supervision dialogues are not isolated or independent from each other. Each contribution to a dialogue is modified in relation with the other partner's contribution (Lyra, 1999).

Supervision dialogues can be expected to include different intentions when it comes to supporting student teachers' sense making in the context of teacher education. On the one hand, supervision dialogues can be seen as functional for discussing sensed continuity in student teachers for reasons of well-being (Sani, 2008). Exploring a sense of continuity seems appropriate as it has been found to enhance self-efficacy and positively contributes to enduring challenging developmental trajectories (cf. Zembylas, 2003). Elaborating on skills and capitalizing on personal qualities (Korthagen, 2001) can serve to explore sensed continuity.

On the other hand, supervision dialogues can be expected to include intentions toward exploring sensed discontinuity to acknowledge and tackle tensions during teacher education, avoiding a so-called "practice shock" upon entering the profession (e.g., Stokking, Leenders, De Jong, & van Tartwijk, 2003). Unraveling tensions, identifying effective and non-effective teacher behavior (Meijer, 2011), or assessing the persistence of negative characteristics (Murray, Swennen, & Shagrir, 2009) can serve to explore sensed discontinuity.

We assume that teacher educators and student teachers both are committed to exploring sensed continuity as well as sensed discontinuity in supervision dialogues. A positive, confident attitude toward development as a teacher (i.e., sensed continuity) is highly valued for further professional development (Onafowora, 2005). It also is considered beneficial, for reasons of resilience, to be are aware of possible challenges or tensions (i.e., sensed discontinuity) that can be part of development as a teacher (Hargreaves, 2005; Johnson et al., 2014).

In the remaining part of this chapter we will analyze in what way student teachers and teacher educators explore both sensed continuity and sensed discontinuity in supervision dialogues as they both can be expected to be functional for dealing with tensions in student teacher development.

Exploring Issues of Dis/continuity in Supervision Dialogues in Teacher Education

For this chapter, we studied 42 supervision dialogues that were audio-recorded in a post-master, 1-year teacher education program at a Dutch research university. We purposefully selected and analyzed problems of the past-type references ($n = 118$) and subsequent responses of both student teacher and teacher educator in those dialogues. We focused on problems of the past-type references (i.e., perceptions of negative characteristics and problems that reflect weak teacher conduct) because these are expected to trigger a discussion of discontinuity as well as attempts to re-establish continuity.

We selected dialogues of six teacher educators with different student teachers, distributed over the first and second practice period of the 1-year program and of a formal and informal (e.g., not related to a portfolio) nature.

Analysis of the problems of the past-type references showed that student teachers and teacher educators both contributed to outweighing and contrasting issues of discontinuity in three ways. Consequently, these processes were described as balancing with time, balancing with content, and balancing with salience. Following, the three processes are described and illustrated with quotes from the supervision dialogues. In the quotes, the contributions of the teacher educator are in italics. All names are pseudonyms.

Balancing with Time

Balancing with time refers to the student teacher and teacher educator together discussing issues of dis/continuity by accentuating specific perceptions of the past in relation to expectations of the future, or vice versa. For example, teacher educator Anna complimented student teacher Michael:

> *I really like the interaction with students when you teach.*
> That is usually the case in my lessons. If we talk about new information, I really let the class do it, I am only facilitating. However, that is dangerous, it could be that not all students cooperate. I could improve that.
> *Yes, but you can also apply it in smaller groups. What you are doing is very good, just expand it a little.*
> For me teaching is not about theory, and sometimes I lack some coherence in my lessons. But, I feel I can teach well.
> *Yes, and the principal of your school agrees, I can tell you.*

In this sequence, the student teacher introduced discontinuity, contrasting the positive appraisal of the teacher educator and indicating that further development as a teacher still was needed.

Balancing with time also appeared when a student teacher and teacher educator reflected on developmental progress. For instance, teacher educator Wilma and student teacher Shirley discussed the difficult task of setting limits in relation to an appraisal of her development as a teacher:

> *How do you value your growth as a teacher? Do you think you are becoming more "teacher-like?"*
> Yes, especially as a counselor, and because I have fun with the students. At first it was more about surviving, and I still feel that anxiety somewhat. But I am liking teaching more and more. My biggest point of interest still is being consequent and knowing better what I tolerate or not in class.
> *Yeah, knowing your limits.*
> In general, I know them, but then something happens, and every situation is different.
> *As such you're doing ok you know.*
> Yeah, but then you start to doubt and you are inclined to react too softly, instead of firm.
> *And then it goes farther than you would like, I get it.*
> I have to take some steps, but I notice teaching is becoming easier. Also preparing lessons. So, I still like teaching a lot.

In this sequence, Shirley reflected on her achievement as a teacher up to now, and she marked the change she had gone through by emphasizing that the phase of surviving is something of the past. Also, at the end of this sequence, Shirley returned to her realized development as a teacher, accentuating that teaching was getting easier. Shirley argued that problems still occurred but had decreased already, with which the likelihood of prior and expected progress of development as a teacher was highlighted.

Balancing with Content

Balancing with content refers to the student teacher and teacher educator discussing issues of dis/continuity by elaborating on other self-attributes. In the sequence of Wilma and Shirley discussed previously, we also can find an example of balancing with content. Student teacher Shirley extended her progress in development as a teacher by elaborating on preparing lessons and the progress made on that account. By doing this, Shirley included pedagogical skills in the constellation of self-attributes relevant to teaching.

Similarly, teacher educator Bianca and student teacher Zoe discussed teaching in the second practice period.

> I will be expected to teach lessons of 70 minutes, that will be a challenge. But, the peda-gogical concept of the school (Montessori MvR) ensures that the students are used to organizing their work themselves. That will be nice, I hope.
> *That's exciting. Do you picture yourself succeeding?*
> Yes, it is going to be all right. I'm someone who likes to be well prepared, and now I'm going to make sure that I have a good relationship with the students in my classroom.

Although the student teacher and teacher educator acknowledged that the new situation could include difficulties, confidence in development as a teacher was accentuated, and the student teacher elaborated on what she knew she could do to deal with the difficult situation. Other examples of balancing with content were student teachers and teacher educators discussing a successful relationship with individual students to counterbalance problems with classroom management, and stressing difficulties with teaching students in the upper classes to contrast an easy relationship with younger students.

Balancing with Salience

Balancing with salience refers to the student teacher and teacher educator together discussing issues of dis/continuity by exploring the relative worth of self-attributes and/or intentions by elaborating on their weight in light of other self-attributes and the demands of the profession. For instance, in the dialogue of teacher educator Jeff and student teacher Jessica:

> I was allowed to teach my first lesson, but I thought classroom management was very bad.
> *You will need some tools for that. All in all, it was quite ok for a first lesson, wasn't it?*

My mentor thought so, but I was disappointed because it didn't go as well as I hoped for.
Can you let that go, because it will happen more often this year?
Yes, but it will be very hard; I really hold it against myself.... Wednesday I will be teaching
    this class again. It is really good that my mentor has confidence in me, there is a
    safety-net.

Jeff at first attempted to downsize ("it was quite ok for a first lesson") the severe judgment of Jessica ("classroom management was very bad"), after which Jessica elaborated on her own disappointment despite her mentor's positive feedback. Jeff then asked about the persistency of her appraisal of experiences, and Jessica acknowledged that this could be problematic for the future. Jessica related the perceived problem in this sequence (poor classroom management) to her habit of holding poor behavior against herself. In the support of her mentor Jessica seemed to find courage to continue her development.

Balancing with salience also appeared when student teachers and teacher educators discussed developmental progress. In the supervision dialogue between teacher educator Matt and student teacher Steven poor classroom management was discussed.

Do you recognize it? Or do you disagree? Because that is important of course.
Well, I do recognize it when you're saying that I do not experience it [disruptions in class-
    room MvR] as problematic enough. My threshold is quite high; I never get angry actu-
    ally. A lot should happen for that.
*Yes, I also wonder about your threshold. You do not have a problem with not being taken
    seriously by students. If a student would treat me like this, he would have a problem. You
    remain very friendly and calm.*

In this example Matt hinted that Steven's characteristics of being "very friendly and calm" were hampering his teacher behavior. By relating the problems with classroom management to personal attributes, the need to strive for a profound change was highlighted. Although addressing positive characteristics typically imply continuity in student teacher development, in this case discontinuity was emphasized.

Balancing with salience also appeared in supervision dialogues that focused on intentions toward teaching. Teacher educator Wilma and student teacher Victor discussed the nature of the teacher role.

I am really confronted with the barrier that I really do not see myself in such an enforcing
    role.
Yes, I get that. But you really have to teach it to yourself, that is your role.
But my motivation for teaching was my disliking of such enforcing teachers, to do it
    differently.
*Yes, but in order to be not that kind of teacher you have to be able to act like it....It is a mat-
    ter of taking the lead. You have a lot going for you.*
Yes, I can do it, I'm convinced of it.
*Yes, me too. But at the moment you give the students too much freedom. Students also like
    it when you provide clarity by setting limits.*

In this example, Victor stressed that enforcing behavior was problematic for him, not because he could not do it, but because he really did not like it. In this sequence, student teacher development was somewhat extended through "You have a lot going for you" and "Yes, I can do it" and consequently continuity was implied. The teacher educator concluded, however, that at the moment this problem had to be solved. The argument that students also liked setting limits seemed to scaffold this statement.

In sum, in balancing with salience student teachers and teacher educators reflect on the importance of specific attributes and/or intentions for development as a teacher, thus including a normative perspective on the vocational self-concept by foregrounding one self-attribute over the other.

Discussion

In this chapter, to better our understanding of how to deal with tensions in teacher education, we discussed with what processes student teachers and teacher educators explored both sensed continuity as well as sensed discontinuity in supervision dialogues. We analyzed 118 sequences surrounding problems of the past-type references in 42 audio-taped supervision dialogues in a 1-year, post-master, teacher education program. We identified three types of processes. Common to the processes was that both student teachers and teacher educators contributed to outweighing and contrasting issues of discontinuity, and consequently the processes were referred to as balancing.

The processes identified in this study are illustrative to how student teachers and teacher educators address tensions in student teacher development in supervision dialogues. Furthermore, the processes disclose how the three core aspects of student teachers' sense making (i.e. temporality (Zittoun et al., 2013), self-attributes and their relevance to the vocation (Super et al., 1963)) can be identified in supervision dialogues. As such, the processes assist supervisors and student teachers in addressing *teacher identity* in supervision meetings, while acknowledging its dynamic and variable nature and attending both to beliefs of the student teacher about him or herself in relation to beliefs about the profession (cf. Alsup, 2006; Beauchamp & Thomas, 2009). Specifically, balancing with time is illustrative to how the progress of identity development itself can become a topic in supervision dialogues as reflections on different past and future instances in development are included (c.f. Zembylas, 2003). Balancing with content shows how the complexity of the teaching profession can be discussed by acknowledging different and complementing self-attributes (c.f. Stokking et al., 2003). Balancing with salience illustrates how different beliefs about what it means to be a good teacher can be discussed (c.f. Murray et al., 2009).

We propose that applying the balancing processes explicitly could assist both student teachers and teacher educators, because the processes enable a better understanding of the nature of student teachers' unique sense making patterns. Future research should then be directed at exploring issues such as identifying sensed dis/continuity in student teachers and considerations associated with confronting student teachers with professional identity tensions in supervision.

Future research also is needed to better understand how intentions of both student teachers and teacher educators determine how sensed dis/continuity is addressed in supervision dialogues. For instance, intentions could lean toward examining current problems in view of avoiding a practice shock and consequently initiate the process of balancing with salience. However, intentions also could pertain to sorting out problems in teaching practice for reasons of immediate problem solving and thus initiate the process of balancing with content. Opposing intensions in supervision dialogues could result in misunderstandings and/or trigger resistance, potentially threatening the safety of the learning environment for student teachers (Bronkhorst, Koster, Meijer, Woldman, & Vermunt, 2014). Moreover, resistance ultimately could undermine exploration of the equilibrium between continuity and discontinuity in long-term development as a teacher.

References

Ahonen, E., Pyhältö, K., Pietarinen, J., & Soini, T. (2015). Student teachers' key learning experiences–mapping the steps for becoming a professional teacher. *International Journal of Higher Education, 4*(1), 151–165. https://doi.org/10.5430/ijhe.v4n1p151

Akkerman, S. F., & Meijer, P. C. (2011). A dialogical approach to conceptualizing teacher identity. *Teaching and Teacher Education, 27*(2), 308–319. https://doi.org/10.1016/j.tate.2010.08.013

Alsup, J. (2006). *Teacher identity discourses: Negotiating personal and professional spaces.* Mahwah, NJ: Lawrence Erlbaum Associates.

Beauchamp, C., & Thomas, L. (2009). Understanding teacher identity: An overview of issues in the literature and implications for teacher education. *Cambridge Journal of Education, 39*(2), 175–189. https://doi.org/10.1080/03057640902902252

Beijaard, D., & Meijer, P. C. (2017). Developing the personal and professional in making a teacher identity. In D. J. Clandinin & J. Husu (Eds.), *The SAGE handbook of research on teacher education* (pp. 177–192). London: Sage Publications.

Bronkhorst, L. H., Koster, B., Meijer, P. C., Woldman, N., & Vermunt, J. D. (2014). Exploring student teachers' resistance to teacher education pedagogies. *Teaching and Teacher Education, 40*, 73–82. https://doi.org/10.1016/j.tate.2014.02.001

Caspi, A., & Moffitt, T. E. (1991). Individual differences are accentuated during periods of social change: The sample case of girls at puberty. *Journal of Personality and Social Psychology, 61*(1), 157–168. https://doi.org/10.1037/0022-3514.61.1.157

Conway, P. F. (2001). Anticipatory reflection while learning to teach: From a temporally truncated to a temporally distributed model of reflection in teacher education. *Teaching and Teacher Education, 17*(1), 89–106. https://doi.org/10.1016/S0742-051X(00)00040-8

Ezzy, D. (1998). Theorizing narrative identity. *The Sociological Quarterly, 39*(2), 239–252. https://doi.org/10.1111/j.1533-8525.1998.tb00502.x

Hammerness, K., Darling-Hammond, L., Bransford, J., Berliner, D., Cochran-Smith, M., McDonald, M., & Zeichner, K. (2005). How teachers learn and develop. In L. Darling-Hammond & J. Bransford (Eds.), *Preparing teachers for a changing world: What teachers should learn and be able to do* (pp. 358–389). San Francisco: Jossey-Bass.

Hargreaves, A. (2005). Educational change takes ages: Life, career and generational factors in teachers' emotional responses to educational change. *Teaching and Teacher Education, 21*(8), 967–983.

Hermans, H. J. (2002). The dialogical self as a society of mind introduction. *Theory & Psychology, 12*(2), 147–160. https://doi.org/10.1177/0959354302012002626

Johnson, B., Down, B., Le Cornu, R., Peters, J., Sullivan, A., Pearce, J., & Hunter, J. (2014). Promoting early career teacher resilience: A framework for understanding and acting. *Teachers and Teaching, 20*(5), 530–546. https://doi.org/10.1080/13540602.2014.937957

Korthagen, F. (2001). Specific instruments and techniques for promoting reflection. In F. A. Korthagen, J. Kessels, B. Koster, & B. Lagerwerf (Eds.), *Linking practice and theory: The pedagogy of realistic teacher education* (pp. 207–231). Mahwah, NJ: Routledge.

Lyra, M. C. (1999). An excursion into the dynamics of dialogue: Elaborations upon the dialogical self. *Culture & Psychology, 5*(4), 477–489. https://doi.org/10.1177/1354067X9954006

Meijer, P. C. (2011). The role of crisis in the development of student teachers' professional identity. In A. Lauriala, R. Rajala, H. Ruokamo, & O. Ylitapio-Mäntylä (Eds.), *Navigating in educational contexts: Identities and cultures in dialogue* (pp. 41–54). Rotterdam, The Netherlands: Sense.

Murray, J., Swennen, A., & Shagrir, L. (2009). Understanding teacher educators' work and identities. In A. Swennen & M. van der Klink (Eds.), *Becoming a teacher educator: Theory and practice for teacher educators* (pp. 29–43). Dordrecht, The Netherlands: Springer.

Onafowora, L. L. (2005). Teacher efficacy issues in the practice of novice teachers. *Educational Research Quarterly, 28*(4), 34–43.

Pillen, M., Beijaard, D., & den Brok, P. (2013). Professional identity tensions of beginning teachers. *Teachers and Teaching, 19*(6), 660–678. https://doi.org/10.1080/13540602.2013.827455

Polkinghorne, D. E. (1996). Explorations of narrative identity. *Psychological Inquiry, 7*(4), 363–367. https://doi.org/10.1207/s15327965pli0704_13

Rodgers, C., & Scott, K. (2008). The development of the personal self and professional identity in learning to teach. In M. Cochran-Smith, S. Feiman-Nemser, D. J. McIntyre, & K. E. Demers (Eds.), *Handbook of research on teacher education: Enduring questions and changing contexts* (pp. 732–755). New York: Routledge.

Sani, F. (Ed.). (2008). *Self continuity: Individual and collective perspectives*. New York: Taylor & Francis.

Stokking, K., Leenders, F., De Jong, J., & van Tartwijk, J. (2003). From student to teacher: Reducing practice shock and early dropout in the teaching profession. *European Journal of Teacher Education, 26*(3), 329–350. https://doi.org/10.1080/0261976032000128175

Super, D. E., Starishevsky, R., Matlin, N., & Jordaan, J. P. (1963). *Career development: Self-concept theory*. New York: College Entrance Examination Board.

van Rijswijk, M., Akkerman, S. F., Schaap, H., & van Tartwijk, J. (2016). Past perceptions and future expectations: Sensed dis/continuity at the start of teacher education. *Teaching and Teacher Education, 58*, 99–108. https://doi.org/10.1016/j.tate.2016.05.002

van Rijswijk, M., Akkerman, S. F., Bronkhorst, L. H., & van Tartwijk, J. (2018). Changes in sensed dis/continuity in the development of student teacher throughout teacher education. *European Journal of Teacher Education, 41*(3), 282–300. https://doi.org/10.1080/02619768.2018.1448782

van Tartwijk, J., van Rijswijk, M., Tuithof, H., & Driessen, E. W. (2008). Using an analogy in the introduction of a portfolio. *Teaching and Teacher Education, 24*(4), 927–938. https://doi.org/10.1016/j.tate.2007.11.001

Zembylas, M. (2003). Emotions and teacher identity: A post-structural perspective. *Teachers and Teaching: Theory and Practice, 9*(3), 213–238. https://doi.org/10.1080/13540600309378

Zittoun, T., Valsiner, J., Salgado, J., Gonçalves, M. M., Vedeler, D., & Ferring, D. (2013). *Human development in the life course: Melodies of living*. Cambridge, UK: Cambridge University Press.

Chapter 10
Mentor Teachers. Contributions to the Development of Preservice Teachers' Identity

Mahsa Izadinia

The process of identity formation is usually considered as a process of meaning making about one's self (Hung, Lim, & Jamaludin, 2011). The answers we find to questions like who am I as a teacher?; What kind of teacher do I want to be?; And how good am I at teaching (Beijaard, Meijer, & Verloop, 2004; Cook, 2009) would determine our perseverance and success in teaching. In my article (Izadinia, 2013) I defined teacher identity as teachers' perceptions of their cognitive knowledge, sense of agency, self-awareness, voice, confidence, and relationship with colleagues, pupils and parents. I elaborated that the fluctuation in each of these components determine how strongly teachers feel about their teacher identity. Developing a strong sense of teacher identity, in turn, sustains teachers' interest in teaching, broadens their skills and knowledge, and motivates them to become active contributors to their learning-to-teach process. In other words, as Wenger (1998) argued there is a close connection between identity and practice. If preservice teachers manage to develop a strong sense of teacher identity, one which conveys an attitude of "I can teach", their teaching practices would be inspired by their teacher identity and subsequently become more effective.

The factors contributing to development of teacher identity are varied including both internal and external factors. For instance, it is believed that motivation (Schepens, Aelterman, & Vlerick, 2009) and prior experiences (Olsen, 2008), as internal variables, influence the process of identity formation. There are also different external factors at play that change our experiences and shape the person we are. In my own research on teacher identity (2013–2016), I found that, for instance, significant others such as parents and teachers played a determining role in construction of professional identity (Izadinia, 2015, 2017). I was fascinated to know one of the main reasons preservice teachers participating in my research had for opting for teaching was simply receiving positive comments from significant others

M. Izadinia (✉)
School of Education, Edith Cowan University, Joondalup, Australia
e-mail: rose@circle.education

© Springer International Publishing AG, part of Springer Nature 2018
P. A. Schutz et al. (eds.), *Research on Teacher Identity*,
https://doi.org/10.1007/978-3-319-93836-3_10

on their teaching skills; comments like 'Oh you are really good at explaining things, you should be a teacher'. Such comments sparked their interest and motivation to have a go at teaching in later stages of their life. I also found that growing up in a family of teachers, where there had been inspiring role models and a passion for teaching, could be a driving force to become a teacher. These observations have led me to conclude people with whom we have a close connection impact our perception of who we are and inadvertently push us in certain directions that would gradually shape our sense of identity and our attitude that 'Yes, I can do this', or 'No, this is not me'. That is why the process of identity formation, from a social constructivist perspective (Vygotsky, 1986), is believed to occur not in individual isolation but rather in a social-community context.

In the context of teacher education, preservice teachers are surrounded by significant others such as university teachers, peers, and mentor teachers at schools. The one-on-one relationships they form with each of these parties can shape their understanding of the process of becoming a teacher and how effective they can be at teaching. For instance, mentor teachers, who are defined as those who supervise preservice teachers in their practicum setting (Beck & Kosnik, 2000), are one of the most influential parties in professional practice unit. Mentor teachers play different roles including carer, helper, and sharer (Baird, 1993). Their role can also change from showing empathy and giving advice to empowering the mentees and highlighting their personal strengths (Pascarelli, 1998). For sure one of the key responsibilities of mentor teachers is to instil a sense of confidence, power, and agency (Liu & Fisher, 2006; Ticknor, 2014) so that preservice teachers develop a strong teacher voice and feel motivated and inspired throughout the practicum experience and long afterwards. In other words, mentor teachers can definitely impact the process of teacher identity formation but the question is how?

The quality of interactions between mentors and preservice teachers is an important issue to consider and it requires constant evaluation and reconsideration throughout the mentoring process. The literature on mentoring abounds with studies on components of good mentoring relationships. For instance, researchers have highlighted issues such as communication, authenticity, encouraging gestures, honesty, trust, constructive feedback, and emotional and academic support (Beck & Kosnik, 2002; Izadinia, 2016) as the key components of mentoring. Below I present principles that mentor teachers can apply in their mentoring practices to contribute to the development of a robust teacher identity on the part of preservice teachers. Each principle will be followed by realistic scenarios that are derived from my own research on teacher identity and mentoring relationships (2013–2016). I also present useful examples and tips for effective mentoring conducive to the development of teacher identity and draw upon the literature to support the ideas presented here.

Principle 1: Building and Maintaining Strong Relationships

Positive and strong relationships based on trust and mutual respect are key to a successful mentoring experience (Izadinia, 2016; Nevins Stanulis & Russell, 2000). In a practicum setting mentor teachers are usually swamped with different tasks they need to perform as a mentor and might consider spending extra time for personal interactions with their mentees not much of a priority. However, preservice teachers need to connect to their mentors at a personal level so that they perceive their mentors not only as someone who is there to guide and assess them but someone who they can trust and open up to in case they experience emotional challenges. Preservice teachers participating in my own research repeatedly mentioned that even a small chit-chat with their mentors here and there and generally receiving an impression that their mentors cared to know more about them would help them feel included and welcome, which would impact their practicum experiences. Consider the scenarios below, which emerged from the data of my research (please refer to author 2013–2017 for more on preservice teacher identity development during practicum):

> Scenario 1: *Ben is an experienced teacher who values interpersonal relationships. Ben and Alex, a preservice teacher, have developed a close personal relationship. Ben usually asks Alex to help him out in arranging concerts for after school activities and they go for burgers and drinks afterwards. Ben takes an interest in knowing Alex's plans for his future and life objectives. Alex is very satisfied with his practicum experience and thinks their positive and close relationship has hugely contributed to the success of this block.*

> Scenario 2: *Tess is Sarah's mentor and an active teacher and an artist. Tess has to manage many different activities during school hours and after that she has to quickly leave to attend different musical events. Hence, Tess is usually too busy to have time for Sarah and they barely know each other. At times Sarah thinks she does not have a mentor and feels unwelcome.*

As shown above, Ben and Tess are different in their approaches to mentoring in that one is willing to spend time on creating a bond with his mentee and the other is busy with her own schedules and everyday routines. As evident by feelings Alex and Sarah express, their experiences of their first block practicum is very different, which could considerably influence their attitudes towards the teaching job and how suitable it is for them. Mentor teachers are encouraged to make time for having friendly conversations with their mentees to get to know them. Such conversations could occur at different stages of the mentoring especially at the outset when mentors plan for their mentoring practices and teaching strategies. The conversations should focus on mentees' learning approaches, needs, expectations, their strengths and what they need to improve from their own point of view. This information will help mentors to not only build strong and friendly relationships with their mentees but also identify the mentees' professional and emotional needs to adjust their teaching approaches accordingly. Also mentors can consider developing strategies to strengthen their one-on-one relationships. For example, as shown in Scenario 1 above, participating in out-of-school activities, which interest both parties, can serve as a rich opportunity for making personal connections conducive to a better evaluation of mentees' skills and potentials. It goes without saying that highlighting and recognizing mentees' skills and abilities demonstrated in different occasions would enhance their enthusiasm, confidence, and motivation to teach. Hence, by maintaining a positive relationship with their mentees, one which is based on mutual trust, clear expectations and effective communication, mentor teachers can greatly facilitate their mentees' professional identity construction. In other words, the strength of the relationships preservice teachers maintain with others indicates the development of their teacher identity (Cattley, 2007). Being successful in maintaining positive relationships with mentors and students and being inspired to do so would convey the message that "Yes, you are able to bond with students and colleagues" and "Yes, you CAN be a teacher" to preservice teachers.

Principle 2: Offering Support and Encouragement

Support as a key element in mentoring has been identified as instructional and psychological while the former refers to the knowledge, strategies, and skills given to student teachers and the latter refers to enhancing their self-efficacy, confidence, and feelings of effectiveness (Gold, 1996). Both kinds of support have been identified as the main component of mentoring relationships in different studies (Beck & Kosnik, 2002; Izadinia 2016). Consider the two scenarios below:

> Scenario 1: *Adam has just started his first practicum. He lacks confidence and at times ideas for how to teach students, whom he feels are close to his age, and how he can discipline them. His mentor Tom has made himself available after hours and weekends so Adam can contact him anytime he needs help. Tom offers Adam ideas as to what he could be teaching so that Adam has some direction. But at the same time Tom gives Adam freedom to choose whatever he wants to teach. When they do lesson planning Tom is like "What about you do this?" and then if Adam has an idea Tom is like, "Oh yeah, that is great."*

> Scenario 2: *Mary likes to have a go at trying out her ideas but Kath, her mentor, encourages her to closely imitate her teaching approaches because she "knows what the school wants and advocates". Kath is like "Here you go, see how you go with this technique, I am here if you have any questions.". Also, Mary feels her confidence is shrinking because she receives few positive comments from her mentor. The comments from Kath mainly focus on what went wrong in the classroom and Kath fails to recognize Mary's hard work and achievements.*

As preservice teachers start their practicum experience, they are filled with anxiety and stress originating from their perceived inability to function as competent teachers, how they can control and interact with the pupils, how to implement what they have learnt, and how much leniency they could employ, to name a few. However, although preservice teachers lack ideas and strategies for effective teaching, they should not be spoon-fed with details so much so that they feel paralysed to test their ideas as shown in Scenario 2. A reasonable amount of instructional support given at an appropriate time is more effective than bombarding mentees with details and techniques.

As important as the academic and instructional support is, preservice teachers need constant emotional support. One form of emotional support can be designing strategies to boost mentees' confidence as a boost in confidence help preservice teachers to take risks and experiment in the classroom (Rajuan, Beijaard, & Verlo, 2007). A few effective strategies mentor teachers can implement to develop their mentee's confidence include:

- Showing warmth and interest in their ideas and teaching approaches;
- Encouraging and approving their teaching progress;
- Highlighting their strengths;
- Recognizing their prior knowledge and skills;
- Providing opportunities for them to test their ideas while the mentor is there so if they fail, the mentor can pick them up;
- Complimenting them in front of others including staff and pupils about their teaching skills and success.

It is also important for mentor teachers to discuss with their mentees how much support they need to receive, in what areas, what format and how often. A key point to remember is that preservice teachers have different expectations depending on their academic and emotional needs. Having a discussion about the support they need could prevent disappointment and misunderstanding between mentors and mentees and lead to a higher level of satisfaction on their part.

The degree of self-confidence demonstrated by preservice teachers at different stages of their learning process has been regarded as an indicator of the progression of teacher identity (Cattley, 2007). The support and encouragement preservice teachers receive from their mentors can cultivate that sense of self-confidence. In particular, research shows if mentor teachers provide ongoing emotional and instructional supports and exhibit openness to preservice teachers' ideas, they develop confidence in their teaching practices and find their teaching voice through experimentation and risk-taking (Izadinia, 2016; Rajuan, et al., 2007).

Principle 3: Providing Ongoing Feedback

The importance of feedback in mentoring cannot be overstressed as it has been frequently considered as fundamental to a successful mentoring relationship (Bates, Drits, & Ramirez, 2011; Leshem, 2012). However, not all feedback is constructive. Consider the scenarios below:

Scenario 1: *Mark believes in the important role of feedback in improving mentees' teaching practices and professionalism. He engages his mentees in a continuous cycle of letting the mentee have a go and giving him feedback. After a lesson, he always starts off with a comment about how the lesson went. Then he provides a whole sheet of feedback and goes through it and makes sure his mentee understands the points. He also tries to give feedback in a way that the mentee feels affirmed rather than put down.*

Scenario 2: *John often cannot attend the classes his mentees lead, which he believes is a good thing because his mentees can feel a sense of ownership of the classroom. Hence, John tries to provide one general debrief at the end of each week. Also, instead of giving specific feedback on their teaching and where they need to improve, he prefers to use general comments like "Do not worry too much about the details, you are improving, you just need time to learn things". He thinks the mentees will eventually learn how to teach so why should he spend much time on going through the details and highlighting their mistakes.*

Preserve teachers regard their mentors as a reliable source of knowledge and professionalism and hence feel an urgent need to receive their constant comments and feedback throughout practicum. However, as shown above there is a difference between the quality of feedback mentors provide. There are mentor teachers like John who avoid negative feedback as they think it might demotivate and disappoint their mentees. Also some mentors tend to provide only positive comments out of fear of jeopardizing the relationship. However, first and foremost, mentors should bear it in mind that constructive feedback is honest feedback (Glenn, 2006). Although feedback should not in any way intend to demoralize mentees, it cannot facilitate progress if not focused on both strengths and weaknesses.

One of the best ways to provide feedback is to start with positives. Mentors can begin with highlighting the achievements mentees have meaning their problem solving, cooperation, and persistence and only then move on to the areas where improvement is required and discuss weaknesses. Mentors also need to make sure mentees clearly understand the comments and how they can address their weaknesses. As such, it is best if feedback follows a reflection on what can be done, as will be explained below. In addition, continuity of feedback counts as well. Although the feedback provided might be more detailed at the beginning given the range of skills mentees need to develop, it is acceptable if it shrinks in size as mentees progress. The following diagram shows the steps involved in constructive feedback (Fig. 10.1):

A smooth transition between each of the stages mentioned above can guarantee the effectiveness of feedback. However, above all, mentors need to consider that feedback should be given in an appropriate spirit and manner (Beck & Kosnik, 2002) so that mentees feel more motivated and affirmed to have another go and strengthen their weaknesses. Providing ongoing feedback would encourage preservice teachers to constantly reflect on their own progress, evaluate their teaching practices, reconstruct their learning and teaching, and subsequently develop their sense of self-awareness.

Self-awareness is another component of teacher identity and essential to possess because without knowing about one's beliefs, preservice teachers are unable to refine and develop their teaching practices (Fung, 2005). Hence, the more time mentor teachers devote to feedback and reflecting on the feedback, the more likely preservice teachers are to acknowledge their own weaknesses and strengths, gain a heightened awareness of the teacher they are, and take responsibility for their own development.

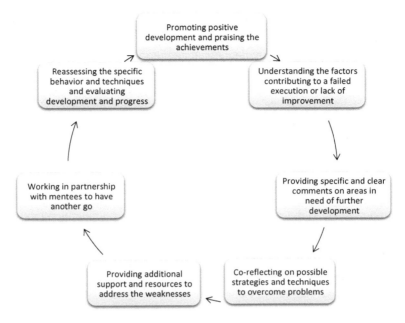

Fig. 10.1 Constructive feedback cycle

Principle 4: Making Time for Reflective Activities

As Shor (1992) believed, in constructivism, knowledge about self, everyday experience, and society is built through reflection and meaning making. In other words, through inquiry and not through blind acceptance of the pre-existing knowledge new opportunities for democratic and critical learning experience arise for students. As such it has been discussed to engage preservice teachers in reflective activities (Cattley, 2007; Vavrus, 2009; Webb, 2005) to help them critically examine their own development and be in charge of their learning process. Consider the following scenario:

> Scenario: *Tom, an experienced mentor, engages Dan in a continuous process of teach, feedback, and reflect. When Dan executes a lesson, Tom says, "Let's reflect on this lesson. Take a step back, take a broader view, Okay, so what can we do?" He gives Dan time to come up with ideas and strategies to address the problem he had faced. Then they collaboratively reflect on Dan's ideas and come up with a solution. He recaps and says "next time you walk in there and something happens like this, try just this one thing." Dan reflects on that, learns from it and adds it to his list of useful tools in the classroom. At the next session, Tom is like "Right, now you have done this, now I want you to do further". He tries to build on the knowledge Dan has already acquired and take it to the next level.*

Reflecting on one's teaching practices either individually or collaboratively helps not only to identify gaps and problems but also to test ideas and techniques to find effective solutions, address the weaknesses, and improve the teaching skills and practice. A reflection session with mentees should involve the following steps:

- Identifying what mentees are doing well and recording them as effective strategies in their repertoire
- Isolating problematic areas
- Evaluating their own understanding and impression of what went wrong
- Pinpointing the probable causes of the problem
- Examining the problem in light of effective teaching strategies to discover the differences and gaps
- Finding solutions and strategies collaboratively with mentees to address the problem through utilizing key resources
- Putting into practice the developed strategies to examine their effectiveness

Mentor teachers are encouraged to effectively stimulate joint reflective activities in their mentoring practices, set an example of how they can reflect on their teaching practice, and highlight the benefits they can earn. The reflection process, as explained above, can follow a feedback session, however, it goes beyond simply discussing the weaknesses and strengths. The aim of reflective activities should be enabling mentees to develop the habit of constantly evaluating their teaching and finding solutions to address the problems they face to improve. When mentees are familiar with the processes involved in a reflective cycle, they can proceed to conduct self-reflection, where they individually write down their own observations, solutions and evaluations of their own teaching. However, mentors should still have an active presence to observe and supervise the process and provide feedback.

The importance of relfection in supporting the development of teacher identity has been widely discussed and emphasised (Sutherland, Howard, & Markauskaite, 2010; Vavrus, 2009). Researchers argue that teachers' voice, as an indicator of teacher identity, develops when preservice teachers examine and reexamine their experiences through the process of reflection (Sutherland, et al., 2010). Cattley (2007) also suggests preservice teachers are more likely to shape a strong sense of teacher identity if they are constantly encouraged to reflect on the breadth of their roles.

Principle 5: Creating a Positive Environment

Creating a positive environment encompasses the two principles discussed above namely, building and maintaining strong relationships and offering support and encouragement as there will not be any positive environment without the element of a healthy and friendly relationship characterized by constant and strong support from members. However, there is another important aspect to a positive environment and that is open communication between members based on respect and trust. An effective mentoring provides equal opportunities for mentors and mentees to engage in ongoing dialogue to negotiate ideas and establish expectations and goals collectively. However, given that mentoring relationships are inherently laden with unequal power relations (Martinovic & Dlamini, 2009), they are likely to result in silence, a level of self-censoring and subsequently lack of learning on the part of mentees (Patrick, 2013) if mentees are constrained and intimidated by their mentors' judgment. In that case, mentees would shrink away from sharing their ideas and having an active participation in the learning process. Consider the following scenarios:

> Scenario: *Kath is a young teacher who has recently been assigned her first mentee, Luke. Luke wished his mentor to be like a friend whom he could open up to and bounce ideas off. However, Kath is not comfortable with making personal connections with Luke and thinks in order to be professionals they need to have a formal relationship. Kath also believes she is in a higher position and her job is only about providing Luke with detailed and step-by-step instructions to follow. Luke feels their relationship is strictly hierarchal and his mentor is a distant and unfriendly person who is not open to ideas. Although Luke is very unhappy with the mentoring he is receiving, he does not want to discuss his dissatisfaction with his mentor and cause any conflict.*

Working in a positive environment promotes feelings of security and fosters a sense of belonging and connectedness. On the contrary, environments that are stressful, unpleasant, and unsupportive can cause negative outcomes such as job anxiety, passivity, and loss of interest and motivation to complete activities. As shown in the above scenario, Luke's feelings of disappointment and discouragement were caused by the mentor's top-down approach that did not allow for negotiation of ideas. Creating an open line of communication allows mentees to freely discuss their viewpoints and hence feel heard and recognized. One way to establish a positive environment is offering ample opportunities to pause and evaluate the process together with the mentee throughout the practicum. Having a friendly discussion about the process, the objectives and what is working or not creates an atmosphere of trust and friendliness supportive of each party's needs and expectations. Hence, mentor teachers are recommended to allow for negotiation of ideas throughout the process and create the impression that their mentee can freely express their ideas and viewpoints about their mentoring experiences without worrying about their mark and assessment.

Studies suggest that the negative feelings and tensions preservice teachers experience can cause damaging consequences for their learning and functioning and hence jeopardize their professional identity. For instance, unlike typical beginning teachers' problems which are solvable, Pillen, Beijaard, and Brok (2013) argue, professional identity tensions such as those related to preservice teachers' beliefs, feelings, and perceptions are not easy to fix. A trusting and positive environment, where preservice teachers learn how to cope with their feelings of hoplessness, anger, and frustrations, can turn tensions into learning moments.

Concluding Remarks

In this chapter, I highlighted the role of mentor teachers in the development of pre-service teachers' teacher identity. Drawing upon the realistic scenarios based on my own research, I showed that the mentoring preservice teachers receive could define their understanding and perceptions of who they are a teacher. In other words, as I explained, teacher identity entails teachers' perceptions of their cognitive knowledge, sense of agency, self-awareness, voice, confidence, and relationship with colleagues, pupils and parents. I tend to believe the more positive preservice teachers' mentoring experiences are, the more positive their views towards each of these components will become and the stronger their sense of teacher identity would be. This is supported by the findings of the research which shows the influence mentor teachers have on preservice teachers' professional development and growth is both significant and meaningful (Ambrosetti, 2010; Garza, Duchaine, & Reynosa, 2014). The principles I presented in this chapter are designed to create a positive learning experience for preservice teachers to enhance preservice teachers' perceptions of each of the above-mentioned components of teacher identity.

As Wegner (1998) suggests our direct experiences with others and the nature of these relationships define who we are. Through establishing positive relationships with preservice teachers and incorporating the above-mentioned principles into the mentoring relationships, mentors can create a more positive learning experience for preservice teachers, one which fosters a positive attitude towards teaching and who they can be as a teacher.

References

Ambrosetti, A. (2010). Mentoring and learning to teach: What do preservice teachers expect to learn from their mentor teachers? *The International Journal of Learning, 17*(9), 117–132.

Baird, J. R. (1993). A personal perspective on mentoring. In B. J. C. E. M. A. Carter (Ed.), *The return of the mentor: Strategies for workplace learning* (pp. 45–58). London: The Falmer Press.

Bates, A. J., Drits, D., & Ramirez, L. A. (2011). Self-awareness and enactment of supervisory stance: Influences on responsiveness toward student teacher learning. *Teacher Education Quarterly, 38*(3), 69–87.

Beck, C., & Kosnik, C. (2000). Associate teachers in pre-service education: Clarifying and enhancing their role. *Journal of Education for Teaching: International Research and Pedagogy, 26*(3), 207–224.

Beck, C., & Kosnik, C. (2002). Components of a good practicum placement: Student teacher perceptions. *Teacher Education Quarterly, 29*(2), 81–98.

Beijaard, D., Meijer, P. C., & Verloop, N. (2004). Reconsidering research on teachers' professional identity. *Teaching and Teacher Education, 20*(2), 107–128.

Cattley, G. (2007). Emergence of professional identity for the pre-service teacher. *International Education Journal, 8*(2), 337–347.

Cook, J. S. (2009). "Coming into my own as a teacher": Identity, disequilibrium, and the first year of teaching. *The New Educator, 5*(4), 274–292.

Fung, M. Y. (2005). A philosophy of teaching practicum: Construction of a personal theory of teaching and learning. *Teacher Development, 9*(1), 43–57.

Garza, R., Duchaine, E. L., & Reynosa, R. (2014). A year in the mentor's classroom perceptions of secondary preservice teachers in high-need schools. *International Journal of Mentoring and Coaching in Education, 3*(3), 219–236.

Glenn, W. J. (2006). Model versus mentor: Defining the necessary qualities of the effective cooperating teacher. *Teacher Education Quarterly, 33,* 85–95.

Gold, Y. (1996). Beginning teacher support: Attrition, mentoring, and induction. *Handbook of Research on Teacher Education, 2,* 548–594.

Hung, D., Lim, S. H., & Jamaludin, A. B. (2011). Social constructivism, projective identity, and learning: Case study of Nathan. *Asia Pacific Education Review, 12*(2), 161–171.

Izadinia, M. (2013). A review of research on student teachers' professional identity. *British Educational Research Journal, 39*(4), 694–713.

Izadinia, M. (2015). A closer look at the role of mentor teachers in shaping preservice teachers' professional identity. *Teaching and Teacher Education, 52,* 1–10.

Izadinia, M. (2016). Student teachers' and mentor teachers' perceptions and expectations of a mentoring relationship: Do they match or clash? *Professional Development in Education, 42*(3), 387–402.

Izadinia, M. (2017). From swan to ugly duckling? The role of mentor teachers in preservice teachers' professional development. *Australian Journal of Teacher Education, 42*(7), 65–83. https://doi.org/10.14221/ajte.2017v42n7.5

Leshem, S. (2012). The many faces of mentor-mentee relationships in a pre-service teacher education programme. *Creative Education, 3*(4), 413–421.

Liu, Y., & Fisher, L. (2006). The development patterns of modern foreign language student teachers' conceptions of self and their explanations about change: Three cases. *Teacher Development, 10*(3), 343–360.

Martinovic, D., & Dlamini, S. N. (2009). Is 'good' really good? Exploring internationally educated teacher candidates' verbal descriptions of their in-school experiences. *Language Awareness, 18*(2), 129–146.

Nevins Stanulis, R., & Russell, D. (2000). "Jumping in": Trust and communication in mentor ing student teachers. *Teaching and Teacher Education, 16*(1), 65–80.

Olsen, B. (2008). How reasons for entry into the profession illuminate teacher identity development. *Teacher Education Quarterly, 35,* 23–40.

Pascarelli, J. (1998). A four-stage mentoring model that works. In S. Goodlad (Ed.), *Mentoring and tutoring by students* (pp. 231–243). London: Kogan Page & BP.

Patrick, R. (2013). "Don't rock the boat": Conflicting mentor and pre-service teacher narratives of professional experience. *The Australian Educational Researcher, 40*(2), 207–226.

Pillen, M., Beijaard, D., & den Brok, P. (2013). Professional identity tensions of beginning teachers. *Teachers and Teaching, 19*(6), 660–678.

Rajuan, M., Beijaard, D., & Verloop, N. (2007). The role of the cooperating teacher: Bridging the gap between the expectations of cooperating teachers and student teachers. *Mentoring & Tutoring, 15*(3), 223–242.

Schepens, A., Aelterman, A., & Vlerick, P. (2009). Student teachers' professional identity formation: Between being born as a teacher and becoming one. *Educational Studies, 35*(4), 361–378.

Shor, I. (1992). *Empowering education.* Chicago: University of Chicago Press.

Sutherland, L., Howard, S., & Markauskaite, L. (2010). Professional identity creation: Examining the development of beginning preservice teachers' understanding of their work as teachers. *Teaching and Teacher Education, 26,* 455–465.

Ticknor, A. S. (2014). Negotiating professional identities in teacher education: A closer look at the language of one preservice teacher. *The New Educator, 10*(4), 289–305.

Vavrus, M. (2009). Sexuality, schooling, and teacher identity formation: A critical pedagogy for teacher education. *Teaching and Teacher Education, 25*(3), 383–390.

Vygotsky, L. (1986). *Thought and language* (A. Kozulin, Trans.). Cambridge, MA: MIT Press.

Webb, M. (2005). Becoming a secondary-school teacher: The challenges of making teacher identity formation a conscious, informed process. *Issues in Educational Research, 15*(2), 206–224.

Wenger, E. (1998). *Communities of practice. Learning, meaning, and identity.* Cambridge, UK: Cambridge University Press.

Chapter 11
Student Teachers' Identity Development in Relation to "Teaching for Creativity"

Paulien C. Meijer and Ida E. Oosterheert

In this chapter, we investigate how student teachers develop their professional identities throughout a course that focused on 'teaching for creativity'. Teaching for creativity demands teachers to take up an additional role that is fundamentally different than their role in more traditional ways of teaching, which are still common practice in schools. This implies that this is an excellent context for working on student teachers' professional identity, as theories on identity learning see 'role changes' as opportunities for such learning to occur (e.g. Illeris, 2013). Learning to teach for creativity can then be approached as a process of professional identity development. For aspirant novice teachers this means that they should be kindled and stimulated to engage in learning how to cultivate creativity during their teacher training period, as part of the process of developing an identity as a teacher (see also Meijer & Oosterheert, 2017).

In 2009, Beauchamp and Thomas stated that "we need to more effectively address identity as a component in teacher education" (p.176). The last decade, many pedagogies were developed or proposed in an attempt to do so (see for overviews Leijen, Kullasepp & Anspal, 2014; cf. Meijer, Oolbekkink, Pillen & Aardema, 2014). Central in these overviews is a consensus on teachers' professional identity as the core of who teachers are and what defines them as teachers. It is developed as a result from dealing with both professional and personal tensions, from courage, and from living through professional crises (Illeris, 2013; Alsup, 2006). It is clear that traditional pedagogies do not suffice to support beginning teachers' identity development.

In a parallel process, several developments in society are calling for educational approaches in which pupils acquire not only knowledge and skills, but also learn to apply these to discover, devise, and realize new possibilities (cf. Scardamelia & Bereiter, 2014). To do this, *creativity* is viewed as one of the most important "skills"

P. C. Meijer (✉) · I. E. Oosterheert
Radboud Teachers Academy, Radboud University Nijmegen, Nijmegen, The Netherlands
e-mail: p.meijer@ru.nl; I.Oosterheert@docentenacademie.ru.nl

© Springer International Publishing AG, part of Springer Nature 2018   121
P. A. Schutz et al. (eds.), *Research on Teacher Identity*,
https://doi.org/10.1007/978-3-319-93836-3_11

for pupils to develop (e.g., Ferrari, Cachia, Ala-Mutka & Punie, 2010). As a result, teachers as well teacher educators are facing the challenge to achieve this goal.

Sternberg (2015) and Blamires and Peterson (2014), among others, have observed how little cultivation of creativity has penetrated the average classroom in the USA and the UK, although teachers seem to be motivated to get started on the cultivation of creativity. However, they experience a lack of knowledge and support to do this in a systematic and responsible manner (SLO, 2015). Scardamalia and Bereiter (2014) pointed out that simply passing the label "skill" onto a desired human characteristic (i.e., "creativity") does not make this characteristic teachable. It is therefore not surprising that many teachers today, feel they need to *learn* how to cultivate the creativity of their pupils (e.g. Ferrari et al., 2010; Sternberg, 2015). In this chapter we examine and illustrate how this challenge affects teachers' professional identities. Creativity, according to Jonathan, Plucker, Beghetto, and Dow (2004), can be described as "the interaction among aptitude, process, and environment by which an individual or group produces a perceptible product that is both novel and useful as defined within a social group". Cultivating such creativity in pupils, requires teachers to rethink their role, and even their teacher identity, as they develop from a teacher "who knows the answers" to a teacher "who challenges pupils to produce unknown outcomes". In a literature study on creativity and creative functioning in schools (Oosterheert & Meijer, 2017), we concluded that the cultivation of creativity in primary and secondary education requires more than the addition of a few creative assignments and a supplemental line of instruction. We proposed basic characteristics of a creativity cultivating context which, in subtle and less subtle ways, differ from what most students and teachers are accustomed to. This is the "creativity cultivating context" we propose, in brief (Oosterheert & Meijer, 2017):

A Creativity Cultivating Context

The main *goal* of a creativity cultivating context is to increase the confidence and ability of pupils to tackle creative challenges and contribute to ideas that can be considered new and useful within a given peer group. The second is to help pupils discover the domain(s) in which they want to further develop their creativity. Pupils work on *creative challenges* in which divergent and convergent activities form a meaningful whole, within or across disciplines. They learn to generate ideas and to deal with context boundaries and limitations. The outcomes are often unknown prior to the completion of the process, also to the teacher. *Teachers* create the space pupils need to tackle creative challenges, individually and with peers. They overtly value unconventional thinking and acting, emphasize the pleasure and benefit of creative functioning and discuss what constitutes creative quality within a particular challenge or domain. Pupils know ahead of time just how and for what purpose(s) their creative ideas will be looked at. Teachers curiously watch, from a broad developmental perspective, how pupils' creativity gets cultivated. Teachers are appreciative of pupils' efforts, provide feedback, and offer support. *Pupils* notice that teachers have high expectations for them and appreciate their creative qualities. They also notice that their ideas are given sufficient space and respect, even when they are not particularly creative. Pupils fearlessly put all of their imaginative powers, thinking, practical skills, and courage to work. Pupils discover their own qualities, those of others and how these qualities complement each other. Pupils gradually start to think up their own creative challenges. Pupils are stimulated to take on both little and bigger creative challenges across all subject domains. These creative challenges are elements of *reconstructed parts* of the existing curriculum. Specific creative talents and interests of pupils are given room within the elective and extracurricular components. *Assessment* largely has the character of "evaluating to learn". Summative assessment of creativity occurs on an incidental basis for components of the curriculum for which individual pupils have shown to have some substantive affinity.

Teacher Qualities in a Creativity Cultivating Context Through the Lens of Identity Development

It is evident that teaching for creativity requires specific teacher qualities. Among these are (cf. Oosterheert & Meijer, 2017):

- Creating learning environments with unknown and uncertain processes and outcomes
- Being creative themselves, at least within their major discipline
- Letting go of existing routines
- Having dialogues with pupils on the quality of their processes and outcomes, in this case to help them discover what constitutes creativity (in a domain)
- Perceive their pupils from a broad developmental perspective, not only from their progress in knowledge and skills in one discipline (secondary education).
- Being fine with not being the (only) expert
- Feeling safe (in their school) to experiment and fail

The development of these teacher qualities clearly do not primarily relate to their acquisition of skills and knowledge. Rather, it relates to teachers' attitudes and dispositions regarding 'who am I' and 'what do I identify with' as a teacher, which are central questions in identity development. Also, some qualities, at first sight, seem to conflict with common understandings of the learning-to-teach process. For instance, what does "*letting go* of existing routines" mean for a beginning teacher, who struggles to *build* basic routines? How does "feeling safe to experiment and 'fail'" work for a (student) teacher who feels insecure and vulnerable in front of a new classroom? What about a teacher with a self-perception of not being creative?

From the perspective of identity learning (cf. Meijer et al., 2014), however, such qualities should perhaps not be seen as potentially conflicting with the learning process of a novice teacher. In identity learning, dilemma's and (internal) conflicts are not so much to be avoided, but to be approached as *potential learning opportunities* (e.g., Illeris, 2013). Identity development or learning is a seen as a deep learning process that breaks down routines, involves sensemaking and meaning-making (cf. Geijsel & Meijers, 2005), and often results in personality changes (Illeris, 2013). Several pedagogies in teacher education programs have been developed over the past decades, which have identity development as their central concern (see for an overview Meijer et al., 2014). Among these are pedagogies that view critical incidents and dilemmas as learning opportunities, biography writing, and pedagogies that frame the dealing of professional tensions as inevitable component of teacher identity. All of these refer to the concept of transformative learning, as coined by Mezirow (e.g. 2006) and require a critical rethinking of oneself as teacher, and a breakthrough of routine behavior.

Interesting questions that arise are: Why should novice teachers first develop routines when in a later stage they need to let go of these routines? Why not explicitly stimulate student teachers to develop their cultivating-creativity qualities and professional identity at the same time, right from the start? What happens in teacher education programs based on this idea? These questions formed the incentive of the study described in this chapter.

Identity Formation in the Context of Learning to Teach for Creativity

In this section, we report on a course on teaching for creativity in initial teacher education to illustrate how it challenged student teachers' identity as beginning teachers. Point of departure for the course was that it should challenge beginning teachers' qualities as discussed earlier, when igniting their creative potential to do the same for their pupils. In addition, teacher educators should meet the same creativity cultivating qualities they aim to cultivate in their students. We designed an experimental elective course in a one-year post-master program, aiming to prepare teachers for teaching in (the upper parts of) secondary education. In four sessions of 90 min with 2 weeks intervals, 15 student teachers were challenged to experiment with the cultivation of pupil's creativity in their teaching practice. Throughout the course, they developed their answers on the following questions: What does creativity and the cultivation of creativity mean for (1) your pupils and for your subject area; (2) you as a person and as a teacher and (3) your professional context (colleagues, school)?

During the meetings, student teachers were involved in creative exercises, meant to lure them *out of their comfort zones*, such as crafting ("craft how you see yourself as a teacher") and unexpected questions ('what are we going to do today?'). Alongside, they *read scientific literature* on creativity and *viewed clips and animations* to prepare for the meetings. We *discussed* the purposes and value of education and teachers' role in it. Student teachers *experimented* with fostering pupils' creativity in their own teaching. As teacher educators, we explicitly *modeled* the qualities to be developed as much as possible and often explicitly. For example, we shared on the spot our own discomfort and also how we struggled with understanding the many voices in the scientific literature. In addition, we talked about experiences of *resistance* and overcoming it, and, above all, we shared our own *enthusiasm* about their ideas and classroom experiences. At the final meeting, student teachers presented their learning experiences and outcomes to each other. "Be creative" and "Set your own standard" were the only guidelines given.

After the course, student teachers answered the three course questions (see above) in a learner report. Their answers were analyzed in light of literature on identity formation (e.g., Beijaard & Meijer, 2017; Illeris, 2007, 2013; Meijer, 2011) and we used our own observations to understand some of these more thoroughly. For example, we learned from the data that student teachers often related to the concept of "uncertainty", and described how feeling uncertain, gave them the strength to develop courage to do something new. This relates to the work of Illeris (2007), who described how the feeling of uncertainty is a necessary part of identity learning. Another example is the identification with the teacher profession, as we found student teachers to rethink what it meant, for them, to be a teacher. This relates to the work of Verhaeghe (2012), who described identity as a result of relating to oneself, and relating to significant others (in this case: the teaching profession). Table 11.1 shows the identification aspects we distinguished from the data, along with illustrative quotes.

Table 11.1 shows student teachers' learning outcomes related to several aspects of teacher identity formation. Some of these do not refer exclusively to 'teaching for creativity'. Many outcomes refer to schooling or being a teacher in general. Apparently, the course 'Teaching for Creativity' has stimulated many student teachers to reconsider their role as teachers, the role of students, in their classrooms and in their schools. In addition to these findings, we think it is noteworthy to mention that during the meetings there were, at times, emotional outbursts, positive and negative or sad, from the student teachers. For example, some student teachers suddenly realized how little they have been challenged to use their creativity during their entire educational career. Particularly one student teacher in Physics burst out in tears during the craft assignment. He shared his inner conflict in realizing how much he felt 'trapped' or chained by the ways he had been taught thus far, and firmly stated '… and I NEVER want to feel it again!'. A student teacher claimed during a meeting that creativity plays an important role in her subject (English as a foreign language) and that she pitied teachers in other areas, because 'teaching for creativity in e.g., Biology is impossible.' An experienced biology teacher however, just passing by, responded that she just had her secondary students role-play the menstruation cycle. An exciting and engaging session followed in which student teachers from a variety of subject areas showed a renewed interest in their ideas on fostering creativity in their classrooms. In her learner report, this student teacher in English reported how pleasantly surprised she was about her fellow student teachers. Her experience made her realize that you teach together, with your colleagues. In addition, quite a few student teachers reported learning experiences and learning

Table 11.1 Identification aspects, findings (learning outcomes) and example quotes

Identification aspect	Findings	Examples
Student teachers' identification with the current educational practice in their school	After the course, about 70% of the student teachers spontaneously express their stronger awareness of and willingness to reconsider existing (curricular) structures and habits in their school. The same holds for the educational system as a whole. Through the course, they start to see it 'at a distance' and they feel a need to act upon it more deliberately.	'I may let go more of what seems evident'. 'I have become aware that I can actually question the assessment practices in my school'.
Student teachers' identification with their need for certainty and predictability	About 50% of the student teachers spontaneously report a changing view on certainty and predictability. They want to develop more tolerance of uncertainty and trust in themselves. Making mistakes must be possible. One of these student teachers reports her rediscovery of the importance of pleasure in teaching and her need to stay close to her own strengths; this includes the acceptance of less certainty.	'I want to learn to accept uncertainty and trust that it will be alright in one way or another'. 'I need to let go of my desire for control and regularity. Although that leads to resistance and uncertainty at first, I want to develop the courage to do something deviating, and to let go of restrictive norms'.
Student teachers' sense of professional space and agency in their own practice and in the school	About 90% of the student teachers express their discovery of the possibility of taking up a more proactive role in their classrooms and in their school. They become aware of their compliance and realize that it is just easy to start doing things in a (slightly) different fashion. They become aware that, in a sense, experienced teachers can learn from them as well. They report the necessity to proactively share new ideas and cooperate with colleagues, also from other disciplines. And a willingness to take up more responsibility.	'I can just show my colleagues what I have tried out in my classroom, instead of waiting for some kind of permission'. 'I need to let go of all kinds of control, to develop stamina instead of compliance'. 'I have to keep thinking for myself'

(continued)

Table 11.1 (continued)

Identification aspect	Findings	Examples
Student teachers' (changing) views on what good teaching (for creativity) could be	All student teachers report on new (emerging) views on learning and teaching, such as playful learning, having fun together, using imagination (teachers and students), experiencing more freedom and responsibility and having a lot of interaction. At the same time, sufficient safety and boundaries must be provided. New practice does not require a revolution, it can start small. It resembles the gradual establishment of a new learning culture, with other teachers. Flexibility and teachers' openness to experience is key.	'Teaching for creativity often means luring myself and my students out of our comfort zones'. 'Teaching for creativity is not about collecting new didactic tools; it is rather about the establishment of a new learning environment where students can develop themselves'. 'Students can handle less instructions and also they can think along with teachers about new challenges'. 'I know now that my subject involves so much more that the book or the study planner.'
Student teachers' identification with other teachers	About 40% of the student teachers express their positive surprise about unexpected qualities and ideas of their fellow students, particularly of students from other disciplines. As a consequence, they start to see teaching as a collaborate endeavor and not an isolated task.	'You educate students together, with your colleagues' 'Surprising for me is that so many of my fellow students feel restricted in the current practices in their schools.' 'Creativity can be nurtured in all disciplines'
Student teachers' identification with personal or teacher characteristics	About 60% of the student teachers express (emerging) personal or teacher characteristics they identify with.	'In my teaching I show characteristics of an artist' 'I want to have fun when I teach' 'Teaching for creativity is about freedom; for me and for the students (…). 'The open assignment was so hard for me… being a perfectionist, I am more proud of having done it (with so many open options!) than of the final result. So educative.'

desires such as 'overcoming uncertainty' and 'a desire to develop courage', in their own classrooms as well as in their school as an organization. Third, the open character of the final assignment turned out to be an exciting challenge for the student teachers as well as for us, the educators. Several students initially showed strong frustration and resistance because of this lack of structure and clarity. However, in the end, they saw that it was just this lack of structure that challenged them to think up original presentations that surprised all of us, and sometimes even themselves.

From the point of view of identity development, emotional experiences and even outbursts as described above may indicate a transformative learning process, which goes beyond the development of knowledge or skills towards the intensity of identity development (cf. Toompalu, Leijen & Kullasepp, 2017). Students' emotional system alerts them because (aspects of) their current identity are seriously challenged, which is a fundamentally disturbing experience for them. In this respect, Illeris (2013) states that "This learning implies what could be termed personality changes, … a break of orientation that typically occurs as the result of a crisis-like situation caused by challenges experienced as urgent and unavoidable, making it necessary to change oneself in order to get any further" (p.14). The outburst as described above can be seen as such a "crisis-like situation" (cf. Meijer, 2011) and, as such, labeled as identity learning. Also Pillen (2013), using the phrase "professional identity tensions" referred to the role of emotion in identity development. In her study, beginning teachers appeared to frame their most powerful learning to take place in the form of tensions, which kept them awake at night, made them uncertain and involved emotions. This confirms Illeris' model, who defines identity learning as to include a cognitive, an emotional and a social dimension.

Conclusions & Discussion

This study departed from the idea that learning to teach for creativity should be foremost conceived and approached as a process of professional identity development (Oosterheert & Meijer, 2017). A course was developed to bring these ideas into practice and to investigate, in an exploratory study, its processes and outcomes.

The findings indicate that the course 'Teaching for Creativity', based on pedagogies such as creating (and dealing with) uncertainty and dilemmas and with 'teach as you preach' as a major didactic approach, challenged student teachers' professional identities. It made student teachers actively consider various aspects of their emerging identities as teachers, such as their teacher roles, the purpose of schooling and student roles therein, and personal and teacher characteristics. Most student teachers evolved towards more trust in their students' ability to learn (creatively) and in their capacity to create space to learn (creatively). The results also indicate a grown 'sense of agency' as young professionals in a school context, which is not self-evident for Dutch (student) teachers (e.g. Oolbekkink-Marchand et al. 2017). In line with these findings, the study indicates that '*learning* to teach for creativity' indeed entails a process that goes beyond the acquisition of new knowledge and skills and the breaking through routines. In this study we found student teachers to refer to changes that went much deeper and included (a wish for) personality changes. The study provides some evidence that the cultivation of teaching for creativity during teacher training should be approached *as part of the process* of developing an identity as a teacher.

Particularly considering the relatively short duration of this course, we conclude that the course is promising; identity formation can be kindled and stimulated when 'Teaching for Creativity' is the challenge and when 'Teach as you Preach' is a major didactic ingredient. At the same time, just because of the relatively short duration of the course, we estimate that the observed learning outcomes, for the most part, indicate preliminary changes in student teachers' professional identities. It is uncertain whether these changes will be strengthened and further developed in everyday school life. Longer interventions, such as, for example, a whole teacher education program (Oosterheert & Meijer, 2017), are needed to ensure sustaining effects on student teachers professional identity formation.

References

Alsup, J. (2006). *Teacher identity discourses. Negotiating personal and professional spaces.* New York: Routledge.

Beauchamp, C., & Thomas, L. (2009). Understanding teacher identity: An overview of issues in the literature and implications for teacher education. *Cambridge Journal of Education, 39*(2), 175–189.

Beijaard, D., & Meijer, P.C. (2017). Developing the personal and professional in making a teacher identity. In D.J. Clandinin & J. Husu (Eds.), The SAGE handbook of research on teacher education (pp. 177–192). London: SAGE.

Blamires, M., & Peterson, A. (2014). Can creativity be assessed? Towards an evidence-informed framework for assessing and planning progress in creativity. *Cambridge Journal of Education, 44*(2), 147–162.

Ferrari, A., Cachia, R., Ala-Mutka, K., & Punie, Y. (2010). *Creative learning and innovative teaching: Final report on the study on creativity and innovation in education in EU member states.* Institute for Prospective and Technological Studies, Joint Research Centre.

Geijsel, F., & Meijers, F. (2005). Identity learning: The core process of educational change. *Educational Studies, 31*(4), 419–430.

Illeris, K. (2007). *How we learn: Learning and non-learning in school and beyond.* New York: Taylor and Francis.

Illeris, K. (2013). *Transformative learning and identity. London.* New York: Routledge.

Leijen, Â., Kullasepp, K., & Anspal, T. (2014). Pedagogies of developing teacher identity. In C. Craig & L. Orland-Barak (Eds.), *International teacher education: Promising pedagogies, Part A* (pp. 311–328). Bingley, UK: Emerald Publishing.

Meijer, P. C. (2011). The role of crisis in the development of student teachers' professional development. In A. Lauriala, R. Rajala, H. Ruokamo, & O. Ylitapio-Mäntylä (Eds.), *Navigating in educational contexts: Identities and cultures in dialogue* (pp. 41–54). London: SensePublishers.

Meijer, P. C., Oolbekkink, H. W., Pillen, M., & Aardema, A. (2014). Pedagogies of developing teacher identity. In C. Craig & L. Orland-Barak (Eds.), *International teacher education: Promising pedagogies (Part A), 293–309.* Bingley, UK: Emerald Group Publishing Limited.

Meijer, P.C. & Oosterheert, I.E. (2017). *Challenging student teachers' professional identities through immersion in 'teaching for creativity'*. Symposium paper presented at AERA 2017, San Antonio, USA.

Oolbekkink-Marchand, H. W., Hadar, L. L., Smith, K., Helleve, I., & Ulvik, M. (2017). Teachers' perceived professional space and their agency. *Teaching and Teacher Education, 62*(2), 37–46. https://doi.org/10.1016/j.tate.2016.11.005

Oosterheert, I.E., & Meijer, P.C. (2017). Wat creativiteitsontwikkeling in het onderwijs behoeft. [What it takes to cultivate creativity in education]. *Pedagogische Studiën, 94*, 196–210.

Pillen, M.T. (2013). *Professional identity tensions of beginning teachers*. Doctoral thesis, University of Eindhoven, the Netherlands.

Plucker, J. A., Beghetto, R. A., & Dow, G. T. (2004). Why isn't creativity more important to educational psychologists? Potentials, pitfalls, and future directions in creativity research. *Educational Psychologist, 39*(2), 83–96.

Scardamelia, M., & Bereiter, C. (2014). Knowledge building and knowledge creation: Theory, pedagogy, and technology. In K. Sawyer (Ed.), *The Cambridge handbook of the learning sciences* (pp. 397–417). New York: Cambridge University Press.

SLO. (2015). *21e eeuwse vaardigheden in het curriculum van het funderend onderwijs*. [21st century skills in the curriculum of primary and secondary education]. Enschede: SLO.

Sternberg, R. J. (2015). Teaching for creativity: The sounds of silence. *Psychology of Aesthetics, Creativity, and the Arts, 9*(2), 115–117.

Toompalu, A., Leijen, Ä., & Kullasepp, K. (2017). Professional role expectations and related feelings when solving pedagogical dilemmas: A comparison of pre- and in-service teachers. *Teacher Development, 21*(2), 307–323.

Verhaeghe, P. (2012). *Identiteit* [Identity]. Amsterdam: de Bezige Bij.

Part IV
Teacher Identity Development in the Content Areas

Chapter 12
"I'm Not Just a Math Teacher": Understanding the Development of Elementary Teachers' Mathematics Teacher Identity

Dionne Cross Francis, Ji Hong, Jinqing Liu, and Ayfer Eker

For years policy makers have sought to establish stringent accountable measures to encourage high quality teaching in schools. Such policies are grounded in the belief that effective teachers play a direct role in improving students' outcomes (Darling-Hammond & Youngs, 2002). Researchers (e.g., Cross & Hong, 2012) have shown, however, that to become and remain "effective" requires more than learning or adapting certain roles or specific instructional strategies. To develop and maintain teaching expertise often necessitates transformative change and development across cognitive, affective, and motivational dimensions. This requires changing teachers' sense of self so they can effectively respond to challenges and changes over time (Day & Gu, 2010). Given this perspective, teacher identity has been a useful construct for providing insight on how effective teachers develop, how teachers navigate induction during the early years of teaching, and how they negotiate the discrepancy between their personal and professional selves.

Teacher identity has been studied across various fields including teacher education (e.g., Beijaard, Meijer, & Verloop, 2004), educational psychology (e.g., Schutz, Crowder, & White, 2001), and educational leadership and policy studies (e.g., Lasky, 2005). It has been acknowledged as a critical factor that shapes and is shaped by teachers' professional lives, quality of their teaching, motivation to teach, career decision-making and their willingness and capacity to sustain commitment (Day, Elliot, & Kington, 2005). Although the increasing number of studies on teacher identity has broadened our understanding about the nature, characteristics and process of teacher identity development, little attention has been paid to content area specific identity development. Focusing on this aspect of teacher identity is critical

D. Cross Francis (✉) · J. Liu · A. Eker
Department of Curriculum and Instruction, Indiana University, Bloomington, IN, USA
e-mail: dicross@indiana.edu; jinqliu@iu.edu; ayeker@iu.edu

J. Hong
Department of Educational Psychology, University of Oklahoma, Norman, OK, USA
e-mail: jyhong@ou.edu

© Springer International Publishing AG, part of Springer Nature 2018
P. A. Schutz et al. (eds.), *Research on Teacher Identity*,
https://doi.org/10.1007/978-3-319-93836-3_12

133

as particular disciplines provide guidelines for the role of the teacher in the instructional context. For example, the National Council for Teachers of Mathematics' [NCTM] (1991) *Professional Standards for Teaching Mathematics* provides a set of standards for professional mathematics teaching. Such documents thereby shape teachers' perspectives on who they should be and how they should act when teaching. As such, in this chapter, we discuss how the mathematics education community frames the role of the teacher in the mathematics classroom, the tensions teachers experience in identifying as mathematics teachers, and how they describe these tensions.

The Role of the Mathematics Teacher

NCTM is the largest mathematics education organization in North America focused on supporting mathematics teachers. The organization provides clear descriptions of effective mathematics teaching practices and the beliefs that support them. Such practices are supported by both the numerous NCTM documents published (e.g. Principles to Action: Ensuring Mathematics Success for All (NCTM, 2014); Professional Standards for Teaching Mathematics (NCTM, 1991)) and research in the field.

Effective mathematics teachers view students as constructers of their own mathematical knowledge (Cai & Wang, 2010; Philipp, 2007), engage students in worthwhile tasks and utilize student-centered teaching methods to guide their learning (Mewborn & Cross, 2007). This includes promoting equity by ensuring all students have access to high-quality curricula and instruction, and the resources they need without discriminating based on students' levels of success, gender, race, and socioeconomic status (NCTM, 2000). A mathematics teacher knows that to be effective, she must know her students' needs and the most productive ways to address them. This requires extensive knowledge of mathematical content and ambitious teaching practices (Confrey, Maloney, & Corley, 2014; Lampert et al., 2013). Creating safe psychological spaces where students can make mistakes and become producers of mathematical ideas is essential; thereby requiring a delicate balance between "allowing students to pursue their own ways of thinking *and* providing important information that supports the development of significant mathematics" (Hiebert et al., 1997, p. 9).

This perspective on the role of the mathematics teacher serves as a guide for many mathematics teacher education and professional development (PD) programs across the U.S. Since the publication of the NCTM's *Professional Standards for Teaching Mathematics* (1991) and *Principles and Standards for School Mathematics* (1991) and more recently the *Principles to Action: Mathematics Success for All* (2014), teachers have received a fairly consistent message about the nature of their role in the mathematics classroom.

Teacher Identity Tension

Teacher identity is a teacher's sense of self as a teacher, which encompasses one's personal, professional, socio-political, and cultural dimensions. Teacher identity is considered a dynamic, continually changing, and active process which develops over time through interaction with different policy, school, and classroom environments and those who work in them (Watson, 2006). Currently many researchers tend to assume that identity is relational (e.g., Day, Kington, Stobart, & Sammons, 2006). That is, identity is continually being formed and reshaped based on how we internalize the external environment, negotiate the interactions, and present ourselves to others. For these researchers, although professional identity is shaped by prior experiences and beliefs, it is situated within a specific context, which creates a dynamic that is consistent with or in conflict with the professional standards, work demand, or the cultural context of the school. Although it is a commonly agreed notion that identity is changing and developing (e.g., Day, Chap. 6, this volume; Buchanan & Olsen, Chap. 17, this volume) not much is known about the *process* of change, which Meijer (2011) referred to as a "black box". Studies have focused on exploring the developing and dynamic nature of identity through the concepts of "tensions in learning to teach" (Smagorinsky, Cook, Moore, Jackson, & Fry, 2004), "identity shifts in the boundary space" (Beauchamp & Thomas, 2011), and "professional identity tensions" (Pillen, Beijaard, & Den Brok, 2013).

These frameworks emphasize that teachers' beliefs, values, or dispositions that have been shaped through their personal biographies, past schooling experiences, teacher education program, and teaching experiences are likely to be in tension or conflict with the ideals and ideology from various social contexts including educational policy, the professional communities' norms and vision for teaching, curriculum change, relationships with school administrators and colleagues, and students' learning processes and outcomes. When teachers' existing sense of what being a teacher means to them is challenged, teachers tend to question their identity as a teacher.

When teachers experience identity tensions, it can be potential sources of both challenge and professional growth. If teachers actively manage challenges, then the experience of tension and disequilibrium becomes a source for learning. As Jones and Nimmo (1999) commented, "Transformative change, genuine learning, happens only through disequilibrium, through the discovery that 'what I thought I knew isn't enough to deal with this new situation' (p. 8)." However, not all teachers navigate these tensions effectively. In fact, persistent and increasing tensions accompanied by lack of support often leads to teachers' decisions to leave the profession (Borman & Dowling, 2008). Thus, it is critical to unpack the nature and sources of identity tensions in order to extend our understanding of teachers' identity development processes, and identify proper ways to support and empower teachers.

Although an increasing number of studies have addressed teachers' identity tensions, what has been missing in the literature is in-service teachers' identity tensions related to discipline-specific teaching. Most studies related to identity tensions have focused on student teachers, or the transition from pre-service to in-service teaching (e.g., Beauchamp & Thomas, 2011; Pillen et al., 2013). Not much is known about in-service teachers' identity tensions, especially the tensions related to elementary teachers' mathematics teaching. Thus, in this chapter we discuss the tensions of elementary teachers' experiences in developing their mathematics teacher identity.

Context

Following the adoption of the *No Child Left Behind Act* (2001) and subsequently *Every Student Succeeds Act* (2015), the accountability mechanisms instituted in schools have placed pressure on teachers to ensure high student achievement in core academic subjects, namely mathematics and English/language arts. To support school districts and teachers in achieving these goals, there have been initiatives at both the federal and statewide levels to support schools and teachers. For example, professional development (PD) programs, research exploring the efficacy of reform-based curricular, and transformational leadership programs.

Our exploration into elementary teachers' mathematics identity took place within the context of a 2-year, state-funded PD program implemented by teacher educators from a neighboring university. The teachers were selected by their principals to participate. This is particularly relevant as the teachers were involved in activities designed to support them in transforming their practices to align with a problem-solving, inquiry-based approach to mathematics instruction. Also, their school districts volunteered them because they were seeking to transform mathematics instruction in their schools to ultimately improve scores on high stakes achievement tests. So, through involvement in this program, the participants were receiving messages directly and indirectly about what constitutes high-quality mathematics instruction and the role(s) they need to take on in order to meaningfully engage students mathematically and to teach effectively.

Teaching in student-centered ways tends to be challenging, particularly for elementary teachers as it requires deep knowledge of content, knowledge of students' mathematical thinking and an arsenal of instructional strategies to attend to the learning needs of a range of students. Unlike secondary level teachers, elementary teachers' educational training spans several content areas (including mathematics) and is not subject-specific.

To discuss the tensions elementary teachers experience in developing a mathematics teacher identity we draw from semi-structured interviews conducted with 18 elementary teachers who were involved in a PD program designed to improve their knowledge of mathematics and effective teaching practices.

Experiencing Tensions

Teachers seemed to struggle with four main tensions considering their roles as mathematics teachers, specifically related to their perceptions of professional roles as (i) a generalist (teacher of all subjects) versus being a subject-specific teacher (teaching framed around one subject); (ii) a grade-level teacher versus a mathematics teacher; (iii) a teacher with deep knowledge of mathematics versus a teacher with emerging mathematical knowledge; and (iv) a teacher of the whole person versus a teacher of academics. In the sections below we describe these tensions.

Generalist Versus Math Specific Teacher Several of the teachers fully embraced the identity of an elementary generalist, a teacher with a comprehensive understanding of the knowledge and skills needed to teach mathematics, science, language arts, reading, social studies and fine arts (Indiana Department of Education [IDOE], 2016). A generalist is expected to know the content of each subject area, in addition to being able to identify and use effective strategies, including technology, to effectively support students in learning the respective concepts in these subject areas.

Lily[1] captured these sentiments well when asked how closely she identified with being a math teacher, she stated "I wouldn't say I was just a math teacher. I'm a teacher of math and reading and writing and science and social studies and – that's how I would identify myself." She saw herself as not only a teacher of mathematics but of all the core subjects. When asked about her comfort level with being referred to as a math teacher, Whitney described her teacher role as wearing many hats.

> I am somewhat comfortable because I'm not just a math teacher. It's that it takes a village. So even though I'm wearing my math teacher hat right now I've got to put on my writing teacher hat … my reading teacher [hat], and science teacher [hat], and social studies teacher [hat].

This perspective of being a teacher of multiple subjects aligned with that of Amelia and Taylor who preferred the label 'teacher' and not aligned with a specific subject. Amelia described why she was not comfortable with the label 'math teacher' as, "I don't really identify myself as a math teacher – just a teacher. Because when I'm in the classroom, I'm teaching all the subjects, not just one or two."

Not all the teachers rejected the label 'math teacher'. Others, although they did see themselves as teachers of multiple subjects, also identified with the subject-specific label of math teacher. Jenna expressed ease with the label stating: "I feel confident saying that, yes, I'm a math teacher. I feel confident in the way I teach math." Interestingly Jenna aligned her comfort with identifying as a math teacher with her perception of her mathematics teaching ability – she feels confident about

---

[1] All names are psuedonyms.

her math teaching so she feels confident with the title of math teacher. Both Aria and Julia described how they initially identified more closely as a teacher of multiple subjects or another subject, and that the math teacher identity came along later. Aria explained,

> I can be identified as a math teacher. I can be identified as a reading teacher, a history teacher. I believe I can identify myself in those areas as well because of my initial background [training as an elementary generalist]. So prior to even identifying myself as a math teacher, I identified myself as a history teacher.

Grade-Level Teacher Versus Math Teacher Teachers also saw themselves as grade-level teachers. Based on years of experience teaching students at a specific grade level, they developed an identity as a teacher of that content and students within that grade. Taylor had over 10 years experience teaching first grade. Although in some years she was assigned to another grade level, she still saw herself as a first grade teacher. She explained,

> I'm a first grade teacher probably at heart first. I know that encompasses everything. This is the first time since 2004 that I haven't looped back down to first grade, and I'm struggling with that. So I think at heart, I'm a first grade teacher. It's who I am. It's what I do.

Also a veteran teacher of 24 years, Ava, had only taught 3rd grade for the past 6 years. In describing how she identified in her teaching role she stated, "I think I'm not just a math teacher. I'm a third grade teacher I guess." These remarks indicate they feel more comfortable and confident to identify themselves as a specific grade level teacher.

Teacher with Deep Content Knowledge vs. Teacher with Emerging Knowledge It is believed that in order to teach mathematics effectively, teachers need to be equipped with strong content knowledge (Hill, Rowan & Ball, 2005). There is also a widely accepted view that mathematics is one of the more challenging disciplines. As such, to be a teacher of this content implies that one must be highly competent with deep knowledge of the content. Several of the teachers held this view which served as a barrier to them embracing a mathematics teacher identity.

Bella explained that her view of a math teacher was a teacher who could teach higher level math, like trigonometry. She knew she was not strong enough in math to teach beyond elementary school, so she was not comfortable wearing the label 'math teacher'. Bella explained,

> I think I am not nearly qualified to be identified as a math teacher. To me, a math teacher is somebody that can teach trig [Trigonometry] in high school, and not fourth grade math. So it's a more specialized label than I would be willing to put on myself.

Leah also considered a math teacher as one with strong knowledge of mathematics which she did not think she had. The teacher educators in the PD program further supported this image of a mathematics teacher in the conversations they had with the teachers and also in the activities the teachers engaged in. Leah explained why she did not think of herself as a math teacher,

> I don't know if I would say a math teacher. To me, that's different from teaching math. So I wouldn't overly identify as that, because I don't think I know enough about math all around, like Donna [one of the professional developers] was talking about.

Teacher of the Whole Person vs. Teacher of Academics Teaching all core subjects meant spending a lot of time with their students. As a result, they knew their students quite well – including their students' strengths, struggles, interests, and needs. They knew the whole child and tended to assume responsibility to nurture not only academically, but psychologically, emotionally, and physically. Ava described how she prioritized educating the whole-being in discussing what she valued about teaching.

> I am more than just a teacher of academics. So, I think I'm a teacher of good choices, and good character, and a lot of life skills as well – not just making sure I have academically talented kids, but making sure that we are helping raise well-rounded, good character, and kids who have problem solving and life skills

Several of the teachers stated that they felt a tremendous responsibility to develop students to be successful and to be good, productive citizens. Both Keylee and Lily described how important it was for them to provide opportunities for their students to grow and thrive holistically. Kennedy emphasized, "I value kids and education, and that they're the future. And I want to make sure that they're going to be productive citizens of life, and that they can be in this community and in life, and get a job, and go to college." Lily echoed this sentiment,

> I think the biggest and most important factor to me, especially in the area that I'm teaching, is providing an opportunity for kids to grow into a responsible and a respectful member of our society, to teach them good citizenship. And that's huge to me. Just a love of kids and what they can grow up to be. And then, after that, it would be the educating part.

All the teachers taught in schools with large populations of students of low socio-economic status. Teachers acknowledged that many of their students come from unstable homes, some unsafe, and often do not get the guidance and support they need to thrive. As shown in Jenna's comments, she wanted to provide a safe, consistent space for their students and to help the students develop holistically. Jenna stated, "The relationships that the students and I make, I value being their safe place- they look for me to be there for them every day. I feel like I'm their one constant in their lives. I don't know – what they need other than just academics."

Unpacking Tensions

Our data showed some of the elementary teachers identified as being math teachers while many of them did not. Teachers who felt comfortable with their math teacher identity described embracing it in connection with an evaluation of their teaching of mathematics as competent. This implies associations between teaching competence, their mathematics teaching efficacy, and the respective identity. For those who did not consider themselves math teachers, they experienced at least one of the four types of core tensions, described above.

Although teachers are exposed to both subtle and direct messages about the importance of developing math expertise, they seemed to be more cognizant of these expectations during the PD program. This was not particularly surprising as their school administrators consistently underscored the importance of high student achievement on standardized tests and teachers' accountability for these positive student outcomes. For example, the teachers explicitly described mathematics teachers as teachers with deep knowledge of the content having a level of expertise they considered deeper and broader than their own. This sentiment was communicated by the professional developers and explicitly aligned with positive student outcomes. As such, participating in the PD program increased their experience and awareness of tensions – a difficult but necessary and important aspect of teachers' identity development. As Marcia (1980) addressed, the strength of identity can be acquired "only through vulnerability" (p. 110). When teachers experience tensions, the lack of stability of their identity is likely to elicit a sense of vulnerability. Thus, it is critical to provide a safe and supportive environment where teachers can learn, seek help, take risks, and develop their math teacher identity in order to reduce the likelihood they will suppress concerns or withdraw from participation. The PD program gave the teachers access to the resources they needed to improve their knowledge. Having access to the necessary resources and knowing that their professional learning would be beneficial for students' achievement would suggest that the tensions experienced may promote growth.

In contrast, the ways in which the teachers identified closely with being a grade level teacher and as a generalist created tensions that may be particularly challenging to resolve. Within the mathematics education and school-based communities, although elementary teachers are not subject-specific teachers and are required to teach the four core subjects, the expectation is that they should take on the role of mathematics teachers when engaging in mathematics instruction. Further, elementary teachers are generally licensed to teach grades kindergarten through sixth grade and should be able to transition from grade to grade flexibly. In this regard, embracing a professional identity that aligns one with a specific grade level, specific content, and specific aged students – although the teacher will likely become more competent with teaching at that level – becomes problematic when changes occur, as we observed with several teachers in the study. When such changes occur in a top-down manner and teachers have no agency in the decision-making process, this exacerbates the struggle. As Ruohotie-Lyhty and Moate (2016) and others (e.g., Alsup, Chap. 2, this volume; Schutz, Nichols & Schwenke, Chap. 5, this volume) emphasized, teachers' sense of agency functions as a resource for their teacher identity development. When teachers exercise agency, their capacity to regulate their learning and make decisions "forms professional identity and establishes its maintenance and transformation" (Vähäsantanen, 2015, p.15). In the same vein, when teachers loose their power to act, influence their own work, and make effective decisions, their weak sense of agency, which is often coupled with low confidence, is likely to erode their sense of identity and negatively impact their learning and growth (Eteläpelto, Vähäsantanen, & Hökkä, 2015). Thus, when changes occur that diminishes their agency, their sense of empowerment and identity begin to erode and they may feel less capable to achieve set goals or to improve their teaching context.

Additionally, within the wider community of subject-specific educators, for example the mathematics education community, there is the expectation that elementary teachers identify as math teachers in similar ways that secondary math teachers do. In the literature that describes the professional standards, knowledge, and dispositions of teachers of mathematics, there is no distinction between elementary and secondary teachers.[2] We assume this is similar to other disciplines. So although they are responsible for the instruction in at least four core areas, within the mathematics education community they are expected to have strong mathematical content and pedagogical expertise for grades kindergarten through sixth. Within their school districts they should have this level of expertise for all the subjects they teach which means not being a math teacher at the expense of the other subjects; rather, foregrounding a perspective of generalist as expert teacher in all the core subject areas.

These tensions may be particularly difficult to resolve for a couple of reasons. First, there will be significant pushback from the communities in which the teachers are embedded to transform and redefine the identities they currently embrace. In particular, their school-based community may support a "redefining" of generalist to one that serves as an overarching term for a teacher who has deep knowledge of all the core content areas and who wears the relevant discipline-specific "teaching hat" during instruction. Maintaining a coherent and consistent sense of self while orchestrating multiple discipline-specific "teaching hats" is important identity work in developing a balanced and competent teacher identity, or what Akkerman and Meijer (2011) called "unity of self". However, the data showed that teachers tended not to consider themselves knowledgeable enough to embrace the math teacher identity. Based on their licensure, teachers should be open to movement across grades, and administrators tend to expect this flexibility. Being wedded to a grade level will heighten the tension and decrease likelihood of achieving "unity of self". Second, embracing a math teacher identity in absence of the other subject-related teacher identities is not expedient given the expectation of competence across all core areas. However, to some extent this expectation of broad and deep knowledge across the core subjects is highly improbable. As such, it posed extraordinary challenges given that there were no resources readily available to support advancement in these other areas.

In relation to the fourth tension of teacher of the whole person versus teacher of academics, O'Connor (2007) describes the caring aspect of teaching and the high value teachers place on it. For many teachers caring becomes deeply embedded in their professional identity. The messages these teachers were receiving seemed to

---

[2] Elementary teachers are expected to have deep and broad knowledge of K-6 math content in similar ways that secondary level teachers are expected to have strong knowledge of 9–12 math content.

be interpreted as the teacher should have a core focus on academics *or* on nurturing the whole child. From a policy and ideological perspective neither communities in which the teachers were embedded viewed these as opposing perspectives; rather, that there should be a delicate balance with the teacher's core responsibility being to nurture the child academically, psychologically and emotionally. Achieving this balance would minimize possible negative emotion, burnout or attrition, which is likely to positively impact their identity development.

This study showed that elementary teachers experience various identity tensions in identifying themselves as mathematics teachers. These tensions can be sources for either challenge or growth, depending on how the tensions are addressed and managed. Thus, teacher educators, professional developers, school leaders, and policy makers need to be mindful about teachers' identity tensions and to provide access to necessary resources, build supportive work environments, and make decisions in ways to acknowledge and empower teachers' sense of agency and identity, especially during this time of heightened accountability related to mathematics achievement.

References

Akkerman, S. F., & Meijer, P. C. (2011). A dialogical approach to conceptualizing teacher identity. *Teaching and Teacher Education, 27*, 308–319.

Beauchamp, C., & Thomas, L. (2011). New teachers' identity shifts at the boundary of teacher education and initial practice. *International Journal of Educational Research, 50*, 6–13.

Beijaard, D., Meijer, P. C., & Verloop, N. (2004). Reconsidering research on teachers' professional identity. *Teaching and Teacher Education, 20*(2), 107–128.

Borman, G. D., & Dowling, N. M. (2008). Teacher attrition and retention: A meta analytic and narrative review of the research. *Review of Educational Research, 78*(3), 367–409.

Cai, J., & Wang, T. (2010). Conceptions of effective mathematics teaching within a cultural context: Perspectives of teachers from China and the United States. *Journal of Mathematics Teacher Education, 13*(3), 265–287.

Confrey, J., Maloney, A. P., & Corley, A. K. (2014). Learning trajectories: a framework for connecting standards with curriculum. *ZDM Mathematics Education, 46*(5), 719–733.

Cross, D. I., & Hong, J. Y. (2012). An ecological examination of teachers' emotions in the school context. *Teaching and Teacher Education, 28*(7), 957–967.

Darling-Hammond, L., & Youngs, P. (2002). Defining "highly qualified teachers:" What does "scientifically-based research" actually tell us? *Educational Researcher, 31*(9), 13–25.

Day, C., Elliot, B., & Kington, A. (2005). Reform, standards and teacher identity: Challenges of sustaining commitment. *Teaching and Teacher Education, 21*(5), 563–577.

Day, C., & Gu, Q. (2010). *The new lives of teachers.* London: Routledge.

Day, C., Kington, A., Stobart, G., & Sammons, P. (2006). The personal and professional selves of teachers: Stable and unstable identities. *British Educational Research Journal, 32*(4), 601–616.

Eteläpelto, A., Vähäsantanen, K., & Hökkä, P. (2015). How do novice teachers in Finland perceive their professional agency? *Teachers and Teaching: Theory and Practice, 21*(6), 660–680.

Every Student Succeeds Act. (2015). *Every student succeeds Act of 2015.* Pub. L. No. 114-95 § 114 Stat. 1177 (2015–2016).

Hiebert, J., et al. (1997). *Making sense: Teaching and learning mathematics with understanding.* Portsmouth, NH: Heinemann.

Hill, H. C., Rowan, B., & Ball, D. L. (2005). Effects of teachers' mathematical knowledge for teaching on student achievement. *American Educational Research Journal, 42*, 371–406.

Indiana Department of Education. (2016). *REPA educator standards*. Retrieved from http://www.doe.in.gov/licensing/repa-educator-standards

Johnson, E., & Nimmo, J. (1999). Collaboration, conflict, and change: Thoughts on education as provocation. *Young Children, 54*(1), 5–10.

Lampert, M., Franke, M. L., Kazemi, E., Ghousseini, H., Turrou, A. C., Beasley, H., et al. (2013). Keeping it complex: Using rehearsals to support novice teacher learning of ambitious teaching. *Journal of Teacher Education, 64*(3), 226–243.

Lasky, S. (2005). A sociocultural approach to understanding teacher identity, agency and professional vulnerability in a context of secondary school reform. *Teaching and Teacher Education, 21*(8), 899–916.

Marcia, J. E. (1980). Identity in adolescence. In J. Adelson (Ed.), *Handbook of adolescent psychology* (pp. 159–187). New York, NY: Wiley.

Meijer, P. C. (2011). The role of crisis in the development of student teachers' professional identity. In A. Lauriala, R. Rajala, H. Ruokamo, & O. Ylitapio-Mäntylä (Eds.), *Navigating in educational contexts: Identities and cultures in dialogue* (pp. 41–54). Rotterdam, The Netherlands: Sense Publishers.

Mewborn, D. S., & Cross, D. I. (2007). Mathematics teachers' beliefs about mathematics and links to students' learning. In *The learning of mathematics* (pp. 259–269). Reston, VA: National Council of Teachers of Mathematics.

National Council of Teachers of Mathematics. (1991). *Professional standards for teaching mathematics*. Reston, VA: The National Council of Teachers of Mathematics.

National Council of Teachers of Mathematics. (2000). *Principles and standards for school mathematics* (Vol. 1). Reston, VA: National Council of Teachers of Mathematics.

National Council of Teachers of Mathematics. (2014). *Principles to actions: Ensuring mathematical success for all*. Reston: National Council of Teachers of Mathematics.

NCLB. (2002). *No child left behind Act of 2001*. P.L. 107–110, 20 U.S.C. § 6319 (2002).

O'Connor, C. J. (2007). Magnetochemistry – Advances in theory and experimentation. *Progress in Inorganic Chemistry, 29*, 203–283.

Philipp, R. A. (2007). Mathematics teachers' beliefs and affect. In F. K. Lester Jr. (Ed.), *Second handbook of research on mathematics teaching and learning* (pp. 257–315). Charlotte, NC: Information Age Publishing.

Pillen, M., Beijaard, D., & Den Brok, P. (2013). Professional identity tensions of beginning teachers. *Teachers and Teaching: Theory and Practice, 19*(6), 660–678.

Ruohotie-Lyhty, M., & Moate, J. (2016). Who and how? Preservice teachers as active agents developing professional identities. *Teaching and Teacher Education, 40*, 94–103.

Schutz, P. A., Crowder, K. C., & White, V. E. (2001). The development of a goal to become a teacher. *Journal of Educational Psychology, 93*(2), 299–308.

Smagorinsky, P., Cook, L., Moore, C., Jackson, A., & Fry, P. (2004). Tensions in learning to teach: Accommodation and the development of a teaching identity. *Journal of Teacher Education, 55*(1), 8–24.

Vähäsantanen, K. (2015). Professional agency in the stream of change: Understanding educational change and teachers' professional identities. *Teaching and Teacher Education, 47*, 1–12.

Watson, C. (2006). Narratives of practice and the construction of identity in teaching. *Teachers and Teaching: Theory and Practice, 12*(5), 509–526.

Chapter 13
Elementary Science Teacher Identity as a Lived Experience: Small Stories in Narrative Analysis

Lucy Avraamidou

Identity and how it develops has been of interest for a few decades now in various fields of studies, such as education, philosophy, psychology, sociology and anthropology (e.g., Gee, 2000; Moore, 2008; Stets & Burke, 2000). Broadly summarized, identity has been used to refer to the characteristics of *Self:* who someone is and the ways in which she/he presents her/him-self in everyday life (Goffman, 1956). In identity theory, the core of an identity is the categorization of the self as an occupant of a role, and the incorporation, into the self, of the meanings and expectations associated with that role and its performance (Stets & Burke, 2000). In this study occupant role is seen as the role of a science person meaning someone who can self-identify with science and engage in scientific practice and scientific discourse.

The construct of identity is greatly important especially when studying women's engagement with science (as in this study) given that identity offers itself as a tool for examining the ways in which gender identity might influence how women see themselves as science persons. In a review study about girls' participation in science, Brotman and Moore (2008) asserted that the development of a science identity is the most recently emerged theme in the gender and science literature. As they recommended "schools, as well as society in general, need to make room for identities that defy commonly held, stereotypical norms about both gender and science" (p. 21). These ideas surfaced in the findings of this study as evident in different episodes where the participant of this study was filtering her science experiences through her gender identity.

Science identity has been defined in the literature as the view of self as a successful science learner and/or a future scientist (Carlone & Johnson, 2007). More specifically, science identity has been defined as consisting of three dimensions: (a) *competence*: knowledge and understanding of science content; (b) *performance*:

L. Avraamidou (✉)
Institute for Science Education and Communication, University of Groningen,
Groningen, The Netherlands
e-mail: L.Avraamidou@rug.nl

© Springer International Publishing AG, part of Springer Nature 2018   145
P. A. Schutz et al. (eds.), *Research on Teacher Identity*,
https://doi.org/10.1007/978-3-319-93836-3_13

social performances of relevant scientific practices, such as collecting and analyzing authentic data using scientific instruments and, (c) *recognition*: recognizing oneself and getting recognized by others as a science person (Carlone & Johnson, 2007).

The study reported in this chapter is framed within this model of science identity as it examines how these three dimensions intertwine to characterize Anna's, a beginning elementary science teacher, emerging science identity. As such, in exploring Anna's science identity, I provide evidence for Anna's competency as a learner/ teacher of science, her performance as a science learner/teacher, and how she recognizes herself and is recognized by others as a science person.

Identity Through Life-History

In this chapter, I frame Anna's story in relation to science within a life-history or biographical perspective. Knowles and Holt-Reynolds (1991) use the terms biography and personal histories interchangeably to refer to the many and varied experiences that pre-service teachers bring with them to teacher education, and which have influenced the ways they think about teaching. But, why does life-history provide a useful lens for examining teachers' science identity development? Goodson and Sikes (2001) argued that the stories people tell about their lives provide useful and important insights into big questions of social life because they offer evidence of how individuals negotiate their identities and, consequently, experience, create, and make sense of the rules and roles of the social worlds in which we live in.

For the purposes of this chapter, identity is conceptualized as a *lived experience* (translated from the Russian term *perezhivanie*, coined by Vygotsky) which is used to describe the ways in which people perceive, experience, and process the emotional aspects of social interactions. As such, *lived experience* presents a dynamic, fluid, and complex unit of analysis between personality characteristics and environmental characteristic. Lived experience, in this study, is used to emphasize that: (a) cognition/thinking/meaning are inextricable from feelings/emotions/ meaning; and, (b) learning and experience are intrinsically situated in a matrix of life trajectories and ecological transactional aspects throughout one's life. In doing so, science identity is conceptualized as a *dynamic process of becoming* instead of a product, and an emphasis on the affective domains of the pathways through which teachers come to form their science identities. The centrality of emotions is found in the concluding pages of *Thinking and Speech*, where Vygotsky discusses the dialectical relationship between thought, affect, language, and consciousness: "Thought has its origins in the motivating sphere of consciousness, a sphere that includes our inclinations and needs, our interests and impulses, and our affect and emotions" (1935/1987, p. 282).

By conceptualizing identity as a lived experience, emphasis is placed on the affective domains of a science teacher's identity development and on the ways in which their emotions throughout their life histories as science learners might influence their developing science identities. For the purpose of this study, in analyzing

Anna's life history in relation to science I looked for the presence of achievement emotions, defined as emotions tied directly to achievement activities or achievement outcomes (Schutz & Pekrun, 2007), within the various experiences that might have impacted the development of her identity. A life history perspective then is used both as a theoretical framework and a data collection tool for this study. By adopting a life history perspective, emphasis is placed on the historicity of identity or how identity is developed over time within various kinds of contexts. By using life history as a data collection tool, emphasis is placed on the stories that teachers make out of their experiences, and how those can be used as data for exploring their developing science identities. In examining these stories, the three dimensions of science identity serve as a unit of analysis across time and within contexts: competence, performance, and recognition.

Teacher Identity Research

There is a growing interest in the construct of science teacher identity with an increasing number of studies exploring science teachers' identities and experiences that impact their formation (e.g., Avraamidou, 2016; Moore, 2008; Rivera-Maulucci, 2013; Varelas, 2012). Researchers have viewed teacher identity in terms of: how teachers view themselves and are recognized by others (Gee, 2000); the stories that teachers create and tell about their teaching lives (Connelly & Clandinin, 1999); the communities in which teachers participate, learn and develop (Wenger, 1998); a gender perspective (Carlone & Johnson, 2007); and, through a positionality lens (Moore, 2008). My work is situated in Connelly and Clandinin's (1999) conceptualization of identity, who proposed the use of personal histories to frame teacher identity and referred to teachers' professional identity in terms of "stories to live by" (p. 4). In doing so, my work is framed within the notion of narrative inquiry, which is premised on the idea that, as human beings, we come to understand and give meaning to our lives through stories. As Connelly and Clandinin argued, a teacher's knowledges are "narratively composed, embodied in them and expressed in practice" (Clandinin & Connelly, 2000, p. 124) in the form of stories.

To examine these stories Clandinin and Connelly (2000) developed the Three-Dimensional Space Narrative Structure, which is defined by three major dimensions: (a) interaction; (b) continuity; and, (c) situation. *Interaction* refers to two aspects of experience: personal – look inward to internal conditions such as desires, feelings, and hopes; and, social – look outward to existential conditions in the environment with other people and their intentions, purposes, assumptions, and points of view. *Continuity* refers to the idea that experiences have a past, a present, and a future reference. Lastly, *situation* places an emphasis on the context where events take place and experiences take hold. Clandinin and Connelly's conceptualization of teacher identity in terms of stories has been used as an analytical framework for the study reported in this chapter aiming to examine how Anna's narratively-composed science identity is embedded in her life history. Hence, I explore her narrative in relation to science in terms of its continuity through three different times: past, present, and future. In doing so, I filter her narrative through three analytical lenses that comprise the dimensions of a science identity: *competence, performance,* and *recognition.* As such, the main research question that guided the analysis of Anna's story in relation to science is the following:

- What kinds of lived experiences throughout childhood, schooling, university, and first-years of teaching shaped Anna's science identity?

On the Where and How of the Study

The study is situated in Southern Europe and Anna is a middle-class Caucasian, 25 years old, who went through a typical 4-year elementary teacher preparation program and took three science content followed by a methods course. At the time she entered this study, Anna had 2 years of teaching experience and she was enrolled in a graduate master's program in science education. Anna was a motivated, average-ability (by GPA means) graduate student, with no special interest in science. In a sense, Anna offers a profile of a typical elementary teacher in the context where this study took place, and that is why she was chosen to participate in this study to provide a more representative case.

Several kinds of data were collected for the purpose of exploring Anna's life history in relation to science: a detailed science-biography, three brief biographical assignments, a personal philosophy of teaching statement, and a 2-h long interview. The data were collected over a period of a year during which Anna was enrolled in the master's program. To analyze the data, I first organized those chronologically: past experiences through schooling as a science learner, current views about science teaching and experiences at the university, and vision of self as a teacher. In doing so, I was looking for data that would help me examine the impact of various experiences Anna had throughout her life on the development of her identities. In what follows, I narrate Anna's story in a chronological order, starting from her childhood experiences and ending with her professional teaching experiences.

Anna's Story in Relation to Science

I narrate Anna's life-history in relation to science by framing it through the Three-Dimensional Space Narrative Structure. Her story is structured in a chronological sequence starting from her early life experiences, navigating through the present while looking into the future. Throughout this narration I exemplify how different experiences were influential to shaping the three dimensions of Anna's science identity: competence, performance and recognition.

Elaborating on her childhood memories, Anna stated that she always wanted to become a teacher, even at the age of 6. The following extract from her interview reads as follows:

> To become a teacher for me was life dream, which started from a very young age. From kindergarten already, when I was asked what I wanted to be when I grow up, I would say: "a teacher"! (Anna, interview)

A critical influence on her decision, as she described, was the fact that both of her parents were teachers.

> Both my mom and my dad were teachers, so I had an understanding of what their job was about and how it looked like on an everyday basis. But, most importantly, I remember how the rest of the family and the community had a big sense of admiration for them. (Anna, interview)

It's interesting to notice in this above extract how Anna pointed to the fact that her parents were recognized by others alongside a sense of admiration from the community. A possible assumption is that implicitly Anna was thinking how she would be *recognized* in the same way by her family and community, if she followed the same career path as her parents. Another influence from her family environment were Anna's grandparents who were farmers and who provided her with ample opportunities to experiment in nature. Below is an extract from her autobiography:

> My grandparents were farmers, they had a farm with animals and were also growing potatoes, tomatoes, and other vegetables. I used to spent a couple of months in the summer at the farm helping them out, so I learned a lot of things about the weather, animals, and plants. (Anna, autobiography)

From this exract, another dimension of science identity is starting to surface: *competence*. As evident in Anna's words with the use of "I learned a lot of things", she was developing a sense of a competent science learner.

Going to elementary school, Anna felt that she had more knowledge about the natural world because of these experiences, than the rest of the classroom. Elaborating on her experiences as a science learner, she shared positive memories of experimenting with science:

> I was really excited about science, we were studying very interesting topics, and we used to go on field-trips quite often. I remember visiting a dam, an environmental center, and also a museum about water. During these visits we had opportunities to take scientific measures, such as for example, the temperature of the water of the dam. I was very excited about these experiences, especially the use of real scientific instruments! (Anna, biographical assignment)

It becomes clear in this extract how Anna's *competence* was matching her *performance* as a science learner, another dimension of science identity. This extract illustrates that not only did she feel competent as a science learner she also developed the necessary skills for the *performance* of relevant scientific practices (e.g., application of scientific tools).

In secondary school, as Anna noted in a biographical assignment, her interest in science started to decline because the lessons became more theoretical:

> Science became one of the most boring lessons. I was not excited about science no more. I
> don't remember carrying out any experiments. I remember having to read and write a lot,
> which I hated actually. (Anna, biographical assignment)

It's interesting to notice here the shift on Anna's interest in science but also her emotions towards science learning. The choice of words 'boring' and 'not excited' serve as evidence of the negative impact of these schooling experiences on her interest in science. Besides the fact that students were not involved in experimentation, Anna commented on the characteristics of her science teacher:

> Our science teacher was very strict. It looked like he was obsessed with physics and mathematics, very knowledgeable but he wasn't able to explain things to us. Each time I would pose a question he would respond with a sarcastic comment implying that my question was stupid. So, I started feeling anxious, and I stopped asking questions (Anna, biographical assignment).

Three things become of great interest in this extract. One is related to science stereotypes (e.g., a man who is obsessed with physics, inability to communicate ideas to others), the other one is related to how Anna was being *recognized* as a science learner (e.g., the teacher's response making her feel that she was stupid) and how Anna's emotions influenced her performance (e.g., feeling anxious, stopped asking questions). These ideas might imply issues related to gender and women's engagement in science. First, it might be possible that this teacher did not enact gender inclusive practices and did not make an effort to support female students' participation in science (though there is not explicit evidence in the data to assert this), but it is also possible that Anna filtered these experiences through her gender identity. As will become apparent later on, she was better able to relate with her female university instructors, even though those instructors used contemporary approaches to science teaching as well, which makes it difficult to tease out whether gender alone had an influence on her identity trajectory.

Similarly to the above extract, Anna again chose the words 'feeling anxious' which point to her emotions as a learner of science. In the interview, I asked Anna to elaborate on this and so she described what a typical lesson looked like. She responded as follows:

> ...he would start a lecture about a new subject. From time to time he would stop and ask if
> we had any questions. Nobody ever had any questions of course because it was so hard to
> follow him but also because we also felt intimidated. (Anna, interview)

It becomes apparent through Anna's words that these experiences impacted in a negative way not only her interest in science and *competence* (i.e., felt intimidated) but also her *performance* as a science learner (i.e., not asking questions). It is interesting to note in this description how Anna referred to feeling intimidated by this teacher, which can be traced back to her science identity as a learner of science. Going to high school, Anna experienced science even in worse ways. She described very difficult and theoretical lessons, and very strict teachers. As a result, by the end of high school she lost any interest she had for science completely. In describing one of her teachers, many science stereotypes came to surface:

> When he entered the class for the first time, we were all shocked. He looked like Einstein – he was bald, and enormous eyebrows. He would usually say things like science is the best discipline...he was arrogant, and rude, and a really bad teacher. Science lessons felt like a nightmare by the end of high school. (Anna, interview)

Anna's interest in science was revived when she went to university after completing a set of compulsory science courses. Even though, as she said, she dreaded the day that she would have to take a set of mandatory science courses, she enjoyed all science content courses as well as the methods course that she took. Because of these experiences she decided to specialize in science education. In describing her experiences as a preservice teacher, she shared memories of experimentation, projects, examination of socio-scientific issues, and interdisciplinary approaches. In a journal she wrote:

> First, I learned a lot so I feel confident in my content knowledge. But, I also enjoyed the ways in which the lessons were taught because we were always engaged either in experimentation or in large-group discussions. The classroom climate was friendly and we all felt comfortable in asking questions, especially because all of our teachers were younger women, and so we were not intimidated. (Anna, journal entry)

It becomes clear in this quote how Anna's science identity was shaping because of how her *competence* as a science learner was being supported (i.e., confidence) but also her *performance* was enhanced (i.e., engaged in experimentation and classroom discourse). It's also interesting to notice the choice of various words that point to her emotions such as, feeling comfortable, enjoyment, not being intimidated, which indicate a positive shift in her identity as a learner of science, especially on her competency. Also, it's interesting to note that Anna made an explicit reference to the gender of her instructors (who were women), which again might imply the role of gender in filtering these science experiences.

In the interview, Anna shared similar positive experiences and emphasized the impact that the science methods course had on her:

> I loved the science methods course. Through the course, we saw in practice how contemporary approaches to science teaching could be applied in practice, such as for example scientific inquiry. I felt that the course prepared me to be an effective teacher...but, most importantly it made me gain confidence in myself as a future science teacher. (Anna, Interview)

It's clear in this extract that her university experiences impacted Anna's developing science identity and specifically her *competency* (i.e., confidence in self).

Sharing her experiences as a beginning teacher, Anna reflected on her experiences as a learner of science to pinpoint how those experiences shaped her views about science teaching and learning, and how children learn science.

> I realize now how my practices have been influenced by my past experiences as a science learner. I do not want to be that teacher who puts students off science, who scares them away, who intimidates them. I want to make them realize the value of science to their lives and to make them passionate about science, as my university instructors did for me! (Anna, interview)

These words speak directly to Anna's *performance* as a science teacher. These reveal a strong science identity of a teacher who has a clear vision of how she aspires to be. Additionally, these words might also imply how Anna would like to be *recognized* by her students, as an inspiring and passionate teacher, the same way that she recognized her university instructors.

When I asked her to explain how she tries to achieve this goal, she said:

> I always engage them in some kind of experiment or activity, I try to make connections between what we learn in class and their everyday lives. But, most of all, I try to create a fun and friendly learning environment, I want them to feel excited to be there. This is the kind of teacher I aim to be! (Anna, interview)

This extract illustrates a sense of Anna's high *competence* and *performance* as a science teacher. Her words reveal a high self-efficacy and confidence as a science teacher who is able to perform or enact specific practices to achieve her goals. What's also interesting to observe here is the emphasis that Anna places on creating a fun and friendly learning environment, which implies her attention to developing a positive emotional climate in her classroom. In her personal philosophy statement, Anna described the kinds of approaches and strategies that she uses in her practices, which serve as evidence of her performance as a science teacher:

> I engage them in inquiry-based investigations, in field-studies, in examination of real-life issues like, for example, the quality of air. Of course, I engage them in experimentation and in using technology applications, such as mobile games. Most importantly, I try to engage them in discussions about the value of science to society and the work of scientists. (Anna, personal philosophy of teaching)

Various contemporary ideas about science teaching become apparent in this extract that reveal Anna's strong science identity through her *competency* and *performance*: enactment of inquiry-based science, use of modern technology applications, establishing links between science and society as well as addressing science stereotypes. These ideas featured centrally not only in Anna's personal philosophy but also in her journal entries as well as her interview, which provides evidence of the maturity and consistency of these ideas.

Conclusions and Implications

What the story of Anna tells us is how complex beginning elementary teachers' identity trajectories are, influenced by various kinds of experiences throughout their life histories. As evidenced in Anna's story, she viewed herself as a successful science teacher, one who uses contemporary approaches to science teaching and serves as a positive role model for her students. Anna was recognized as a successful learner of science by her family, and she also performed well in science, as a young learner in science. That, however, was not the case in secondary and high school, when Anna experienced science teaching through teacher-centered approaches and came across teachers that impacted her emotional trajectory as a learner of science in negative ways. During that chronological period two things surfaced: she was not recognized as a successful learner of science by her teachers, and as a result, she did not feel competent and did not perform well as a science learner. It was not until Anna went to university that her interest in science was revived because she experienced science in personally meaningful ways, and she came across strong female role models. At that time, Anna was also recognized as a successful science learner by her instructors, she performed well and viewed herself as a competent science learner and future teacher.

In describing her experiences with science from her childhood through her first-years of teaching, Anna placed emphasis on affective domains of her development, which points to the role of the emotions on her identity trajectory. In several instances she described her emotions as a learner of science (e.g., scared, excited, bored) which were directly connected to her science identity. Moreover, the possible role of gender in filtering her science experiences appeared to emerge in different instances, even though this was not conscious and she never made any explicit statements about that. However, in describing her science teachers in secondary and high school she emphasized that those were "strict men" and when describing her university instructors she emphasized that they were "young women". These references deserve further attention. Gender and its role to the development of a science identity has featured centrally in various studies that range from examining women scientists' identities (Carlone & Johnson, 2007) and young girls' participation in science (Brickhouse, Lowery & Schultz, 2000).

Drawn within the findings of this study, and building upon existing literature on science teacher identity, the study provides evidence for the need of conceptualizing teacher identity as a lived experience, the value of life-histories in examining identity development, and the role of emotions in teachers' identity development. A few other researchers in science education have argued about the affective domains of teachers' learning and development and the central role of emotions in teacher identity and identity development (e.g., Rivera-Maulucci, 2013; Zembylas, 2005). Rivera-Maulucci (2013) argued that "emotions influence the goals teachers set and indicate the intensity of their relationships to ideas, to their beliefs about science, to others, and to science teaching" (p. 137). In agreement with this view, Tobin and Llena (2012) stated that emotions are constituents of a teacher's identity as well as enactment. Likewise, Zembylas (2005) stated, "the ways in which teachers understand, experience, perform, and talk about emotions are highly related to their sense of identity" (p. 937).

The findings of the study showed how Anna's identity trajectory shifted and reformed through teacher preparation, and provide evidence of the significant impact of the elementary methods course in supporting Anna reflecting on her prior experiences as a learner and developing contemporary ideas about science teaching and learning. Specific aspects and experiences within teacher preparation appeared to have a critical impact, and which have implications for the design of teacher preparation programs. These are as follows:

- Understanding that a science teacher's identity has multiple dimensions that go beyond cognitive domains of learning and address these through teacher preparation;
- Providing opportunities for preservice teachers to be recognized as successful science leaners and/or future teachers;
- Paying attention to the emotional experiences and how these interrelate with teachers' identity trajectories;
- Examining preservice teachers' personal histories in relation to science as they enter a preparation program to better understand and address their needs as future teachers;
- Providing opportunities for identity shaping and re-shaping, as well as offering opportunities for self-reflection on life histories

This chapter presents my narration of Anna's narrative or life history in relation to science, which consists of a series of stories that took place throughout her life. My narration is, in fact, a selection of small stories that construct and reconstruct her narrative. As any other narration, this one as well, is bounded within my subjective interpretations of Anna's story. It is, therefore, likely that through my subjective interpretations I have highlighted certain dimensions, experiences, and events over others concerning Anna's emerging identity as a science teacher. As such, this narration is composed by the pieces or small stories that I chose to put together to articulate how Anna's science identity was shaped and what kinds of experiences were critical to its development.

References

Avraamidou, L. (2016). Intersections of life histories and science identities: The stories of three preservice elementary teachers. *International Journal of Science Education, 38*(5), 861–884.

Brickhouse, N. W., Lowery, P., & Schultz, K. (2000). What kind of a girl does science? The construction of school science identities. *Journal of Research in Science Teaching, 37*, 441–458.

Brotman, J. S., & Moore, F. M. (2008). Girls and science: A review of four themes in the science education literature. *Journal of Research in Science Teaching, 45*(9), 971–1002.

Carlone, H. B., & Johnson, A. (2007). Understanding the science experiences of successful women of color: Science identity as an analytic lens. *Journal of Research in Science Teaching, 44*, 1187–1218.

Clandinin, D. J., & Connelly, F. M. (2000). *Narrative inquiry: Experience in story in qualitative research.* San Francisco: Josses-Bass.

Connelly, F. M., & Clandinin, D. J. (1999). *Shaping a professional identity: Stories of educational practice.* New York: Teachers College Press.

Gee, J. P. (2000). Identity as an analytic lens for research in education. *Review of Research in Education, 25*, 99–125.

Goffman, E. (1956). *The presentation of self in everyday life.* New York: Doubleday.

Goodson, I., & Sikes, P. (2001). *Life history research in educational settings: Learning from lives.* Buckingham, UK: Open University Press.

Knowles, J. G., & Holt-Reynolds, D. (1991). Shaping pedagogical through personal histories in preservice teacher education. *Teacher College Record, 93*(1), 87–11.

Moore, F. M. (2008). Positional identity and science teacher professional development. *Journal of Research in Science Teaching, 45*(6), 684–710.

Rivera Maulucci, M. S. (2013). Emotions and positional identity in becoming a social justice science teacher: Nicole's story. *Journal of Research in Science Teaching, 50*(4), 453–478.

Schutz, P. A., & Pekrun, R. (2007). *Emotions in education*. San Diego, CA: Elsevier.

Stets, J. E., & Burke, P. J. (2000). Identity theory and social identity theory. *Social Psychology Quartely, 63*(3), 224–237.

Tobin, K., & Llena, R. (2012). Colliding identities, emotional roller coasters, and contradictions of urban science education. In M. Varelas (Ed.), *Identity construction and science education research: Learning, teaching, and being in multiple contexts* (pp. 141–156). Rotterdam, The Netherlands: Sense Publishers.

Varelas, M. (2012). *Identity construction and science education research*. Rotterdam, The Netherlands: Sense Publishers.

Vygotsky, L. S. (1935/1987). Thinking and speech. In R. Rieber & J. Carton (Eds.), *The collected works of L. S. Vygotsky, Volume 1. Problems of general psychology* (pp. 39–285). New York: Plenum Press.

Wenger, E. (1998). *Communities of practice. Learning, meaning, and identity*. Cambridge, UK: Cambridge University Press.

Zembylas, M. (2005). Discursive practices, genealogies, and emotion rules: A poststructuralist view on emotion and identity in teaching. *Teaching and Teacher Education, 21*(8), 935–948.

Chapter 14
Becoming a Language Teacher: Tracing the Mediation and Internalization Processes of Pre-service Teachers

Vesna Dimitrieska

Interest in language teacher identity development has surfaced in second language teacher development in the past two decades (Borg, 2003; Miller, 2009). Its emergence as a theme corresponds to the shift "in learning theory from cognitive to social perspectives" (Pennington & Richards, 2016), when features of identity began to be seen as relational, interactional, and constructed in a specific context (Miller, 2009). Thus, examining the wider picture, the sociocultural and sociopolitical dimensions of teaching, (e.g. Pennycook, 2001) is crucial, as to understand language teaching and language learning, one needs to understand teachers.

Investigations into the combined role of personal and social dimensions along with the professional context are an emerging line of research as they can be detrimental in one's identity formation (Tsui, 2007). Previously, these dimensions were examined separately without looking at teacher identity development holistically and as it is contoured both during formal teacher preparation and in post-training contexts. It is difficult to define effective language teaching as conceptions about what constitutes good teaching vary across cultures (Tsui, 2009). The Western language teaching perspective posits that an English as a foreign language (EFL) teacher needs to develop proficiency in the target language, content knowledge, teaching skills, contextual knowledge, learner-focused teaching, pedagogical reasoning skills, membership in a community of practice, and professionalism (Richards, 2011). However, to understand language teaching, it should be approached as "situated" in a specific context as it depends on the teacher's view of good teaching, their personal and cultural background, and the student profiles (Richards, 2011).

Language teacher cognition plays a crucial role in EFL teachers' identity development. It is defined as what teachers know, believe, and think about teaching, whereas teacher learning is "the unobservable dimensions of teaching" (Borg, 2003,

V. Dimitrieska (✉)
School of Education, Indiana University, Bloomington, IN, USA
e-mail: vdimitri@umail.iu.edu

© Springer International Publishing AG, part of Springer Nature 2018
P. A. Schutz et al. (eds.), *Research on Teacher Identity*,
https://doi.org/10.1007/978-3-319-93836-3_14

p.81). Both concepts have been perceived as having impact on language teachers' instructional practices and students' language learning (Burns & Richards, 2009). Borg (2003) acknowledged the complex nature of teacher cognition due to the multiple layers that constitute or influence it: teachers' mental lives, prior language learning experiences, teacher education, teachers' beliefs, their classroom practices, and the teaching contexts. However, efforts to conduct research on language teacher cognition and teacher learning in relation to language teacher identity have been scant. To fill the gap in research, in this chapter, I examine language teacher identity in relation to the change in EFL trainee teachers' conceptualizations during and after an intensive teacher training course. EFL teachers' identity formation does not only happen during their teacher training courses. Consequently, examining how their language teacher identity is shaped as they engage in social activities during teacher training and as soon as they enter their respective teaching contexts is crucial in order to reach a deeper understanding of the issue at hand. Vygotsky's (1978) sociocultural theory provides a useful lens for understanding identity (Penuel & Wertsch, 1995) since it highlights the interconnectedness of the cognitive and the social, and emphasizes the crucial role participation in social activities plays in human cognition development.

Mediation and internalization are some of the primary psychological constructs of Vygotsky's theory. Mediation refers to humans' acting with the environment (i.e., intermental domain) through the use of certain tools that can be physical (e.g., textbooks) or symbolic (e.g., metaphors about teaching) (Johnson, 2009). In second language teacher education, the type and quality of mediation that language teachers receive play a critical role in understanding and improving teaching expertise development (Johnson & Golombek, 2011). Internalization is the developmental process through which learning is internalized and shifts from the intermental to the intramental front (Swain, Kinnear, & Steinman, 2011). Making explicit the types of mediation and the symbols that help EFL teachers develop is crucial in order to understand how EFL teachers form the conceptualizations they have about language learning and language teaching and, in turn, how those conceptualizations affect their instructional practices and students' outcomes. In this chapter, I will use two pre-service EFL teachers to unpack the mediation and internalization processes and their identity development in more detail.

Mediation Processes

Emma and Anna, two pre-service EFL teachers, were followed during the 1-month intensive teacher training course and for 1.5 years in their post-teacher training contexts. They both completed the Certificate of English Language Teaching to Adults (CELTA) course, one of the most widely recognized EFL teaching qualifications. Both were native speakers of English and interested in pursuing language teaching careers abroad. Emma had no prior language teaching experience whereas Anna had some experience teaching EFL in Korea.

On their path to becoming language teachers, Emma and Anna engaged in distinct mediation processes. Within mediation, a distinction is made between concrete and symbolic tools (Vygotsky, 1978). *Asking questions* emerged as concrete mediation tools for both Emma and Anna, as, by definition, they are externally oriented, (i.e., they were directed to other people – their tutors, their peers, and their students). By being able to ask questions, Emma and Anna were affecting change in their own and their peers' conceptualizations about language learning and language teaching. They were able to either confirm what they knew, for example, from their previous experiences as language learners, or reconsider and modify their previous knowledge about language learning and language teaching. Thus, they were developing their content knowledge, teaching skills, and pedagogical reasoning skills. Additionally, *"modeling"* emerged within Emma's mediation processes and functioned both as a tool (used by the teacher educator as a model) and a sign (aimed at improving oneself, as a teacher). Emma's mediation was manifested through her *using examples from teaching practice.*

Teacher Identity Development Through Asking Questions

By asking a range of questions and asking different people those questions Emma's conceptualizations of language learning and language teaching developed and contributed to her becoming a more confident language teacher. She asked trainer-directed, peer-directed, and student-directed questions (Table 14.1).

Even though Emma asked a wider array of questions, compared to Anna, the greatest takeaway in her teacher identity development was not their type but the sole process of asking them and the need to engage in constructive dialogue with her tutors and peers. By tracking the manner in which Emma interacted with knowledgeable others, we see the pivotal role the process of asking questions as a mediational tool played in the development of her language teacher identity (Johnson, 2009). The question-asking process contributed to her identity development as she started to feel more confident as a legitimate member in her community of teachers.

Similarly to Emma, Anna was asking questions and most of them were directed towards her tutors. However, Anna's way of *asking questions* differed from Emma's as, by engaging in this activity, she attempted to reconstruct some of her previous understandings gained through her prior teaching experience and construct novel ways of thinking about effective language classroom practices. Asking the tutor for confirmation and for clarification were the most commonly used questions by Anna (Table 14.1). Also, she was providing answers to tutors' prompts as another mediational process. By engaging in this social activity and dialogue with her tutors and peers (Johnson, 2009), she demonstrated that she had appropriated the practices promoted in the course. The types of interaction Anna had with her tutors and peers correspond to the sociocultural perspective on teacher learning as "situated in the actual practice of the participating teachers" and the discussions were "concept-based

Table 14.1 Types of questions asked by Emma (E) and Anna (A)

Types of questions	Who was she asking?	Examples from the data
Clarifying questions (E, A)	Tutors	A: "So, do I do the same thing then?" (Debriefing #1)
Procedural questions (E)	Tutors	E: "Are we making those little six pairs again?" (Debriefing #4)
Asking for permission (E)	Tutors	E: "Can we call on people individually and comment?" (Debriefing #2)
Housekeeping questions (E, A)	Tutors	E: "So, not the transcriptions, but what the students have?" (Debriefing #3)
Asking for approval/ confirmation (E, A)	Tutors	A: "And then to check, you would put this sheet up?" (Debriefing #4)
Asking for an opinion (E)	Tutors	E: "…That's fine for outside of class, but here, we want you to ask questions, it's OK to make a mistake." I'm curious to hear what you have to say about that." (Debriefing #6)
Asking for metalanguage (E)	Tutors	E: "…when someone is in the chair the whole time, you have a nice word for that?" (Debriefing #7)
Asking for rationale for one's actions (E)	Peer trainee teachers	E: "Is that because you were trying to cut down on time or is that how you had planned it?" (Debriefing #3)
Concept checking questions (E)	Language learners	E: "It may, but do you have to be driving?" "No." "Can you be somewhere else?" "Yes." (Debriefing #2)
Asking for more specific information (E, A)	Tutors Peers	E: "Can you give me a specific example before my brain goes blank?" (Debriefing #8)

and meaning making in orientation" (Kiely & Davis, 2010, p. 278). Anna's and Emma's teacher identity was shaped as a result of being a part of the dialogue that directly addressed issues arising from their own teaching context. Such an opportunity to elaborate on their own instructional practices allowed Emma and Anna to further access and unpack their language learning and language teaching conceptualizations. Their own language proficiency, content knowledge, teaching skills, and pedagogical reasoning skills unquestionably affect what they would do under specific circumstances in an EFL classroom and, ultimately, the type of EFL teacher they will become.

Teacher Identity Development Through "Modeling"

Emma's various types of "modeling" had strong agency in her own teacher identity growth. Modeling is most typically associated as a practice that teacher educators perform and is considered their professional competency, (i.e., the ability to explicitly model for their students, the thoughts and actions that underpin one's pedagogical approach) (Loughran & Berry, 2005). Even though Emma was not a teacher educator, her own practices resembled teacher educators' modeling practices. Hence, I distinguish between modeling (i.e., what teacher educators do) and "modeling" (i.e., what Emma, a teacher-in-training used). Emma's "modeling" can be understood as "an ability to be explicit about what one is doing and why" and is improved by "systematically inquiring into learning through experience (self-study) so that the relationship between knowing and doing might be more accessible" (Loughran & Berry, 2005, p.194). Through the act of "modeling", Emma was engaging in the activity of self-study. Two types of "modeling" emerged: *thinking aloud* (i.e., verbalizing her thinking so that others can hear it) and *proper modeling* (i.e., providing models of actual talk/thinking that serve as a preferred model/example). When giving feedback on her peers' lessons, during the group debriefing sessions, Emma said:

> I thought there were several instances when your ICQs were not there. Like for the 3rd person singular task, and for the one word when they were finding similar person task. I think, ... instead of saying "what are we doing?", 'cuz that's a lot of questions you need to break down differently, so, you know, like super-simple. Sometimes when I write these things, but then I don't remember to use them, I feel like, "Oh my God, they must think that I feel that they are stupid or something, I'm like "Are you writing or listening? Are you this or that?" Ummm, but in that way, you don't have that problem of "what are we doing" and like hear crickets and then somebody chirps in, one of the students and says "this, that", "yes, go", and the rest of them are like "Uh?" [showing that the students might have not caught that]. (Debriefing #4)

After identifying that the instruction checking questions (ICQs) in her peer's lesson were missing, Emma used her peer's exact words and explained why they were not effective. Then she provided the strategy that she uses, scripting the instruction checking questions, followed by her own models of those questions that her peer could use. By providing her own initial internal conflict associated with asking those simple, broken down questions, followed by the realization of the value of asking close-ended questions during the task setup stage, Emma's teacher identity strengthened. Her teacher identity development was evident by her willingness to share how she acknowledged the utility of instruction checking questions as an important teaching skill.

Teacher Identity Development Through Using Examples from Teaching Practice

Drawing on specific instances from her and her peers' teaching, Anna used these examples as a means to construct and reconstruct some of her language teaching conceptualizations. Thus, those examples functioned as mediational tools:

> So, when you started, they were like really happy to talk about it, and very interested in mystery. And at the end, too, they all were talking, and, you know, you could tell that there was interest. But the vocabulary was intense and even, like, I know that wasn't our fault, but I feel like it could've been more effective if it would have been adapted, 'cuz for the article,

they did need to know what "a tenement" is. Also, the part in which they were trying to find if they had "access to economic mobility"- that's like college-level. (Debriefing #9)

By referring to specific examples from her peer's lesson, Anna was prompting her peer to reconstruct what she thought she knew about adapting authentic materials for classroom use. Additionally, by engaging in this exchange with her peer, Anna was re-affirming her own knowledge and the entire process helped her build her confidence and further develop her teacher identity. Her own efficacy empowered her to positively impact her peer's learning and thus proportionately develop her own teacher identity.

Internalization Processes

Vygotsky (1978) refers to the process of appropriating the symbols (e.g., participants' asking questions, "modeling" and using examples from CELTA teaching practice) as a part of their cognitive domain and as the point when their learning to teach is internalized. Emma's and Anna's internalization processes occurred during and after the course and were manifested as *making connections, tensions*, and *noticing*. They all shaped their language teacher identity.

Making Connections

For Emma, initially emerging in the second half of the course and continuing to develop in her post-CELTA teaching context, she was making connections between various aspects of teaching English: *making connections between her lesson aims and student performance; making connections through noticing cause and effect; and making connections between her own learning experience on the CELTA and the new teachers' practices in her school.* In her post-course teaching context, Emma commented on the following:

And it's really interesting, when I observe a new teacher for their demo lesson, when I see people doing the wrong thing, I go, "A-ha! I remember! I've done this! And they [tutors] said, 'Don't do that!' (Interview #2)

The type of connection in this example can be referred to as reflection-within-reflection as she was imagining what her CELTA tutors would have said in that situation. She was simultaneously reflecting about the observed teacher's practices and connecting those to similar situations that she experienced as a trainee teacher.

Anna's manifestation of *making connections* as an internalization process was in terms of discussing causal relationships. By being able to explain how specific actions influenced subsequent actions and students' response to both, Anna was starting to see the stronger relationship between the two. Discussing those causal relationships helped Anna see the bigger picture as she was making additional connections of her and her peers' classroom practices and their effect on the learning of language students. For example, she was making connections between ineffective setup of activities and subsequent student participation in the task:

> I really liked the listening. I just noticed when I was reading the second time, you told them to write down answers, and I was trying to read slow, but they didn't hear you say "write down", so they were just listening to me. So, when it was time to switch, they didn't have anything on the paper, so they gave it to the other people. (Debriefing #8)

Even though discussing causal relationships is most commonly found to be a characteristic of novice teachers (Tsui, 2009), Anna was going a step beyond by seeing the bigger picture of those causal relationships through connecting her or her peers' classroom practices to the effect those had on their language students. Thus, awareness of her own language students started to play a role in Anna's EFL teacher identity development. She has internalized the impact of language teachers' classroom practices on the students themselves.

Tensions

Tensions appeared as another way of internalizing what Emma and Anna were learning and thus advancing their own understanding of sound language teaching practices. Emma perceived these conflict-like situations with her peers and tutors as opportunities to clarify possible misunderstandings and grow from the entire experience. These tensions were potential loci for change or learning (Engeström, 1999). By deciding to initiate and resolve tensions and conflict-like situations, one is more prone to experience learning and growth.

In Anna's experience, tensions took the shape of challenging other people's actions (i.e., what her peers/tutors did/said). She was confident enough in her understanding of language teaching to doubt certain procedures or activities and openly express it. By questioning their actions/thinking, she advanced her own thinking about language classrooms (i.e., her internalization) which had an impact on the construction/reconstruction of knowledge of her peers (i.e., external, socially mediating what her peers were learning about teaching). On one occasion, she commented on not seeing the rationale behind her peer's actions in his lesson:

> I'm getting confused a little bit, 'cuz you said you needed to cut that one, you weren't sure, but then you had like a little bit of extra time, and you didn't want to do it. Why didn't you do error correction at that time? (Debriefing #8)

By initiating the tension, Anna was internalizing what she had started to learn about including error correction stages in one's teaching, especially when one had sufficient time. The discussion around and the overall appropriation of error correction techniques as another teaching skill further contributed to Anna's development of her EFL teacher identity. Error correction techniques started to be a part of her language teaching skills.

Noticing

Both Emma and Anna used *noticing* as an internalization process but there were differences in terms of what each of them noticed. Most commonly, Emma noticed change in herself, peers, and her students. Compared to Gusky's (2002) model of types of change, Emma's instantiations of change could be identified as most frequently noticing change in classroom practices, less frequently noticing change in students' learning outcomes and rarely noticing change in her own or peers' attitudes and beliefs. Noticing change in her students was evident in the following excerpt:

> Brian's guided discovery for TP#7 was a leap of faith that paid off; students were engaged for the entire lesson, and demonstrated their learning through correctly answering CCQs and completing follow-up activities. (Reflective Assignment)

In her peer's lesson, Emma noticed the levels of engagement and the amount of learning that took place because of her peer's using guided discovery as an approach to teaching grammar.

For Anna, noticing featured dominantly as an internalization process throughout the course. Not only was she noticing her peers' practices but she was showing that she noticed those practices. This may be interpreted as her own growth. She may have had fragmented knowledge about certain practices, but when she started to notice them, that knowledge was reconstructed and internalized into her existing knowledge. The noticing of practices was most visible in the following aspects of classroom management: her peer's performance during different parts of the lesson: "Good CCQs and monitoring constantly." (Debriefing #8); peer's good timing in the first part of the lesson: "The first half [of the lesson], I think, the timing was really good." (Debriefing #8); peer's inappropriate teacher talk and instructions: "You were always monitoring, except, I think the efficacy would've been higher if they already understood the directions in the target language." (Debriefing #8); peer's good drilling technique: "I thought it was good, you really, really doing the drilling a lot." (Debriefing #9). By expanding the repertoire of classroom management areas that she noticed, Anna was shaping her own EFL teacher identity. She started to notice areas of classroom management that she did not notice prior to the course.

Discussion

The analysis of Emma's and Anna's trajectories revealed the usefulness of examining language teacher identity from a sociocultural perspective. The sociocultural framing allowed a look into the way the intersubjective, socially situated domain (i.e., their interactions with peers and tutors) plays out and affects how the knowledge and skills they are exposed to become appropriated, internalized, and integrated into the teachers' own knowledge and teaching skills repertoire. Since internalization is "not the straightforward appropriaton of concepts, knowledge, or skills from the outside in", human agency plays a role in deciding what is internalized and how the internalization process "shapes new understandings and new ways of engaging in activities" (Johnson, 2009, pp.18–19). This framing provides a glimpse into the processes and tools that are driving growth in language teachers' identity. By becoming cognizant of the platforms that afford the occurrence of those mediation and internalization processes one can reach a deeper understanding of the language teacher's identity development and work towards making those platforms more available in professional development contexts beyond formal teacher training.

Additionally, their manner of mediating and internalizing what they learned about language teaching and language learning was triggered by events that took place in real contexts, (i.e., their language classrooms during and after the course). Those events were context-generated and the related discussions were context-specific. By reacting to real events and actions from their own classrooms both Emma and Anna had the opportunity to personalize the knowledge and skills they were exposed to. Consequently, they were able to advance their conceptual, theoretical, and practical knowledge by initially activating what they know, through engaging in the activity of teaching, and attending to problematic aspects of their practice in structured discussion with peers and tutors, and reaching a more refined understanding of what effective language teaching entails.

The similarities in the mediation processes between Emma and Anna revealed that *asking questions* was a common tool that helped them mediate what they were learning during the course. A second mediational tool that helped shape Emma's and Anna's teacher identities was *"modeling"* and *using examples from the teaching practice*, respectively. These two were rooted in specific events that occurred in their own or their peers' teaching practice and were included in the discussions that Emma and Anna had with their peers and the tutor, (i.e., the external, socially mediated activities). By referring to real examples, Emma and Anna mediated their own and their peers' learning as those "models"/examples were then reconstructed and subsequently helped advance their understanding of the classroom practices of which they were a part. Not only were those "models"/examples and the resulting discussions the driving force for the teachers to modify their teaching practices but they also affected change in terms of their more general conceptualizations related to language teaching and teacher learning. Thus, they had an immediate and a more lasting effect on their teacher identity through the change they caused in their instructional practices and their language teaching conceptualizations. More specifically, the individual (i.e., intrapersonal realization about the utility of certain techniques), led both Emma and Anna to adopt those techniques and use them in their subsequent teaching.

To develop their teacher identity, Emma and Anna experienced similar internalization processes. First, tensions played an important role in the way their teacher identity was shaped during and after the course. Those tensions may have been negative and uncomfortable experiences but they were also a springboard for them to experience change in the teaching practices and their conceptualizations. Tensions or contradictions are impetus to learning (Swain et al., 2011) and imperative to reaching a higher cognitive level in language teaching and language learning. Second, Emma and Anna were making connections as another tool necessary to internalize the skills and knowledge they were acquiring. Third, noticing featured prominently as a part of the internalization they experienced even though they were noticing various aspects (e.g., Emma was noticing change, whereas Anna was noticing practices). Fourth, Anna used expressing as an internalization tool as she first had to express what/how she felt before she could experience change in any of the target areas. The different internalization processes might be considered "internal mediation controlled by the individual teacher", following after the "externally, socially mediated activities" (Johnson, 2009, p.17). The external and the internal mediation comprise a complex progressive movement that is associated with the processes of teacher learning and, ultimately, teacher identity development. Internalization cannot be approached as a simple transfer or replacement or "appropriation of concepts, knowledge, or skills from outside in", but rather a complex "dialogic process of transformation of self and activity" (Johnson, 2009, p.18). Thus, the participants were transforming their own selves (i.e., their teacher identity) as well as the activity of language teaching. The different routes they took were influenced by the mediation and internalization processes that further helped them become the teacher they wanted to be.

Conclusion

This study examined the mediation and internalization processes that shape the teacher identity trajectory of two pre-service language teachers. Since the path of becoming and being a teacher hinges on factors, conditions, and processes that materialize in a range of contexts, every individual teacher has a unique path with its own mediation and internalization processes. By following the participants for 1.5 years, during and after the formal training, the practices and spaces that allowed the participants to grow as language teachers were documented. Being able to ask questions, refer to models/examples from their teaching practice, and resolve tensions helped the participants change their instructional practices and readdress the language teaching conceptualizations they held at the beginning of the course.

The mediation and internalization processes are not linear but rather complex and intertwined. Emma's trajectory of becoming a language teacher was largely driven by her own agency in deciding what to internalize when learning how to become an EFL teacher. Over the 1.5 years, she appropriated a range of specific teaching skills (e.g., effective ways to set up tasks, asking instruction checking questions and concept checking questions, etc.). The mediation and internalization processes resulted in more nuanced undertones in Anna's conceptualizations about language learning, and language teaching. During the course and as soon as she started teaching in Mexico, Anna grew to be even more aware of what she needed to do and how to do it in order to become the teacher she wanted to be. Being aware of the areas that needed to change and teachers' willingness to change were crucial in the process of experiencing growth in their language teacher identity.

The sociocultural framing allowed for the understanding of the situated nature of identity development and the role of context in trainee teachers' path of becoming a teacher (Richards, 2011). Additionally, language teachers' own flexibility to use and adapt what they know about language learning and language teaching guide their trajectory and growth as an EFL teacher. Knowledge of the multiple varieties of English across the world along with the affordances and constraints of the language learning/teaching context determine EFL teachers' identity development and the cognitive and social processes they experience in the process of learning to teach (Johnson, 2009). Investigating language teacher identity is an issue that is best examined if approached holistically and with careful consideration of the context in which the interaction between the teacher learning process and the language teaching conceptualizations appears. Thus, pre-service teachers benefit from opportunities to engage in the activity of teaching, reflecting, and engaging in collaborative dialogue with peers, tutors, and other experts. As a result of these three practices, they become more aware of what they need to do in order to continue to grow once they return to their language classrooms.

This study attempted to contribute to the body of research on language teacher identity development and the relational, contextual, and individual factors that shape it. More research is needed to examine the growth of language teachers' identity beyond their first year of formal training and in relation to their respective post-training contexts. Specifically looking at the role of other knowledgeable others (e.g., other teachers, professionals, and even the students themselves) as catalysts for formation and transformation in one's teacher identity would provide deeper understanding of the process.

References

Borg, S. (2003). Teacher cognition in language teaching: A review of research on what language teachers think, know, believe, and do. *Language Teaching, 36*, 81–109.

Burns, A., & Richards, J. C. (2009). *The Cambridge guide to second language teacher education*. New York: Cambridge University Press.

Engestrom, Y. (1999). Innovative learning in work teams: Analyzing cycles of knowledge creation in practice. In Y. Engestrom, R. Miettinen, & R.-L. Punamaki (Eds.), *Perspectives on activity theory* (pp. 377–404). Cambridge, UK: Cambridge University Press.

Guskey, T. (2002). Professional development and teacher change. *Teachers and Teaching, 8*(3/4), 381–391.

Johnson, K. (2009). *Second language teacher education: A sociocultural perspective*. New York: Routledge.

Johnson, K., & Golombek, P. R. (2011). *Research on second language teacher education: A sociocultural perspective on professional development*. New York: Routledge.

Kiely, R., & Davis, M. (2010). From transmission to transformation: Teacher learning in English for speakers of other languages. *Language Teaching Research, 14*(3), 277–295.

Loughran, J., & Berry, A. (2005). Modeling by teacher educators. *Teaching and Teacher Education, 21*, 193–203.

Miller, J. (2009). Teacher identity. In A. Burns & J. C. Richards (Eds.), *The Cambridge guide to second language teacher education* (pp. 163–171). New York: Cambridge University Press.

Pennington, M. C., & Richards, J. C. (2016). Teacher identity in language teaching: Integrating personal, contextual, and professional factors. *RELC Journal, 47*(1), 5–23.

Pennycook, A. (2001). *Critical applied linguistics: A critical introduction*. Mahwah, NJ: Lawrence Erlbaum Associates, Inc.

Penuel, W. C., & Wertsch, J. V. (1995). Vygotsky and identity formation: A sociocultural approach. *Educational Psychologist, 30*(2), 83–92.

Richards, J. C. (2011). *Competence and performance in language teaching*. New York: Cambridge University Press.

Swain, M., Kinnear, P., & Steinman, L. (2011). *Sociocultural theory in second language education: An introduction through narratives*. Bristol, UK: Multilingual Matters.

Tsui, A. (2007). Complexities of identity formation: A narrative inquiry of an EFL teacher. *TESOL Quarterly, 41*, 657–680.

Tsui, A. (2009). Distinctive qualities of expert teachers. *Teachers and Teaching: Theory and Practice, 15*(4), 421–439.

Vygotsky, L. (1978). *Mind in society*. Cambridge, MA: Harvard University Press.

Chapter 15
Teacher Identity and Political Instruction

Wayne Journell

It is widely acknowledged that the overarching purpose of social studies education is to prepare students for civic life. Although multiple interpretations exist for how best to achieve that goal, one aspect common to most approaches is engagement with the political world in which students live (Kahne & Middaugh, 2009). While contemporary politics may be most visible in civics and government courses, all aspects of the social studies curriculum are inherently political, and discussions of controversial political issues are never too far removed from one's instruction (Journell, 2017b).

One aspect of K-12 political instruction that has received little attention from scholars is the role teacher identity plays in how teachers broach politics in their classes. In this chapter, I explore this relationship between identity and political instruction by looking at ways in which social studies teachers' race/ethnicity, gender, sexual orientation, religious beliefs, and political ideologies may influence their pedagogical decisions when confronted with current political issues. My purpose is not to explicitly define how teachers' identities influence their political instruction; rather, I view this chapter as a call for increased attention to the role teacher identity may play in K-12 political instruction.

W. Journell (✉)
Department of Teacher Education and Higher Education, University of North Carolina at Greensboro, Greensboro, NC, USA
e-mail: awjourne@uncg.edu

© Springer International Publishing AG, part of Springer Nature 2018
P. A. Schutz et al. (eds.), *Research on Teacher Identity*,
https://doi.org/10.1007/978-3-319-93836-3_15

A Brief Overview of Political Instruction in the United States[1]

It is important to contextualize this discussion with what the field already knows about broaching politics in K-12 education. First, many teachers shy away from controversy in their classes for a variety of reasons. Those who do engage their students in discussions of controversial issues often do so with trepidation. This trepidation leads most to attempt a neutral stance when broaching political issues in their classrooms, despite research that suggests students prefer to know their teachers' political stances, provided that they do not feel as though their teachers are trying to persuade them to adopt a particular position (Hess & McAvoy, 2009; Journell, 2011c).

Hess (2005) has called the decision whether to disclose one's political opinions to students a "dilemma" that teachers face as part of their instructional decision making. While there is theoretical and empirical support for disclosure (e.g., James, 2009; Journell, 2011c, 2016a, 2016b; Kelly, 1986), most teachers choose not to disclose under the guise of remaining neutral, even when they are presented with theoretical arguments advocating the merits of disclosure (Miller-Lane, Denton, & May, 2006). Yet, research has found that supposedly neutral teachers regularly do or say things that indicate their political leanings, although it is often unclear the extent to which their students view these political statements as facts or their teachers' opinions (e.g., Goldston & Kyzer, 2009; Journell, 2011a, 2011c, 2016b; Niemi & Niemi, 2007).

One limitation of this literature base is that it tends to paint teachers, and the challenges they face in broaching politics in their classrooms, with broad strokes. While there are certainly issues related to teaching political issues that are likely common to all teachers, it also makes sense that aspects of teachers' identities play a part in their decisions to address certain issues in their classrooms or disclose their personal opinions to students. The remainder of this chapter will take a closer look at how various aspects of teachers' identities may influence one's political instruction.

Teacher Identity and Teaching Politics

I frame this chapter using Holland, Lachicotte, Skinner, and Cain's (1998) definition of identity as "self-understandings" that are a "key means through which people care about and care for what is going on around them" (p. 5). Teaching about politics forces teachers to balance how they view the world and their feelings about how society should function with their professional obligation to create spaces in

---

[1] It is important to note that this discussion is focused on the teaching of political issues in the United States. While much of what I discuss in this chapter may also apply to other democracies, research suggests that many issues associated with teaching controversial issues are conceptualized and enacted differently in other parts of the world (e.g., Ho, Alvair-Martin, & Leviste, 2014).

which a variety of rational opinions are valued. Space limitations prohibit an exhaustive discussion of the ways in which teachers' identities may influence their political instruction; however, for the purposes of this chapter, I will focus specifically on the ways in which teachers' race, gender, sexual orientation, religion, and political ideologies, as well as the intersectionality of those various identities, may shape their instructional decision making with respect to political issues.

Race

Race and politics are often interconnected within American political discourse. For example, the alarming number of African-American men killed by police officers in recent years is a political issue. It is a societal problem in which political solutions (e.g., increased training for officers, mandatory body cameras) have been posited and deliberated. Yet, attempting to assess this issue solely as a problem with police violence does not show an understanding of the overarching message articulated by the Black Lives Matter movement and other civil rights activists—that police violence against African-Americans is just the most recent, high-profile example that Black lives are valued less in the United States than those of White citizens (King, Warren, Bender, & Finley, 2016).

The hesitancy of White teachers to discuss issues of race has been well documented (e.g., Bolgatz, 2005). Therefore, it should come as no surprise that many White teachers are also hesitant to broach political issues that intersect with race. For example, during the 2008 Presidential Election, I studied the instruction of six high school civics teachers; five of the teachers were White, and one was African-American. As one might have expected, the historic candidacy of Barack Obama was a topic of conversation in all six classrooms, particularly the questions of whether the United States was ready for a Black president and what impact Obama's race would have on his ability to get elected.

The White teachers in the study largely tried to avoid these issues. For example, one of the White teachers, Mr. Leander, positioned himself as a political expert in class, and it was unusual for him not to weigh in on whatever aspect of the election was being discussed on any given day (Journell, 2011a, 2011b). However, there were several times throughout the semester when his more conservative students would raise issues related to Obama's race and its effect on the election, and Mr. Leander would be uncharacteristically silent. Similarly, in three of the five classes taught by White teachers, students raised the possibility that, should he be elected, Obama would be assassinated because of the racism held by "others" in the United States; yet, none of the teachers questioned students about this assertion or attempted to discuss racism present in the United States (Journell, 2011a).

The African-American teacher in the study, Mr. Harrison, on the other hand, regularly facilitated candid discussions about the racial aspect of Obama's candidacy and how it would impact the election. The fact that Mr. Harrison was an African-American perhaps created a level of comfort in talking about Obama's candidacy, even though he supported McCain in the election. As I will discuss later in the chapter, Mr. Harrison did not disclose his preference for McCain to his students due to the political climate of his school and the surrounding community; however, the fact that, as an African-American, Mr. Harrison was willing to criticize Obama's policies and actions during the campaign seemed to resonate with his students. As Alberto told me in an interview, "Mr. Harrison didn't care that Barack Obama was an African-American; he cared about what [the candidates] were talking about," and another student noted that she respected Mr. Harrison because he wasn't "the type to just vote for Obama because he is Black" (Journell, 2011a, p. 369).

Mr. Harrison's willingness to discuss racially-infused political issues went beyond questions related to Obama's race. Mr. Harrison realized that immigration was an issue about which his predominately Latino/a class was passionate. As a result, he restructured his curriculum so that he used immigration as a springboard to a variety of political and civic topics throughout the semester. Instead of sanitizing the issue like many textbooks and curriculum standards often do (Hilburn, Journell, & Buchanan, 2016; Journell, 2009), Mr. Harrison had his students consider the way immigration affected them and their families based on their race and citizenship status, again reaching a level of depth that the White teachers in the study never achieved when talking about racially-infused political issues (Journell & Castro, 2011).

While a teacher's race may make them more or less hesitant to broach certain political issues in class, research also suggests that one's race may influence how they frame certain issues in their classes. Vickery (2017), for example, studied African-American women social studies teachers and found that their backgrounds and experiences living as Black women shaped their civic and political instruction. Their personal experiences contrasted with the civic narratives found in the formal curriculum, and instead, they offered a different approach that reflected the realities of their lived experiences.

Another example can be found in Dabach's (2015) study of one civics teacher's experience teaching classes with students of mixed citizenship status. This teacher, Mrs. Aguilar, prided herself on being politically neutral in her classes for reasons discussed above. However, when it came to issues related to immigration and deportation policies, issues with which she personally identified and advocated for on behalf of her students, Mrs. Aguilar felt compelled to break from her neutrality stance and disclose to her students that she was opposed to policies that sought to deport undocumented students and their families.

Gender

Much has been written about how gender stereotypes influence Americans' political decision making (e.g., Han & Heldman, 2007; Koch, 2000), but research on how gender plays out within political discussions in K-12 contexts is limited. As with political issues that intersect with race, there is some research to suggest that teachers' gender may influence how they choose to address political issues that relate to topics associated with gender.

For example, although the 2008 Presidential Election is remembered for Obama's historic candidacy, Sarah Palin's inclusion on the Republican ticket also brought gender into the public discourse in a pronounced way. Interestingly, none of the teachers or students in my study raised any concerns regarding Americans' willingness to vote for a female vice president. Yet, Palin's candidacy was subject to overt sexism and regular comments about her physical appearance, which rarely occurred with the male candidates running in the election.

Neither the male nor female teachers spoke against this overt sexism in their classes. Yet, there was a difference in how the different genders responded to such comments when they did occur. When the female teachers heard comments related to Palin's physical appearance, such as when students in Ms. Wilkinson's class said "She is fine" during a video of the candidate, they often responded with silence (Journell, 2011a, p. 374). The male teachers, on the other hand, tended to respond candidly to these types of sexist comments, and oftentimes, their comments served to further trivialize or objectify Palin and the other women in the campaign. Even beyond comments directed at female candidates' physical appearances, the male teachers often made sexist comments that suggested women were not as emotionally suited for political office as men. For example, Mr. Leander described Palin's debate performance as a success because she did not "run crying from the stage," and Mr. Pierce told his class that Palin's popularity created the scenario for a "cat fight" with Hillary Clinton (Journell, 2011a, p. 375).

Unfortunately, little empirical research exists that explores how teachers' gender affects their willingness or ability to broach specific political issues, even issues that implicate topics related to gender. One exception can be found in Engebretson's (2013) study of how preservice social studies teachers responded to the issue of sexual violence. She found that many of the preservice teachers, irrespective of gender, were conflicted about whether they would include issues related to sexual violence in their curriculum. Of those who stated that they would teach issues related to sexual violence, all but one identified as female. Unfortunately, as of this writing, I could find no existing research that discusses how teachers who identify as transgender broach political issues in their classes.

Sexual Orientation

The research on how teachers' sexual orientation influences their political instruction may be even more limited than that on the influence of gender. In a study of preservice teachers, Brant and Tyson (2016) found that they lacked self-efficacy in teaching content, including contemporary political issues, related to the LGBTQ movement. However, Brant and Tyson did not aggregate their data based on the reported sexual orientations of their participants.

The only study I could find that even referenced teachers who identified as LGBTQ and how they broached political issues came from Mayo (2007), who observed seven gay teachers in a conservative area of the United States. It is worth noting that only one of Mayo's participants was openly gay, although two described themselves as "implicitly gay," meaning that they were perceived to be gay by some students and other faculty but they had not openly corroborated those beliefs. Despite the conservative nature of their school community, Mayo found that the teachers did not shy away from teaching political issues, including issues that addressed LGBTQ themes, such as marriage equality and hate crime legislation for violent acts against members of the LGBTQ community.

Religion

In some ways, the influence of teachers' religious convictions on how they address controversial topics that contradict their spiritual worldview is well-documented. The field of science education, for example, has extensively explored how religious teachers struggle with teaching evolution in biology classrooms (for an overview of that literature, see Journell, 2013). However, the research on how religion influences teachers' political instruction, broadly speaking, is limited.

Research suggests that for devoutly religious educators, their religious identity often supersedes other aspects of their instructional decision-making. In a study of preservice social studies teachers, for example, James (2010) found that her religious students often refused to participate in class discussions pertaining to issues that they perceived to be settled from a religious standpoint. For these preservice teachers, simply deliberating multiple perspectives about such issues was a dangerous proposition because it provided secular arguments the same legitimacy as their religious worldview.

In my study of the 2008 Presidential Election, two teachers, Mr. Ryan and Mr. Harrison, both identified as devout Christians. Yet, they also strived to have their classrooms be spaces where multiple viewpoints were valued and vibrant discussions of issues could occur. Generally, I found them to be successful in this endeavor, except when issues intersected with the teachers' religious beliefs. Both teachers, for example, openly disclosed that they did not believe that a Muslim should be allowed to run for the presidency, despite the fact that the Constitution offers no religious litmus test for presidential candidates. Moreover, they made these comments in a way that left little room for opposing viewpoints (Journell, 2011a).

Yet, it would be an oversimplification to say that devoutly religious teachers cannot separate their religious convictions from discussions of political issues. In that same study, I observed two teachers who worked at a private Catholic school. Both teachers were religious and adhered to the school's Catholic mission; yet, both teachers also encouraged students to take stances on political issues that deviated from official Catholic doctrine (Journell, 2011a). Although they may not have personally advocated for secular positions on political issues, they gave those same positions legitimacy within classroom discussions, a finding that has been observed among religious teachers in other contexts (e.g., Orlowski, 2017). In other words, it appears that religious identity plays a role in teachers' political instruction, but it is unclear to what extent. For some teachers, religious conviction supersedes other considerations related to teaching political issues, but for others, religious beliefs appear to have less influence on their instruction.

Political Identity

Although more Americans identify as political independents than as Democrats or Republicans (Pew Research Center, 2015), the nation has become increasingly politically polarized over the past several decades (Abramowitz, 2010). One product of this polarization is that those identifying as liberal or conservative often develop uncompromising political identities of themselves—and of those holding opposing views—that are reinforced by cable news, social media, and other political outlets (Chambers & Melnyk, 2006). Yet, despite this increasing solidification of Americans' political identities, teachers' political identities have received scant attention within the literature on political instruction.

Teachers are political beings, and it is unreasonable to expect them to completely censor their political identities once they enter their classrooms (Journell, 2016a, 2016b). Yet, researchers have shown that most teachers do attempt to remain neutral in their classrooms, even if research suggests that those attempts are in vain (e.g., Hess & McAvoy, 2009; Journell, 2011c). This decision whether to disclose one's political beliefs to their students, however, is not always merely a pedagogical decision; rather, it is often predicated by teachers' political identities.

If teachers' political identities are aligned with that of the school and surrounding community, then disclosure does not present as much of a risk. However, teachers whose political identities are in conflict with that of the school or surrounding community often fall into what Noelle-Neumann (1993) termed a "spiral of silence." These teachers are afraid of revealing their political leanings due to the possibility of admonishment from students and colleagues.

This phenomenon is perhaps best illustrated by Mr. Harrison, the African-American teacher I studied during the 2008 Presidential Election. Mr. Harrison worked at a school that was overwhelmingly in favor of Obama and located in a deeply liberal community. As someone who planned to vote for McCain, Mr. Harrison was careful to not reveal his political identity to his students or colleagues. On one occasion, however, he slipped and admitted that he had voted for George W. Bush, and his students reacted with a mixture of shock and disdain. He indicated later that his students' reaction to this accidental disclosure, coupled with the response he received from members of the local African-American community when he revealed to them that he had voted for McCain, renewed his efforts to conceal his political identity while at school (Journell, 2012).

Although Mr. Harrison is an illustrative example, teachers falling into the spiral of silence due to political beliefs that conflict with the community in which they teach has been documented in a variety of contexts (e.g., Goldston & Kyzer, 2009; Journell, 2012, 2016a). More recently, I have found that the spiral of silence may actually manifest itself before teachers even make it into the field. In a study of politically conservative social studies teachers, I found that many reported feeling marginalized for their political beliefs at various points throughout their teacher education programs. Not only did those experiences discourage them from participating in class discussions as preservice teachers, but they also led them to remain discreet about their political identities as practicing teachers (Journell, 2017a).

Yet, sometimes hiding one's political identity becomes impossible. Swalwell and Schweber's (2016) study of Wisconsin social studies teachers during the 2011 public debate over union rights offers an illustrative example of how teachers sometimes cannot avoid identifying with political issues being discussed in class. Wisconsin teachers' unions became the public face of the opposition to Governor Scott Walker's legislation; therefore, it was impossible for social studies teachers throughout the state to completely remove themselves from the controversy. In addition to whatever political beliefs they held about unions, they also identified as teachers, which meant that they were personally invested in the public dialogue surrounding this issue, and for many of the teachers, it was difficult to remain balanced in their classrooms. As Swalwell and Schweber noted, local controversial or political issues may actually pose more significant challenges to teachers because there is a greater chance that they will identify with and be personally affected by those issues.

Final Thoughts

The purpose of this chapter was not to provide an exhaustive list of the ways in which teacher identities influence their political instruction; there are likely other aspects of teachers' identities that impact their political instruction as much, or more, than those included here. Also, it is important to note the intersectionality of these various identities. I separated race, gender, sexuality, religion, and political identity in this chapter to illustrate salient points; however, in reality, teachers' political instruction is influenced by *multiple* identities. For example, Vickery (2017) noted that what made her participants' civic instruction unique was their identity as Black women, which she argued is different from that of simply being Black or being a woman. One can also see this intersectionality at work in the case of Mr. Harrison from my 2008 Presidential Election study. On one hand, as an African-American, he was able to more openly discuss race-related political issues than his White colleagues. However, his identity as a Christian caused him to shut down student dialogue when the political discussion contradicted his religious beliefs, and his identity as a political conservative working in a liberal community forced him to hide his beliefs from his students and colleagues.

A salient takeaway from this chapter is that teachers cannot magically shed their political identities once they walk into a school building, and in some cases, their professional identities come in conflict with their personal beliefs. Moreover, the "fishbowl" nature of the teaching profession also means that teachers need to be cognizant of how they project their political identities in public and on social media, particularly if they teach in a community whose ideology runs counter to theirs. In other words, teachers' professional positions serve as another point of intersectionality that complicate understanding how teachers' identities influence their political instruction.

Context also matters when assessing the role that teacher identity plays in one's political instruction. Periods of heightened political awareness and/or anxiety, such as presidential elections or the aftermath of a national crisis, tend to bring identity to the political forefront. Donald Trump's election, for example, has had ramifications on how politics is discussed in public schools. Trump's inflammatory rhetoric on immigrants, Muslims, and women have been echoed within the walls of K-12 schools across the United States (Castillo, 2016), and one can imagine that teachers who identify with these groups have found teaching politics under Trump particularly challenging.

My hope is that this chapter encourages a more critical look at the ways in which teacher identity affects K-12 political instruction. An increased focus on the role teacher identity plays on teachers' instructional decision-making can help us better understand and critique longstanding beliefs associated with political instruction. For example, given the research cited in this chapter, is it reasonable to believe that K-12 teachers can remain politically neutral in their classes? Perhaps it is time that the field of social studies education, and American society more broadly, rethinks that premise. The influence of teachers' identity on their political instruction lends support to Kelly's (1986) preferred stance of "committed impartiality," in which teachers disclose their political beliefs in tolerant ways and provide explanations for why they hold those beliefs while simultaneously modeling democratic discourse and recognizing contrary beliefs to open issues as equally legitimate.

Finally, although more research on how teacher identity influences political instruction is needed across the board, it is evident that certain areas have a greater need than others. The research base on how teachers' gender or sexuality influence their political instruction, for example, is almost non-existent. In order to improve K-12 political instruction, it is essential that researchers better understand political instruction from *all* points of view, particularly when issues implicate teachers' identities.

References

Abramowitz, A. (2010). *The disappearing center: Engaged citizens, polarization, and American democracy.* New Haven, CT: Yale University Press.

Bolgatz, J. (2005). *Talking race in the classroom.* New York: Teachers College Press.

Brant, C. A. R., & Tyson, C. A. (2016). LGBTQ self-efficacy in the social studies. *Journal of Social Studies Research, 40,* 217–227.

Castillo, M. B. (2016). *The Trump effect: The impact of the presidential campaign on our nation's schools.* Southern Poverty Law Center. Retrieved from http://www.splcenter.org

Chambers, J. R., & Melnyk, D. (2006). Why do I hate thee? Conflict misperceptions and intergroup mistrust. *Personality and Social Psychology Bulletin, 32,* 1295–1311.

Dabach, D. B. (2015). "My student was apprehended by immigration": A civics teacher's breach of silence in a mixed-citizenship classroom. *Harvard Educational Review, 85,* 383–412.

Engebretson, K. E. (2013). Grappling with "that awkward sex stuff": Encountering themes of sexual violence in the formal curriculum. *Journal of Social Studies Research, 37,* 195–207.

Goldston, M. J., & Kyzer, P. (2009). Teaching evolution: Narratives with a view from three southern biology teachers in the USA. *Journal of Research in Science Teaching, 46,* 762–790.

Han, L. C., & Heldman, C. (Eds.). (2007). *Rethinking madam president: Are we ready for a woman in the White House?* Boulder, CO: Lynne Rienner.

Hess, D. E. (2005). How do teachers' political views influence teaching about controversial issues? *Social Education, 69,* 47–48.

Hess, D. E., & McAvoy, P. (2009). To disclose or not to disclose: A controversial choice for teachers. In D. E. Hess (Ed.), *Controversy in the classroom: The democratic power of discussion* (pp. 97–110). New York: Routledge.

Hilburn, J., Journell, W., & Buchanan, L. B. (2016). A content analysis of immigration in traditional, new, and non-gateway state standards for U.S. History and Civics. *The High School Journal, 99,* 234–251.

Ho, L., Alviar-Martin, T., & Leviste, E. N. P. (2014). "There is space, and there are limits": The challenge of teaching controversial topics in an illiberal democracy. *Teachers College Record, 116*(5), 1–28.

Holland, D., Lachicotte, W., Skinner, D., & Cain, C. (1998). *Identity and agency in cultural worlds.* Cambridge, MA: Harvard University Press.

James, J. H. (2009). Reframing the disclosure debate: Confronting issues of transparency in teaching controversial content. *Social Studies Research and Practice, 4,* 82–94.

James, J. H. (2010). "Democracy is the devil's snare": Theological certainty in teacher education. *Theory & Research in Social Education, 38,* 618–639.

Journell, W. (2009). Setting out the (un)welcome mat: A portrayal of immigration in American history standards. *The Social Studies, 100,* 160–168.

Journell, W. (2011a). Teachers' controversial issue decisions related to race, gender, and religion during the 2008 Presidential Election. *Theory & Research in Social Education, 39,* 348–392.

Journell, W. (2011b). Teaching the 2008 Presidential Election at three demographically diverse schools: An exercise in neoliberal governmentality. *Educational Studies: A Journal of the American Educational Studies Association, 47,* 133–159.

Journell, W. (2011c). The disclosure dilemma in action: A qualitative look at the effect of teacher disclosure on classroom instruction. *Journal of Social Studies Research, 35,* 217–244.

Journell, W. (2012). Ideological homogeneity, school leadership, and political intolerance in secondary education: A study of three high schools during the 2008 Presidential Election. *Journal of School Leadership, 22,* 569–599.

Journell, W. (2013). Learning from each other: What social studies can learn from the controversy surrounding the teaching of evolution in science. *Curriculum Journal, 24,* 494–510.

Journell, W. (2016a). Making a case for teacher political disclosure. *Journal of Curriculum Theorizing, 31,* 100–111.

Journell, W. (2016b). Teacher political disclosure as *parrhēsia*. *Teachers College Record, 118*(5), 1–36.

Journell, W. (2017a). Politically conservative preservice teachers and the spiral of silence: Implications for teacher education. *Teacher Education Quarterly, 44*(2), 105–129.

Journell, W. (2017b). *Teaching politics in secondary education: Engaging with contentious issues.* Albany, NY: State University of New York Press.

Journell, W., & Castro, E. L. (2011). Culturally relevant political education: Using immigration as a catalyst for civic understanding. *Multicultural Education, 18*(4), 10–17.

Kahne, J., & Middaugh, E. (2009). Democracy for some: The civic opportunity gap in high school. In J. Youniss & P. Levine (Eds.), *Engaging young people in civic life* (pp. 29–58). Nashville, TN: Vanderbilt University Press.

Kelly, T. E. (1986). Discussing controversial issues: Four perspectives on the teacher's role. *Theory & Research in Social Education, 14*, 113–138.

King, L. J., Warren, C. A., Bender, M., & Finley, S. Y. (2016). #Black lives matter as critical patriotism. In W. Journell (Ed.), *Teaching social studies in an era of divisiveness: The challenges of discussing social issues in a non-partisan way* (pp. 93–109). Lanham, MD: Rowman & Littlefield.

Koch, J. W. (2000). Do citizens apply gender stereotypes to infer candidates' ideological orientations? *Journal of Politics, 62*, 414–429.

Mayo, J. B. (2007). Negotiating sexual orientation and classroom practice(s) at school. *Theory & Research in Social Education, 35*, 447–464.

Miller-Lane, J., Denton, E., & May, A. (2006). Social studies teachers' views on committed impartiality and discussion. *Social Studies Research and Practice, 1*, 30–44.

Niemi, N. S., & Niemi, R. G. (2007). Partisanship, participation, and political trust as taught (or not) in high school history and government classes. *Theory & Research in Social Education, 35*, 32–61.

Noelle-Neumann, E. (1993). *The spiral of silence: Public opinion—Our social skin* (2nd ed.). Chicago: University of Chicago Press.

Orlowski, P. (2017). The light to the left: Conceptions of social justice among Christian social studies teachers. *Education, 23*, 66–91.

Pew Research Center. (2015, April 7). *A deep dive into party affiliation.* Retrieved from http://www.people-press.org/2015/04/07/a-deep-dive-into-party-affiliation/

Swalwell, K., & Schweber, S. (2016). Teaching through turmoil: Social studies teachers and local controversial current events. *Theory & Research in Social Education, 44*, 283–315.

Vickery, A. (2017). "You excluded us for so long and now you want us to be patriotic?" African American women teachers navigating the quandary of citizenship. *Theory & Research in Social Education, 45*, 318–348.

Part V
Social Historical Contextual Influences on Teacher Identity Development

Chapter 16
Conceptualizing 'Teacher Identity': A Political Approach

Michalinos Zembylas and Sharon Chubbuck

In recent years much literature on teaching and teacher education highlights the importance of *teacher identity* in understanding teaching and teacher development. In the last decade or so there have been several reviews of research on teacher identity (see Beauchamp & Thomas, 2009; Beijaard, Meijer, & Verloop, 2004; Rodgers & Scott, 2008) and numerous books, conceptual papers and empirical studies that essentially make the study of teacher identity a research field on its own (e.g. Akkerman & Meijer, 2011; Alsup, 2006; Beauchamp & Thomas, 2011; Canrinus, Helms-Lorenz, Beijaard, Buitink, & Hofman, 2011; Cohen, 2010; Day, Kington, Stobart, & Sammons, 2006; Hong, 2010; Mockler, 2011; Sfard & Prusak, 2005; Sutherland, Howard, & Markauskaite, 2010; Thomas & Beauchamp, 2011; Timoštšuk & Ugaste, 2010; Zembylas & Chubbuck, 2015). Philosophically and methodologically speaking, teacher identity has been approached in different ways, depending on the issues that become focal points of analysis and the theoretical framework within which these issues are presented. Rodgers and Scott's (2008) review, for example, has a psychological frame, whereas Beauchamp and Thomas's (2009) review has more of a sociocultural and discursive orientation.

Our theoretical framework in this chapter is *political*, namely, we are explicitly concerned about the ways in which politics and power relations figure importantly in teacher identity formation. This proposed political approach is grounded in post-structuralist theories of philosophy and politics (Butler, 1990/1999; Foucault, 1983, 1988, 1990; Rose, 1990, 1998) and critical theories of education (e.g. Britzman, 2003; Cochran-Smith, 2004; Giroux, 2005) and supports the exploration of identity

M. Zembylas (✉)
Program of Educational Studies, Open University of Cyprus, Latsia, Cyprus
e-mail: m.zembylas@ouc.ac.cy

S. Chubbuck
Department of Educational Policy and Leadership, Marquette University,
Milwaukee, WI, USA
e-mail: sharon.chubbuck@marquette.edu

© Springer International Publishing AG, part of Springer Nature 2018
P. A. Schutz et al. (eds.), *Research on Teacher Identity*,
https://doi.org/10.1007/978-3-319-93836-3_16

formation in the context of the social operation of power. To establish this political approach, we first review previous efforts to define teacher identity, showing how the conceptual grounding of each effort shapes the focus and, thus, nature of the definition. Next, we examine four overlapping, interacting aspects of identity in teachers' lives and work, foregrounded in recent research on teacher identity—emotion, discourse and narrative, reflection, and agency/structure (Beauchamp & Thomas, 2009)—highlighting how power relations and politics are central in each aspect. In the third section, we develop a "political approach" that we contend can better illuminate and clarify what constitutes the politicized elements of teacher identity, allowing us to appreciate the experiences requisite to systematically develop critical, transformative teacher practice and professional development. In the final section, we discuss the theoretical and methodological implications of this political approach for studying teacher identity. We hope that the introduction of this explicitly political frame—in addition to Rodgers and Scott's (2008) psychological and Beauchamp and Thomas's (2009) sociocultural/discursive frames—will provide a more *holistic* conceptualization of teacher identity that is beneficial to the profession.

Defining 'Teacher Identity': Conceptual Underpinnings and Key Aspects

Efforts to define teacher identity reveal a complicated task, with shifting and overlapping descriptors, shaped by the orientating framework used by authors. Recent conceptualizations, however, reflect a poststructural perspective, where identity is somewhat commonly seen as dynamic, relational, multiple, and changing over time influenced by a range of individual and contextual factors (Beauchamp & Thomas, 2009; Rodgers & Scott, 2008; Zembylas, 2003a).

In their review of research on teachers' professional identity between 1988 and 2000, Beijaard et al. (2004) acknowledge that while many works show a considerable absence of definition, several authors in education draw on definitions of identity used in the social sciences and humanities. In the review, Beijaard et al. distilled four common characteristics of professional identity marked by their relational quality. First, identity is not a fixed entity, rather the product of an ongoing process of interpretation and re-interpretation of experiences. Second, the interaction of this ongoing process involves both a person and a context, and thus, teacher identity is conceptualized in relation to communities of practice. Third, the formation of teacher identity involves agency, that is, teachers actively pursue professional development and learning in accordance with their goals. And finally, sub-identities, such as race, class, gender, and personal experiences, exist, and interact within a professional teacher identity, especially in the initial steps of a teacher's career, which contribute to a sometimes/sometimes not harmonious whole. Thus, although different understandings of teacher identity exist, often with an unclear distinction between self and identity or between personal and professional identity, Beijaard et al. emphasizes that scholars agree overall that identity, as a multi-faceted, dynamic entity, has a relational nature.

Day et al. (2006) reiterate (while further nuancing) this relational framework of identity by emphasizing that teacher identities are neither intrinsically stable nor intrinsically fragmented; rather, teacher identities are more or less stable and more or less fragmented at different times and in different ways according to a number of life, career, and situational factors. In other words, interrelationships unavoidably exist between the professional and personal identities of teachers. For example, preservice teachers develop a pre-teaching identity on the basis of their student images of teachers, their initial beliefs and concepts of what constitutes a good teacher and their implicit theories of teaching (Flores & Day, 2006). In general, teacher identity involves the complex interplay between personal experience and cultural, social, institutional, and environmental contexts (Sfard & Prusak, 2005). This understanding of teacher identity nuances the relational framework by including sociocultural perspectives where identity is seen as both product (as a result of the sociocultural influences on a teacher) and process (an ongoing interaction within teacher development).

In addition to this relational and sociocultural frame of teacher identity, more developmental perspectives have also been used in studying teachers' professional identity. For example, Rodgers and Scott's (2008) review highlights teacher identity formation through a lens that emphasizes the developmental stages in which teachers make sense out of their experiences. Rodgers and Scott's psychological frame does not deny that identity is relational; in fact, these authors reiterate some of the characteristics identified by Beijaard et al. (2004). However, Rodgers and Scott's emphasis is more on the importance of considering the developmental aspects of teachers' professional identity and the various stages through which teacher identity grows over time (see also, Bullough & Gitlin, 2001).

In the most recent review of literature on teacher identity, Beauchamp and Thomas (2009) similarly reiterate that, while defining teacher identity is challenging, several characterizations of teacher identity recur. Most commonly, these are multiplicity, discontinuity, and social nature, all of which emphasize that identity is not a fixed and stable entity (as it was long perceived), but rather shifts with time and context. Two frameworks that reflect these characterizations of teacher identity are the discursive and the dialogical approaches (e.g. Akkerman & Meijer, 2011; Trent, 2011). The notion of teacher identity-in-discourse acknowledges that identities are discursively constituted, mainly through language. Similarly, within a dialogical approach, teacher identity is conceived as both unitary and multiple, both continuous and discontinuous, and both individual and social. On the basis of this approach, Akkerman and Meijer suggest defining teacher identity as "*an ongoing process of negotiating multiple I-positions in such a way that a more or less coherent and consistent sense of self is maintained throughout various participations and self-investments in one's (working) life*" (2011, p. 315, emphasis in original).

Four Aspects of Teacher Identity Formation

Four key aspects of teacher identity emerge from the survey of the previous and other literature: emotion, narrative and discourse, reflection, and agency and structure.[1] These four aspects illustrate the variety of components of teacher identity seen in both psychological and sociopolitical grounded theory. They also, however, highlight elements of teacher identity formation that warrant a political framework.

The first aspect of teacher identity formation is emotion. Since pioneer work by such scholars as Hargreaves (1998) and Nias (1996) illuminated the influence of emotion in teachers' professional lives and self-understanding, research on emotion as an important aspect of teacher identity formation (Beauchamp & Thomas, 2009; Rodgers & Scott, 2008) has continued to grow (e.g. Cross & Hong, 2009, 2012; Darby, 2008; Hong, 2010; Lasky, 2005; Schutz, Cross, Hong, & Osbon, 2007; Shapiro, 2010; van Veen, Sleegers, & van de Ven, 2005; Zembylas, 2003a, 2005). Collectively, this recent research emphasizes three key themes. First, regardless of the researcher's theoretical framework, emotion and teacher identity are conceptually defined as interrelated and dynamic, seen, for example, in the ways teachers' expressions of emotions of care are guided/shaped by their professional identities. Second, the influential role of emotion in teachers' personal and professional identities seems especially salient in the politicized context of school reform efforts, such as increased managerialism and accountability (Darby, 2008; Lasky, 2005. And third, the emotions experienced in the ongoing construction of teachers' professional identities are deeply connected to their biographies which are, themselves, entangled in the sociopolitical context of their workplace. Clearly, emotional rules, shaped by explicit power relations, influence teachers' identity formation (Zembylas, 2005).

Discourse and narrative are the second aspect of teacher identity formation. The literature on discursive/narrative construction of teacher identity derives from the sociocultural orientation (Beauchamp & Thomas, 2009), emphasizing the multiplicity, discontinuity, and social nature of identity, with several themes emerging. First, discourse—literally the talk within and among teachers—both constitutes identity and is itself constituted through identity (e.g., Cohen, 2010). Second, while narrative identity is often viewed from a psychological framework (e.g. McAdams, 1985, 2001; McAdams & McLean, 2013), in several studies, narrative is seen as a *manifestation* of discourse, both in the teacher and in the institutions/national sociopolitical contexts in which they are located (e.g., Søreide, 2006). Third, discursive identity formation is dialogically relational (e.g., Watson, 2006). Teachers position themselves/their identity in relation to students, other teachers, teacher educators, discourses from programs, schools, and national images—all relational stances which can implicate power relations.

The third aspect of teacher identity formation is reflection, where three themes emerge from the literature. First, reflection in identity is provoked and enriched at

---

[1] For a more detailed discussion of the four aspects, see Zembylas and Chubbuck (2015).

sites of conflict and discomfort, such as the dissonance between one's self-image and how one is perceived by others (Warin, Maddock, Pell, & Hargreaves, 2006). Second, identity development occurs through reflection on multiple trajectories/ images of past experiences and future possibilities, such as "drawing on the past and imagining futures" (Smith, 2007, p. 383), all of which exist in sociopolitical contexts. And third, the context of reflection influences identity formation (Zembylas & Chubbuck, 2015), indicating the complexity of understanding teacher identity (Urzúa & Vásquez, 2008). The role of reflection is seen as multiple factors emerge: prior personal identity, significant community membership, mentoring support, and reflection on actual practice versus theory. In an effort to organize this complexity into a more coherent framework of teacher identity to support professional development, Korthagen (2004) proposes an "onion" model where reflection on "core" layers of identity—mission/identity/beliefs—significantly influences the more tangible outer layers—competencies/behaviors/environment. Thus, those intangible elements of identity most subject to political and power influences can dictate more external practices.

The final aspect of identity development is agency/structure. The term *agency* has been defined as the capacity to achieve one's goals, with the implication being that a self, with (some inherent, others developed in contexts) cognitive and emotional qualities, is the source of such capacity (Beauchamp & Thomas, 2011; Day et al., 2006). *Structure*, in contrast, means there are external influences shaping that process of gaining achievement. In laymen's terms, the tension is seen in the debate over "being born a teacher" versus "becoming a teacher" (Schepens, Aelterman, & Vlerick, 2009). This distinction between teacher identity derived from personal agency and that derived from structures that support becoming a teacher is an important one since it implicates the nature of who may become an effective teacher and even the nature of the teaching process itself (Hoveid & Hoveid, 2008). Additionally, this aspect positions the personal (agency) in reciprocal interaction with the political (structures).

In sum, "identities are a shifting amalgam of personal biography, culture, social influence, and institutional values which may change according to role or circumstance" (Day et al., 2006, p. 613). While highlighting various components of teacher identity development, these four salient aspects lay a groundwork for considering a political framework to further understanding.

Towards a Political Approach in Conceptualizing Teacher Identity

So far, our discussion of teacher identity has focused on its conceptual underpinnings and the major aspects of teacher identity as discussed in the literature (i.e., emotion, narrative and discourse, reflection, and agency/structure). While it is clear from this incomplete review of literature that the political dimensions are an acknowledged part of teacher identity formation, overt attention to a *political frame-work* in conceptualizing and analyzing teacher identity is lacking. Thus, some scholars have recently defined teacher identity within an explicitly political frame of reference (e.g. Clarke, 2009; Mockler, 2011; Zembylas & Chubbuck, 2015). In this model, teacher identity, situated within the broader social and political dimensions of teachers, is at once a complex matter of the social and the individual, of discourse and practice, of agency and structure, and of the singular and the multiple. This political conceptualization of teacher identity compellingly supports analyses of *power* in the process of teacher identity formation, and extends critical social theorists' arguments on governmentality (Butler, 1990/1999; Foucault, 1983, 1988, 1990; Rose, 1990, 1998), that is, how power works in ways that 'discipline' teachers to govern themselves and others in the name of certain regimes of truth (e.g. instrumentality; accountability; professionalism; teachers-as-born vs. teachers-as-made debates; see Sachs, 2009). In addition, by grounding this approach in critical theories of education (e.g. Britzman, 2003; Cochran-Smith, 2004; Giroux, 2005), we suggest that teacher identity formation can be conceptualized as a practical *and* political 'tool' to support teachers in the development of critical transformative agendas that question common sense understandings of teachers' professional practice, supporting the broader critical and transformative aims of education (Mockler, 2011).

Since teacher self-formation involves engagement with both regimes of truth and practices of power (Foucault, 1988; Rose, 1998), teacher identity formation is inevitably a political process. Britzman (2003) makes a similar point when she argues that the politics of identity is essentially about the ways in which the social operation of power, discourses, and social structures shape identities in teaching. Power is, therefore, at the center of teacher identity formation; it produces discourses of truth and induces particular forms of knowledge in teaching practice and teacher development. Power is at work in schools through various technologies (i.e., techniques that provide detailed structuring of space, time, and relations among individuals) which form and perpetuate discourses of truth that are internalized and self-regulating. Thus, teachers play a large part in their own control by embodying certain techniques such as confession, diary writing, and reflection—techniques which are practiced under the actual or imagined authority of some regime of truth. Discourses of truth appear as naturalized bodies of knowledge, yet as critical theorists of education tell us (e.g. Giroux, 2005) these regimes are contested terrains, constantly (re)constructed and (re)invented. This means, for example, that a focus on narrative and discourse or on reflection aspects of teacher identity is at best partial, if it fails to identify the practices within which teacher identities have been fabricated and particular relations with themselves and with others are formed.

The pervasiveness of power relations constituting teachers as particular subjects implies, however, that power is not only repressive—as often assumed—but it is also productive and always exists in relation with freedom (Butler, 1990/1999; Foucault, 1988; Rose, 1998). Attending to the local manifestations of power relations allows one to track resistances, to be critical, and to develop strategies for (re) constituting one's self and identities. "The problem is not changing people's consciousness — or what's in their heads — but the political, economic, institutional regime of the production of truth", as Foucault writes (1990, p. 135). In other words, teachers have choices among various discourses and practices that are available to them; no discourse or practice is inherently liberating or oppressive. Recognizing that teacher identities, like discourses and practices, are not predetermined, but need to be continually renegotiated within specific contexts, opens possibilities for transformations of the encounter with others and with one's self (Clarke, 2009). Such transformative identity work is not easy, as Clarke explains, but requires of teachers that they become social theorists with a critical awareness of the limits that condition them and the ways in which constraints and possibilities are enabled. Based on the recognition that teacher identities are contingent and constructed and are thus open to new creative assemblages, the recognition of the centrality of politics is worthwhile to consider in future theorizations of teacher identity.

All in all, a political approach in conceptualizing teacher identity offers a critical understanding of power and identity in teaching and teacher professional development. Teacher professional identity can serve as a political tool to investigate the role of emotion, narrative and discourse, reflection, and agency/structure aspects in the constitution of power relations in the classroom. For example, an explicit focus on power and its consequences supports examination of the ways dominant and/or resistant discourses about 'best teaching practices' have specific effects on the teaching profession (e.g., suggesting the standardization and internationalization of certain practices or even the resistance to such trends). This implies that teachers with a strong, critical sense of their professional identity and its implications in practice are more likely to be pro-active in the enactment of a transformative vision both within and beyond the school (Mockler, 2011). Thus, an analysis of the reciprocal relationship between politics and teacher identity not only underlines the significance of the political domain in the construction and maintenance of teacher professional identity, but it also recognizes the potential to subvert normalizing practices, discourses and identities in schools.

Implications for Studying Teacher Identity

Taking a political approach in conceptualizing teacher identity has certain implications. We will outline two such theoretical and methodological implications from adopting a political approach towards teacher identity: historicizing identity categories; and enmeshing micro-level and macro-level analysis.

First, a political approach towards teacher identity historicizes identity categories and identity claims by situating the construct of teacher identity within certain historical, cultural, and political contexts. By understanding teacher identity as historically contingent, teachers, teacher educators and researchers have a tool to deconstruct the power relations that normalize the life of teachers in schools. This approach, in other words, *historicizes* (a) the ways in which teacher identities are constituted, (b) their organization into discourses and technologies of power, and (c) their importance as a site of social control as well as resistance. Acknowledging the historicization and politicization of teacher identity helps teachers, teacher educators, and researchers analyze and sort through various discourses about teacher identity, and understand how those discourses operate to fabricate particular meanings about teachers that are circulated through certain practices. For example, the common distinction made between 'personal' and 'professional' identity (see Beijaard et al., 2004) blurs when conceptualizing teacher identity as politicized and historicized; that is, the boundaries between the personal and the professional may not be as clear as one might think, but rather they imply deeper identity politics in relation to race, gender, or class. As Alsup (2006) points out, ideal(ized) versions of teachers as white, male, middle class, and heterosexual are often attached to more professional identities rather than the personal and emotional identities exhibited by women or African-American teachers. A political approach to teacher identity, then, poses an important challenge to normalized views of teachers and teacher development based on their beliefs, their emotions, and their approaches to learning; taken-for-granted assumptions about teachers and teaching are deeply problematized with a political approach to teacher identity.

Second, a political approach towards teacher identity implies paying careful attention to the contextual specificity of the transaction between larger social forces (macro-political level) and the internal psychic terrain of the individual and his or her working conditions (micro-political level), highlighting the ways that identity claims are politicized in specific locales. Within this transactional process of analysis, teacher identities are understood as embedded in culture, ideology, and power relations. Drawing on this perspective on teacher identity foregrounds the cultural, political, and historical context in which identity claims are constituted (Zembylas, 2003a, 2003b, 2005) and thus both micro- and macro-analyses are necessary to capture all the complexities and nuances. Both these analyses, writes Akkerman and Meijer (2011), show "how the macro-context impinges on the teachers' patterned as well as momentary acts, and possibly, how the micro-context may have consequences for the macro-context" (p. 316). This enmeshed micro-level and macro-level analysis enables researchers to study teacher identity in ways that emphasize both *context* and *practice*. This approach restores the concept of identity to its historical sources, thus de-essentializing it.

Concluding Remarks

In this chapter, we have discussed various approaches and conceptualizations of teacher identity. Drawing upon a political approach, our aims have been to introduce an alternative perspective on teacher identity by highlighting the centrality of power relations and their consequences in teaching and teacher development. Thus we have suggested that a political approach in conceptualizing teacher identity can provide a fruitful point of view that adds a productive perspective to existing accounts and approaches of studying teacher identity. We have argued that this approach—which combines poststructuralist perspectives on power and critical theories of education—treats teacher identity as a practical, valuable tool through embracing the political aspects of teaching and teacher development. What follows from a political approach towards teacher identity is a conceptualization of teacher identity as an ongoing political process of negotiation and interrogation of multiple, fragmented and fragile identities.

Although the political perspectives of teacher identity are embedded in the different aspects of teacher identity revisited—i.e. emotion, narrative and discourse, reflection, and agency/structure—what is still missing from the literature and the field is empirical work that explicitly focuses on the value and plausibility of the approach that has been presented here. Many of the claims discussed in this chapter need to be empirically grounded in the context of teachers' work. As an analytical framework, a political approach towards teacher identity can be particularly useful in historicizing identity categories in teaching, enmeshing micro-level and macro-level analysis, and researching teacher identity as a political process that challenges taken-for-granted views about teaching and teachers.

References

Akkerman, S., & Meijer, P. (2011). A dialogical approach to conceptualizing teacher identity. *Teaching & Teacher Education, 27*(2), 308–319.

Alsup, J. (2006). *Teacher identity discourses. Negotiating personal and professional spaces.* Mahwah, NJ: Lawrence Erlbaum Associate, Inc.

Beauchamp, C., & Thomas, L. (2009). Understanding teacher identity: An overview of issues in the literature and implications for teacher education. *Cambridge Journal of Education, 39*(2), 175–189.

Beauchamp, C., & Thomas, L. (2011). New teachers' identity shifts at the boundary of teacher education and initial practice. *International Journal of Educational Research, 50*(1), 6–13.

Beijaard, D., Meijer, P., & Verloop, N. (2004). Reconsidering research on teachers' professional identity. *Teaching and Teacher Education, 20*, 107–128.

Britzman, D. (2003). *Practice makes practice: A critical study of learning to teach.* Albany, NY: State University of New York Press.

Bullough, R., & Gitlin, A. (2001). *Becoming a student of teaching: Linking knowledge production and practice.* London: RoutldgeFalmer.

Butler, J. (1990/1999). *Gender trouble: Feminism and the subversion of identity.* New York/London: Routledge.

Canrinus, E., Helms-Lorenz, M., Beijaard, D., Buitink, J., & Hofman, A. (2011). Profiling teachers' sense of professional identity. *Educational Studies, 37*(5), 593–608.

Clarke, M. (2009). The ethico-politics of teacher identity. *Educational Philosophy and Theory, 41*(2), 185–200.

Cochran-Smith, M. (2004). *Walking the road: Race, diversity, and social justice in teacher education.* New York: Teachers College Press.

Cohen, J. (2010). Getting recognised: Teachers negotiating professional identities as learners through talk. *Teaching & Teacher Education, 26*(3), 473–481.

Cross, D., & Hong, J. Y. (2009). Beliefs and professional identity: Critical constructs in examining the impact of reform on the emotional experiences of teachers. In P. Schutz & M. Zembylas

(Eds.), *Advances in teacher emotion research: The impact on teachers' lives* (pp. 273–296). Dordrecht, The Netherlands: Springer.

Cross, D., & Hong, J. Y. (2012). An ecological examination of teachers' emotions in the school context. *Teaching and Teacher Education, 28*, 957–967.

Darby, A. (2008). Teachers' emotions in the reconstruction of professional self-understanding. *Teaching and Teacher Education, 24*, 1160–1172.

Day, C., Kington, A., Stobart, G., & Sammons, P. (2006). The personal and professional selves of teachers: Stable and unstable identities. *British Educational Research Journal, 32*(4), 601–616.

Flores, M. A., & Day, C. (2006). Contexts which shape and reshape new teachers' identities: A multi-perspective study. *Teaching and Teacher Education, 22*(2), 219–232.

Foucault, M. (1983). The subject and power. In H. L. Dreyfus & P. Rabinow (Eds.), *Michel Foucault: Beyond structuralism and hermeneutics* (pp. 208–226). Chicago: The University of Chicago Press.

Foucault, M. (1988). Technologies of the self. In L. H. Martin, H. Gutman, & P. H. Hutton (Eds.), *Technologies of the self* (pp. 16–49). Amherst, MA: University of Massachusetts Press.

Foucault, M. (1990). *The history of sexuality, volume 3: The care of the self*. New York: Vintage Books.

Giroux, H. A. (2005). *Schooling and struggle for public life: Critical pedagogy in the modern age*. Boulder, CO: Paradigm Publishers.

Hargreaves, A. (1998). The emotional practice of teaching. *Teaching and Teacher Education, 14*, 835–854.

Hong, J. (2010). Pre-service and beginning teachers' professional identity and its relation to dropping out of the profession. *Teaching & Teacher Education, 26*(8), 1530–1543.

Hoveid, H., & Hoveid, M. H. (2008). Teachers' identity, self and the process of learning. *Studies in Philosophy of Education, 27*, 125–136.

Korthagen, F. A. J. (2004). In search of the essence of a good teacher: Towards a more holistic approach in teacher education. *Teaching and Teacher Education, 20*, 77–97.

Lasky, S. (2005). A sociocultural approach to understanding teacher identity, agency and professional vulnerability in a context of secondary school reform. *Teaching & Teacher Education, 21*, 899–916.

McAdams, D. P. (1985). *Power, intimacy, and the life story: Personological inquiries into identity*. Homewood, IL: Dorsey Press.

McAdams, D. P. (2001). The psychology of life stories. *Review of General Psychology, 5*, 100–122.

McAdams, D. P., & McLean, K. C. (2013). Narrative identity. *Current Directions in Psychological Science, 22*(3), 233–238.

Mockler, N. (2011). Beyond "what works": Understanding teacher identity as a practical and political tool. *Teachers & Teaching: Theory and Practice, 17*(5), 517–528.

Nias, J. (1996). Thinking about feeling: The emotions in teaching. *Cambridge Journal of Education, 26*, 293–306.

Rodgers, C., & Scott, C. (2008). The development of the personal self and professional identity in learning to teach. In M. Cochran-Smith, S. Feiman-Nemser, D. J. McIntyre, & K. E. Demers (Eds.), *Handbook of research on teacher education* (pp. 732–755). New York: Routledge.

Rose, N. (1990). *Governing the soul: The shaping of the private self*. London/New York: Routledge.

Rose, N. (1998). *Inventing our selves: Psychology, power and personhood*. Cambridge, UK: Cambridge University Press.

Sachs, J. (2009). Teacher professional identity: Competing discourses, competing outcomes. *Journal of Education Policy, 16*(2), 149–161.

Schepens, A., Aelterman, A., & Vlerick, P. (2009). Student teachers' professional identity formation: between being born as a teacher and becoming one. *Educational Studies, 35*(4), 361–378.

Schutz, P., Cross, D., Hong, J. Y., & Osbon, J. (2007). Teacher identities, beliefs, and goals related to emotions in the classroom. In P. A. Schutz & R. Peckrun (Eds.), *Emotions in education* (pp. 223–241). New York: Academic Press.

Sfard, A., & Prusak, A. (2005). Telling identities: In search of an analytic tool for investigating learning as a cultural shaped activity. *Educational Researcher, 34*(4), 14–22.

Shapiro, S. (2010). Revisiting the teachers' lounge: Reflections on emotional experience and teacher identity. *Teaching and Teacher Education, 26*, 616–621.

Smith, R. G. (2007). Developing professional identities and knowledge: Becoming primary teachers. *Teachers and Teaching: Theory and Practice, 13*(4), 377–397.

Søreide, G. E. (2006). Narrative construction of teacher identity: Positioning and negotiation. *Teachers & Teaching: Theory & Practice, 12*(5), 527–547.

Sutherland, L., Howard, S., & Markauskaite, L. (2010). Professional identity creation: Examining the development of beginning preservice teachers' understanding of their work as teachers. *Teaching & Teacher Education, 26*(3), 455–465.

Thomas, L., & Beauchamp, C. (2011). Understanding new teachers' professional identities through metaphor. *Teaching and Teacher Education, 27*, 762–769.

Timoštšuk, I., & Ugaste, A. (2010). Student teachers' professional identity. *Teaching & Teacher Education, 26*(8), 1563–1570.

Trent, J. (2011). 'Four years one, I am ready to teach': Teacher education and the construction of teacher identities. *Teachers and Teaching: Theory and Practice, 17*(5), 529–543.

Urzúa, A., & Vásquez, C. (2008). Reflection and professional identity in teachers' future-oriented discourse. *Teaching and Teacher Education, 24*(7), 1935–1946.

Van Veen, K., Sleegers, P., & van de Ven, P.-H. (2005). On teacher's identity, emotions and commitment to change: A case study into the cognitive-affective processes of a secondary school teacher in the context of reforms. *Teaching and Teacher Education, 21*(8), 917–934.

Warin, J., Maddock, M., Pell, A., & Hargreaves, L. (2006). Resolving identity dissonance through reflective and reflexive practice in teaching. *Reflective Practice, 7*(2), 233–245.

Watson, C. (2006). Narratives of practice and the construction of identity in teaching. *Teachers & Teaching: Theory and Practice, 12*(5), 509–526.

Zembylas, M. (2003a). Emotions and teacher identity: A poststructural perspective. *Teachers and Teaching: Theory and Practice, 9*, 213–238.

Zembylas, M. (2003b). Interrogating "teacher identity": Emotion, resistance, and self-formation. *Educational Theory, 53*, 107–127.

Zembylas, M. (2005). Discursive practices, genealogies and emotional rules: A poststructuralist view on emotion and identity in teaching. *Teaching and Teacher Education, 21*(8), 935–948.

Zembylas, M., & Chubbuck, S. (2015). The intersection of identity, beliefs, and politics to conceptualizing 'teacher identity. In H. Fives & M. Gill (Eds.), *International handbook of research on teachers' beliefs* (pp. 173–190). New York: Routledge.

Chapter 17
Teacher Identity in the Current Teacher Education Landscape

Rebecca Buchanan and Brad Olsen

To present a situated view of teacher identity, we consider the reform landscape of teacher education and examine its effect on two beginning teachers in California. We treat teacher identity as a social practice-based analytic highlighting how a teacher's self is made, and continually re-made, inside the flow of contextualized practice (Akkerman & Meijer, 2011; Beauchamp & Thomas, 2009; Mockler, 2011; Olsen, 2008, 2014; ,). In this way, teacher identity is both a process and a product. It is the process of self, others, and multiple contexts interacting to create a person's understandings *of* and *for* herself (Olsen, 2014). And it is the always-under-construction product that results (Alsup, 2006; Beauchamp & Thomas, 2009; Beijaard, Verloop, & Vermunt, 2000). By viewing the two student teachers that we profile as both complex products of, and agentive actors inside, the itself complex and multi-faceted current teacher education landscape, we provide a grounded discussion of teacher identity, and simultaneously illuminate what it means to participate in teacher education today.

The Landscape: Practice-Based Teacher Education

Teacher preparation has become contentious (Darling-Hammond, 1994; Goldstein, 2014; Rhee, 2013). Debates concerning who should be teaching, how they should be selected, what knowledge new teachers need, what program models work best, and how new teachers learn are not merely questions of fact, but are rooted in

R. Buchanan (✉)
School of Learning and Teaching, University of Maine, Orono, ME, USA
e-mail: rebecca.buchanan@maine.edu

B. Olsen
Education Department, University of California-Santa Cruz, Santa Cruz, CA, USA
e-mail: bolsen@ucsc.edu

© Springer International Publishing AG, part of Springer Nature 2018
P. A. Schutz et al. (eds.), *Research on Teacher Identity*,
https://doi.org/10.1007/978-3-319-93836-3_17

philosophical and political positions regarding processes of learning and disagreements around purposes of schooling (Berliner & Biddle, 1996; Ravitch, 2010; Rhee, 2013). In fact, over the last 100 years teacher education has been in a nearly constant state of reform, pulled in multiple directions by competing agendas, research programs, and historical events (Clifford & Guthrie, 1988; Cochran-Smith & Fries, 2005; Cuban, 1993). The history of teacher education is marked by differing conceptions of what teachers need to know, what high quality teaching looks like (and how to research it), who is best suited to teach, and who should make decisions about professional preparation.

Over the last few decades especially, teacher education has been the subject of a great deal of public discourse and policy attention, mostly related to the best ways to recruit and train teachers. 1983's *A Nation at Risk*, a report commissioned by the White House, argued that American education in general was in a state of crisis, and framed this crisis as a threat not only to the economy, but also to national security. Two competing teacher education movements responded to this call. One sought to *professionalize* teaching (Carnegie Forum, 1986; Holmes Partnership, 2007). And the other sought to *deregulate* entry into teaching (Ballou & Podgursky, 1997; Finn, 2008; Hess, 2002). Debates between these two agendas have been strident (Darling-Hammond, 1994; Kopp, 1994; Ravitch, 2010; Rhee, 2013) and buried within the debates are differing approaches to a third reform agenda: *social justice*. The social justice agenda fits alongside, and is intertwined with, the other two because both sides argue that their approach leads to better educational opportunities for low-income students and students of color. Many social justice advocates additionally argue that neither side suitably includes critical attention to systems of power and culture (Darder, Baltonado, & Torres, 2003; Kincheloe, 2008).[1]

One currently popular reform on which all three agendas to some extent agree is Practice-Based Teacher Education (PBTE). PBTE is an approach to teacher preparation that centralizes practicing teaching as the main ingredient of teacher education. PBTE takes multiple forms in actual practice and can be thought of more as a discourse about teacher education than a particular program model (Ball & Forzani, 2009; Berry, Montgomery, & Snyder, 2008; Darling-Hammond, 2010; Grossman, 2010; Rust, 2010; Zeichner, 2010). The primary way that PBTE manifests in contemporary programs is a greater emphasis on the student-teaching practicum. The practicum is a kind of crucible that concentrates many aspects of the broader figured world of teaching, and it has been a consistent feature of pre-service teacher preparation since the development of normal schools in the early 1800s (Goldstein, 2014; Herbst, 1989). This makes it a good location for examining teacher identity.

---

[1] The social justice agenda, however, often calls for more than just improved learning opportunities for low-income students and students of color. It often recommends deep overhauls of education in line with transformative learning, critical analyses of traditional and neoliberal views of schooling, redeveloped curricula, and a change in the racial demographics of the teaching workforce (hooks, 2014; Sleeter, 2013).

Teacher Identity: A Social-Practice Theory of Human Development

Teacher identity treats teacher development as holistic and frequently non-linear (Olsen, 2014). As is obvious in this volume, teacher identity can be conceptualized in multiple ways. Our framework draws from socio-cultural practice theory, symbolic interactionism, and sociolinguistics to put forward a grounded model of teachers and their professional learning. We root our view of teacher identity in situated perspectives on development (Lave, 1996) that understand learning to be inextricably linked to context (Greeno, Collins, & Resnick, 1996). Our perspective draws from an ecological model in order to examine the way that macro-influences (like history and culture), meso-forces (such as education policies and school contexts), and the micro-contexts of daily work in actual schools and classrooms are actually *part of* the ongoing learning process, not simply an influence on it (Bronfenbrenner, 1977). As participants construct new understandings they construct new versions of themselves. Learning is inextricably linked to the social location where it happens even as its products are to some degree abstractable or transferrable (Beach, 1999). Such a view understands that social activity with others does not simply result in transmission of closed knowledge and skills from one person to another, but leads to changed selves. Learning changes who a person is and yet, simultaneously, the person affects the shape of the learning.

While this iterative model of human development centers on individual meaning-making processes, it understands those processes as situated within, and therefore co-constructed by, broader cultural, social, and historical contexts. Holland, Lachicotte, Skinner, and Cain (1998), use the term *figured world* to describe each culturally and socially constructed context within which specific identities form. Figured worlds provide parameters against which individuals make decisions, make meaning, and construct understandings of themselves. These figured worlds we inhabit provide ready-made sets of cultural practices that members use in their ongoing identity construction. For example, Holland et al. (1998) describe how members of Alcoholics Anonymous use the narrative structure of telling their story to construct new identities as non-drinking alcoholics. The patterned stories that they tell carry 'ways of being' within the figured world of recovery and, over time, become intertwined with who the person believes she is. Within a community of practice, other non-drinking alcoholics demonstrate use of this narrative practice to novices who, after seeing it modeled, take up the practice themselves and soon become members of the community as they also develop a new way of understanding themselves.

In the same way, the contemporary policy landscape of United States teacher education operates as a figured world within which pre-service teachers make sense of themselves as educators. For reasons introduced earlier in our chapter, the contemporary competing reform agendas and views of education result in a complex and contested "figured world of teaching" which has a reciprocal effect on the development of teacher identities.

Two Examples: Yaotl and Scott

We draw from a recent project investigating how two models of contemporary teacher education—a traditional university program and an alternatively organized program in California—attempt to reconcile the perennial theory/practice divide in the preparation of social justice-oriented teachers. For this chapter, we re-analyzed some of the data to present two short cases from the traditional university program that illuminate teacher identity within the figured world of contemporary teacher education.

Yaotl

Yaotl, a Latina woman in her late twenties, entered her teacher education program in 2014. Her family immigrated to the U.S. from Mexico when she was young. Yaotl had positive student experiences as a young child because she saw herself in her teachers: "I remember amazing experiences as a child with my teachers. I believe that [my positive reaction] was because they looked like [older versions of] me." In college, Yaotl participated in her university's service-learning program, which politicized her prior views of teaching and shaped her commitment to low-income communities. For her, this conjoining of biography with college and her first experience with the explicit politicization of learning initiated a desire to teach. After graduation, she taught preschool for seven years, working primarily with children of Spanish-speaking immigrants. Yaotl decided that she wanted to work with older students so she entered a teacher education program to earn her credential.

Yaotl found the program coursework to be consistent with her prior experiences, and so it reinforced her incoming identity of what a teacher was. The coursework dovetailed with her service-learning work from college and encouraged her to consider how her own personal development had been shaped by broad systems of power and oppression in society.

In our initial interview she articulated an idea of social justice as explicit questioning of societal norms, but she could not describe what that might look like in an actual classroom. Over time and supported by her coursework, she became interested in engaging students in academic content that analyzed how power operates. She looked forward to making her ideas concrete during her practicum; however, she found that once she began student teaching she had few opportunities to actually try out these social justice teaching beliefs.

Yaotl was placed in a kindergarten classroom during her first student teaching practicum and, because of her prior experience as a preschool teacher, it felt comfortable. But when Yaotl entered her second practicum, in a fifth grade classroom, multiple factors of the larger figured world of teaching limited her opportunities to enact the commitments she had been developing. Her cooperating teacher, Carla, adhered tightly to a pre-established curriculum so students would be prepared for

Awareness   Inclusive   Critical   Transformative

Fig. 17.1   Social Justice Teacher Development Continuum

the annual standardized tests they were required to take, which meant that Yaotl had little flexibility to experiment with alternative pedagogies. For Yaotl, the practicum was a conflicting figured space:

> I felt like the challenge as a student teacher is that [you must adhere to] what your cooperating teacher wants. Maybe it's not even what *they* want, but it's what the *school* wants. Then there's what *you* want to do. As you're developing your own ideology, you have to work that into somebody else's already established classroom.

As Yaotl attempted to develop her own lessons for the Teacher Performance Assessment (a series of essays, a curriculum, lesson plans, teaching practice, and post-teaching reflection essays, all of which needed to be revised multiple times and ultimately submitted to the state in order to receive her credential), she was required to use the adopted textbook, fit her lesson into the curriculum Carla had developed, and align the lesson with what she believed were overly rigid state standards:

> The content focus [I'm being asked to address] is on "influential minds of the American Revolution." Originally, I wanted to focus on [women]. I asked my cooperating teacher "Does the standard [stipulate] that students have to know about the *specific* men that are listed?" And she's like, "Yes, that's why I'm having you do them." I was just like, damn it!

This need to fit her social justice teaching goals into an already established curriculum and pre-set instructional practices designed to be politically neutral constrained Yaotl's ability to develop a teacher identity aligned with her early motivations for joining the profession and the stated goals of her university program.

After successfully completing her program, Yaotl entered the classroom as a credentialed teacher but, because of the struggles she faced with the constraints put on her student teaching, she returned to working in a bilingual Pre-K classroom similar to those where she had worked before. As a result of her difficulties with her practicum, her social justice approach also shifted: instead of inviting students into explicit analyses of power and oppression, she focused on providing diverse representations of people. She concluded that this more indirect approach to equity was easier to enact.

We can examine Yaotl's identity development as a social justice educator along a continuum, which was developed using literature on different aspects of social justice education (cited below). Each aspect illustrates a different phase or version of equity-based teaching. See Fig. 17.1.

At the far left is *Awareness* about issues of social and educational inequity—what are frequently called equity-oriented dispositions (Anderson & Stillman, 2012; Garcia & Guerra, 2004). Moving to the right are *Inclusive* practices that affirm student identities by using content that represents diverse backgrounds (Lee, 1995; Moll & Greenberg, 1990). *Critical* pedagogies explicitly examine the way that social structures and practices privilege some groups of people over others (Hyland, 2005; Nieto, 2002), and *Transformative* pedagogies not only critique institutional systems and practices, but also offer students opportunities to engage in reconstructive action (Souto-Manning, 2010; The New London Group, 1996). Yaotl's incoming teacher identity was mostly Awareness, and her program's coursework encouraged her to develop a set of Critical multicultural practices. But, because of the constraints of her practicum, she was not able to integrate her personal identity with her coursework into a coherent beginning teacher identity. Instead of developing an overt, critical, social justice pedagogy—in other words, a Transformational teacher identity—she only got to an Inclusive approach. For example, one unit she taught focused on workers in the community and included published curricular materials she was required to use, yet she removed the picture of a male doctor and covered it with a printout of a female doctor before using it in the classroom.

Scott

Scott, a white male from a middle-class background, was also in his late twenties when he entered the program. Scott grew up in a family of educators and had initially eschewed a career in education because he "didn't want to do what my family [did]." After earning a degree in business, he spent seven years working in retail and service sectors. He grew unhappy with this work, though, and so began substitute teaching; eventually deciding that becoming a full-time teacher would be fulfilling: "There was something missing [in my prior work]. There's this warm feeling at a school—like, everybody has it. I wanted to be a part of that." His mother and sister were elementary school teachers, so Scott believed he knew what teaching entailed.

His teacher education program's coursework was Scott's first formal introduction to social justice and inequity in schools, and he found the readings and discussions powerful. Where the coursework reinforced Yaotl's incoming identity, it collided with Scott's. The year before entering the program, Scott had substitute-taught in a school serving low-income, Latino students. While substitute teaching, he employed the same instructional practices he experienced as a student in his own white, middle-class public school: a pedagogy he called "stand and deliver," which meant lecturing to students and passing out worksheets for them to complete. He also believed good teachers were colorblind. During his graduate-level coursework on social foundations of education and the teaching of English language learners, he realized that his approach was flawed:

> I was totally wrong before… First of all, I was like, "I'm going to be totally colorblind here. We're all the same people. You're the same." That's so anti[thetical to] what they teach us here. Everyone's *not* the same, and you have to acknowledge that and leverage it to enhance the teaching.

His program courses provided Scott with new knowledge about social inequity in schools and, equipped with that knowledge, he tried on a new disposition:

> I thought I knew about [equity before my program], but I realize now I wasn't really thinking about it. Now I totally get it, and it's permeating into my normal life too. I'll see areas like gender inequality. I see social problems—homelessness, things like that—and immediately relate it back to schools and larger forces.

Although he developed an awareness of how society perpetuates inequity, Scott did not wish to teach in a school that served low-income students because he believed that schools serving low-income students paid teachers less and he felt that, given his experience in the business sector, he was worth more.

During his first practicum, in a second-grade classroom, Scott struggled. He had difficultly connecting with his cooperating teacher, who had never worked with a student teacher before. Scott found her expectations ambiguous and he could not figure out how to participate in her classroom but, because Scott disliked confrontations, he never discussed this with her. During his final practicum debriefing these tensions boiled over:

> She threw me under the bus during our meeting at the end. Everything was fine…then the conversation steered in the direction where she was like, "I don't think you were engaged, and a lot of times I feel like you just didn't care."… I got defensive and I felt like quitting the program.

For the second half of the program, Scott was placed in a fifth-grade classroom with a cooperating teacher whose visible identity in many ways matched his own: male, Caucasian, methodical, organized, and liked to surf. For Scott, who (for gendered reasons, we speculate) had previously struggled to imagine himself as an elementary school teacher, this cooperating teacher provided a useful model: "I really lucked out with this guy, Sean, because he's like me. Dresses like me, talks like me, communicates the way I do."

In this second placement, Scott experienced an orderly classroom led by an experienced teacher. However, because Sean did not incorporate diversity or social justice into his instruction, Scott—like Yaotl—could not try out his university's equity-oriented teaching approaches. This was particularly important in Scott's case, since social justice education was new to him and had not yet become part of his identity. It was on his mind and he talked a lot about it in interviews, but he was not offered actual opportunities to incorporate it into his teaching. Like Yaotl's, Scott's cooperating teacher was under external pressure to adhere to an established curriculum and ensure the state standards were covered in preparation for the annual state assessments. This meant that Scott had little freedom, even when planning his solo lessons. When Scott met with Sean to discuss his own state-required Teaching Performance Assessment, Sean simply handed Scott three pre-planned lessons and told him to follow those.

Despite his earlier reluctance, Scott did in fact take a job working with predominantly low-income students of color (not by choice, but because it was the job he was offered). As a first-year teacher, we found that Scott repeatedly slipped into deficit frameworks when describing his students and their families:

We have good teachers here [at this school]. Why is it that our [state standardized test] scores are garbage? I call parents at home. I don't even get calls back… It's like, 'What the heck?' For some of those kids I feel I'm not going to fix it this year. I just have to work around it.

The social justice pedagogy continuum described earlier in this chapter (Fig. 17.1) can be used to examine Scott's teacher identity development, too. From his teacher education program, Scott gained Awareness. He wanted to develop Inclusive classroom practices, but because of practicum constraints, he was not able to. As his program had taught him, he initially resisted accepting student standardized test scores as an accurate measure of student, teacher, or school effectiveness. Once he began teaching he embraced using standardized test scores to measure student and school success, but then he struggled to reconcile his own effort with the students' poor performance and fit this within the social equity frame of teaching from his program. To solve this cognitive dissonance, he mostly discarded his new ideas of equity in favor of longstanding stereotypes around low achievement. Scott believed that the school where he now worked had good teachers. In order to explain why students' test scores remained low, therefore, he employed deficit notions of his students and their families. This allowed him to justify his (and his colleagues') efforts and solved the discontinuity between his self-identity and the student outcomes (Olsen, 2008). While this may seem like an example of equity-oriented dispositions being "washed out" (Zeichner & Tabachnik, 1981) by the pressure of PK-12 school demands, we think instead that it raises questions about the development of social justice dispositions. Without opportunities during the previous year to engage in practices aligned with an equity disposition, Scott was never able to integrate his new ideas around equity into his professional identity.

Concluding Thoughts: The Power of Teacher Identity

Yaotl and Scott entered their program with different incoming teacher identities. They both appreciated the coursework, though each made sense of it differently based on their biographies. Neither teacher was given much freedom during student teaching to try out the culturally relevant pedagogies they were learning. Upon graduation, Yaotl returned to a grade level where she felt comfortable and employed a diluted version of social justice that she felt she could pull off, while Scott—whose previous experience with ideas about social justice had been limited—jettisoned the socially just, multicultural commitment in the face of the external demands and emotional challenges of his work.

Yaotl and Scott's experiences demonstrate how the figured world of teacher education, one's university courses about teaching, and the contours of the student-teaching practicum inter-related to form each pre-service teacher's own beginning teacher identity. What emerges from these two examples are a few salient themes. One is that this teacher education program's goals is at cross-purposes with the schools in which student teaching occurs (Feiman-Nemser & Buchmann, 1985).

Often, teacher education programs' primary objective is to encourage pre-service teachers to think deeply about teaching and learning, to practice enacting research-based pedagogies, and—in the case of the program from which Yoatl and Scott come—learn a particular cluster of social justice and constructivist commitments. However, the local schools and the cooperating teachers' primary objective is often to make sure that their PK-12 students learn the curriculum and perform well on standardized tests, which themselves derive from external demands around account-ability and preset curricula (Costigan, Zumwalt, & Crocco, 2004). This fundamental conflict pulls student teachers in opposing directions and problematizes development of coherent professional identities.

A second, related theme concerns the centralizing of the student teaching practi-cum—something that has become popular in the contemporary figured world of teacher education. In an effort to emphasize learning by doing, PBTE has put more of the onus of teacher learning on the practicum and pushed other aspects (such as learning theory or reflecting on complex topics) to the periphery. This means that, perhaps inadvertently, more of the teacher preparation experience is about strug-gling to please cooperating teachers, attempting to enact other people's lessons, managing high-stakes standardized test pressures, and staying afloat as a beginning teacher. This becomes the new 'hidden curriculum' of teacher preparation and, we found, de-emphasizes deep thinking around culture, power, learning theory, curricu-lum development, and other thorny aspects of becoming a professional educator. Given this, it may not be surprising that both Yaotl and Scott lacked the tools needed to figure out how to adapt their teaching (and professional identities) in the face of contradictory circumstances.

And a third, final theme concerns the larger landscape of teacher education that has been pressuring teacher education programs and PK-12 schools to embrace nar-rowed, standardized views of teaching; focus on what can be easily measured; and reduce theorizing education in favor of nuts-and-bolts, practice-oriented learning. Instead of experiencing the practicum as a place to explore, inquire, and experiment with enacting innovative pedagogies, both Yaotl and Scott were pressured to con-form to practices already in place, whether or not these matched the skills or com-mitments they wanted to develop in themselves. They were tacitly encouraged to act like the teachers they saw around them rather than re-imagine teaching and learning. The contested figured world meant that pre-service teachers received contradictory messages: the university wanted them to transform education, and the schools in which they student taught wanted them to maintain the status quo. Yaotl and Scott and their peers were required to interpret and negotiate these conflicting demands mostly on their own, and the angst that resulted seems to have dominated their teacher identity process. These examples both illuminate the process of teacher ide-nity and point out the complicated nature of contemporary teacher education.

References

Akkerman, S., & Meijer, P. (2011). A dialogical approach to conceptualizing teacher identity. *Teaching and Teacher Education, 27*(2), 308–319.

Alsup, J. (2006). *Teacher identity discourses. Negotiating personal and professional spaces.* Mahwah, NJ: Lawrence Erlbaum Associates, Inc.

Anderson, L. M., & Stillman, J. A. (2012). Student teaching's contribution to preservice teacher development: A review of research focused on the preparation of teachers for urban and high-needs contexts. *Review of Educational Research, 83*(1), 3–69.

Ball, D., & Forzani, F. M. (2009). The work of teaching and the challenge for teacher education. *Journal of Teacher Education, 60*(5), 497–511.

Ballou, D., & Podgursky, M. J. (1997). *Teacher pay and teacher quality.* Kalamazoo, MI: WE Upjohn Institute.

Beach, K. (1999). Chapter 4: Consequential transitions: A sociocultural expedition beyond transfer in education. *Review of Research in Education, 24*(1), 101–139.

Beauchamp, C., & Thomas, L. (2009). Understanding teacher identity: An overview of issues in the literature and implications for teacher education. *Cambridge Journal of Education, 39*(2), 175–189.

Beijaard, D., Verloop, N., & Vermunt, J. D. (2000). Teachers' perceptions of professional identity: An exploratory study from a personal knowledge perspective. *Teaching and Teacher Education, 16*, 749–764.

Berliner, D. C., & Biddle, B. J. (1996). The manufactured crisis: Myths, fraud, and the attack on America's public schools. *NASSP Bulletin, 80*(576), 119–121.

Berry, B., Montgomery, D., & Snyder, J. (2008). *Urban teacher residency models and institutes of higher education: Implications for teacher preparation.* Carrboro, NC: Center for Teaching Quality.

Bronfenbrenner, U. (1977). Toward an experimental ecology of human development. *American Psychologist, 32*(7), 513.

Carnegie Forum on Education and the Economy. (1986). *A nation prepared: Teachers for the 21st century.* New York: Author.

Clifford, G. J., & Guthrie, J. W. (1988). *Ed schools: A brief for professional education.* Chicago: University of Chicago Press.

Cochran-Smith, M., & Fries, K. (2005). Researching teacher education in changing times: Politics and paradigms. In M. Cochran-Smith & K. Zeichner (Eds.), *Studying teacher education: The report of the AERA Panel on research and teacher education* (pp. 37–68). Mahwah, NJ: Lawrence Erlbaum.

Costigan, A. T., Zumwalt, K. K., & Crocco, M. S. (2004). *Learning to teach in an age of accountability.* Mahwah, NJ: Lawrence Erlbaum.

Cuban, L. (1993). *How teachers taught: Constancy and change in American classrooms 1890–1990.* New York: Teachers College Press.

Darder, A., Baltodano, M., & Torres, R. D. (Eds.). (2003). *The critical pedagogy reader.* New York: RoutledgeFarmer.

Darling-Hammond, L. (1994). Who will speak for the children. *Phi Delta Kappan, 76*(1), 21.

Darling-Hammond, L. (2010). Teacher education and the American future. *Journal of Teacher Education, 61*(1–2), 35–47.

Feiman-Nemser, S., & Buchman, M. (1985). Pitfalls of experience in teacher education. *Teachers College Record, 87*, 49–65.

Finn Jr., C. E. (2008). *We must take charge.* New York: Simon and Schuster.

Garcia, S. B., & Guerra, P. L. (2004). Deconstructing deficit thinking: Working with educators to create more equitable learning environments. *Education and Urban Society, 36*(2), 150–168.

Goldstein, D. (2014). *The teacher wars: A history of America's most embattled profession.* New York: Anchor.

Greeno, J. G., Collins, A. M., & Resnick, L. B. (1996). Cognition and learning. In D. C. Berliner & R. C. Calfee (Eds.), *Handbook of educational psychology* (pp. 15–46). New York: MacMillan.

Grossman, P. (2010). *Policy brief: Learning to practice: The design of clinical experience in teacher preparation*. Washington, DC: The Partnership for Teacher Quality.

Herbst, J. (1989). *And sadly teach: Teacher education and professionalization in American culture.* Madison, WI: University of Wisconsin Press.

Hess, F. (2002). Break the link. *Education Next, 2*(1), 22–28.

Holland, D., Lachicotte Jr., W., Skinner, D., & Cain, C. (1998). *Identity and agency in cultural worlds*. Cambridge, MA: Harvard University Press.

Holmes Partnership, The. (2007). *The Holmes partnership trilogy: Tomorrow's teachers, tomorrow's schools, tomorrow's schools of education*. New York: Peter Lang.

hooks, b. (2014). *Teaching to transgress*. New York: Routledge.

Hyland, N. E. (2005). Being a good teacher of black students? White teachers and unintentional racism. *Curriculum Inquiry, 35*(4), 429–459.

Kincheloe, J. L. (2008). *Critical pedagogy primer*. New York: Peter Lang.

Kopp, W. (1994, June). Teach for America: Moving beyond the debate. *The Educational Forum, 58*(2), 187–192.

Lave, J. (1996). Teaching, as learning, in practice. *Mind, Culture, and Activity, 3*(3), 149–164.

Lee, C. (1995). A culturally based cognitive apprenticeship: Teaching African American high school students' skills in literary interpretation. *Reading Research Quarterly, 30*(4), 608–630.

Mockler, N. (2011). Beyond "what works": Understanding teacher identity as a practical and political tool. *Teachers and Teaching, 17*(5), 517–528.

Moll, L., & Greenberg, J. (1990). Creating zones of possibilities: Combining social contexts for instruction. In L. Moll (Ed.), *Vygotsky and education: Instructional implications and applications of sociohistorical psychology* (pp. 319–348). New York: Cambridge University Press.

Nieto, S. (2002). *Language, culture, and teaching: critical perspectives*. Mahweh, NJ: Lawrence Erlbaum.

Olsen, B. (2008). *Teaching what they learn, learning what they live: How teachers' personal histories shape their professional development*. Boulder, CO: Paradigm Publishers.

Olsen, B. (2014). Learning from experience: A teacher-identity perspective. In V. Ellis & J. Orchard (Eds.), *Learning teaching from experience: Multiple perspectives and international contexts* (pp. 79–94). New York: Bloomsbury.

Ravitch, D. (2010). *The death and life of the great American school system: How testing and choice are undermining education*. New York: Basic Books.

Rhee, M. (2013). *Radical: Fighting to put students first*. New York: Harper Collins.

Rust, F. O. (2010). Shaping new models of teacher education. *Teacher Education Quarterly, 37*(2), 5–18.

Sleeter, C. (2013). *Power, teaching, and teacher education: Confronting injustice with critical research and action*. New York: Peter Lang.

Souto-Manning, M. (2010). Challenging ethnocentric literacy practices: (Re)positioning home literacies in a head start classroom. *Research in the Teaching of English, 45*(2), 150–178.

The New London Group. (1996). A pedagogy of multiliteracies: Designing social futures. *Harvard Educational Review, 66*(1), 60–93.

Zeichner, K. (2010). Rethinking the connections between campus courses and field experiences in college and university-based teacher education. *Journal of Teacher Education, 61*(1–2), 89–99.

Zeichner, K., & Tabachnick, B. R. (1981). Are the effects of university teacher education washed out by school experience? *Journal of Teacher Education, 32*, 7–11.

Chapter 18
Preservice Teachers of Color and the Intersections of Teacher Identity, Race, and Place

Tambra O. Jackson

In many geographical spaces in the U.S. public schools have already reached a "new diverse majority" (The Southern Education Foundation, 2010) where students of Color make up the majority of the public school population. Moreover, given the trend of resegregation in public schools, it is highly likely that students of Color attend schools comprised almost primarily of other students of Color (Orfield, Ee, Frankenberg, & Siegel-Hawley, 2016). Despite these demographic developments in K-12 public schools, 73% of students majoring in education are White (U.S. Department of Education, 2016).

For the past few decades, education scholars have written about this racial/ethnic demographic divide between K-12 students and the teaching force (Boser, 2011; Cochran-Smith & Zeichner, 2005; Frankenberg, 2009) and one of the longstanding recommendations has been to diversify the teaching force (Dilworth & Coleman, 2014; Villegas & Irvine, 2010). Undergirding the rationales for increasing the presence of teachers of Color is a subtextual assumption that teachers of Color by virtue of their race and ethnicity have a positive impact on students of Color. While research does establish a positive impact of teachers of Color (Villegas & Irvine, 2010), it is not by advantage of their race/ethnicity alone but other social, contextual, and pedagogical factors (i.e. having high expectations of students of Color; providing culturally relevant teaching; developing trusting relationships with students; confronting issues of racism through teaching; and serving as advocates and cultural brokers). This perspective also assumes that teachers of Color have an intrinsically high level of social justice awareness and are readily concerned with attending to the needs of students of Color. Thus, often times in teacher education programs, particularly at predominantly White institutions (PWIs), the focus of preparing teachers for a diverse student demographic centers on the lived experiences

T. O. Jackson (✉)
Department of Teacher Education, Indiana University –Purdue University Indianapolis, Indianapolis, IN, USA
e-mail: tambjack@iupui.edu

© Springer International Publishing AG, part of Springer Nature 2018
P. A. Schutz et al. (eds.), *Research on Teacher Identity*,
https://doi.org/10.1007/978-3-319-93836-3_18

of White preservice teachers (Sleeter, 2001), facilitating a shift in their beliefs, and developing a teacher identity towards a social justice stance as if preservice teachers of Color already have it figured out. This is a problematic assumption as it allows teacher education programs to overlook the specific needs of preservice teachers of Color and to neglect creating programs of study inclusive of experiences and learning opportunities aimed at developing and equipping socially just and critically conscious teachers of Color.

My assumption is that place (the context of the teacher education program) not only influences the learning environment, but also has an influence on teacher identity development (i.e., the theory, beliefs, and attitudes teachers hold about themselves in relation to their profession). After all, identities develop in part as a response to daily negotiations within social spaces and evolve over time. As noted by Jackson and Bryan (2015),

> Research on the identities of teachers is a growing body of literature that explores how teachers perform identities in school contexts, regulated by cultures, ideologies, sociopolitical histories, and power relations (Barret, 2008; Chong & Low, 2009; Søreide, 2007). Specifically, the notion of 'teacher identity' involves the beliefs one has about teaching and being a teacher, and about how these beliefs influence professional action. Importantly, the ways in which teachers perform their identities have important implications for how they are perceived, both in and out of school contexts. (p. 142)

Miller (2006) further specifies the nuances between *teacher identity* and *preservice teacher identity*.

> A preservice teacher identity is similar to a teacher identity with the exception that the individual is taking on the demands of what it is to be a teacher and the individual is marginally situated in two worlds—that of the inchoate educator who is making meaning of what a teacher is and does and that of student (Britzman, 1991). (p. 165)

Thus, the development of teacher identity for preservice teachers of Color at PWIs occurs in racialized spaces where they are often positioned as the "other" and marginalized even when those programs have a stated commitment to social justice teaching. For preservice teachers of Color, their experiences of marginalization do not begin when they enter teacher education programs, but are part of a collective existence in the larger context of a racialized society that devalues the humanity and contributions of people of Color. Given both the macro and micro factors that influence the experiences of pre-service teachers of Color, an analysis of the ways in which teacher identity development for preservice teachers of Color is influenced by the context of PWIs is warranted. Such analysis will provide better insight into the ways teacher education programs at PWIs can better attend to their needs for promoting critical consciousness as part of their developing teacher identity.

In this chapter I focus on the experiences of preservice teachers of Color, particularly those who attend predominantly White institutions (PWIs) and the ways in which their developing identities as teachers are influenced by the intersections of their racial/ethnic identities and the context (place) of the environment of their teacher education programs. I explore the intersections of race and place by first discussing how preservice teachers of Color describe their decisions to become teachers. Particular attention is given to understanding the ways in which preservice teachers of Color view their initial reasons for entry into the profession and commitments to teaching as a way of understanding their early or beginning teacher identity. Next, I look at their experiences in teacher education programs at PWIs. I specifically focus on the context of PWIs because much of the literature on teacher preparation occurs in these contexts. Thus, the absence of centering the experiences of preservice teachers of Color assumes that these spaces have no or little responsibility for focusing on preservice teachers of Color. I end the chapter with a discussion on how race and place impact the teacher identity development of preservice teachers of Color, particularly in regards to developing socially just and critically conscious perspectives and conclude with implications and recommendations for attending to the critically conscious teacher identity development of preservice teachers of Color.

Critical Consciousness

A key tenet of culturally relevant/responsive pedagogy is the ability to recognize, understand, critique, and work toward eliminating social inequities (Gay, 2000; Ladson-Billings, 1995). Sociopolitical or critical consciousness is necessary in order for teachers to confront the realties of structural inequities in the schooling of students of Color. Teachers of Color, specifically Black women, have a long history of engaging in teaching as a political act and social action on behalf of students of Color (Beauboeuf-Lafontant, 1999; Dixson, 2003).

Teacher education programs may acknowledge in principle the need to prepare teachers for culturally and linguistically diverse populations, but in practice many take a monocultural approach (Melnick & Zeichner, 1997; Zeichner et al., 2006). Thus, Sleeter (2012) posits that culturally responsive teaching has been marginalized due to a persistence of faulty and simplistic notions of what the pedagogy entails. She identifies four simplifications: *cultural celebration* (tends to relegate attention to culture to the margins of instruction with emphasis on cultural celebration as an end in itself); *trivialization* (involves reducing it to steps to follow rather than understanding it as a paradigm for teaching and learning); *essentializing culture* (means assuming a fairly fixed and homogeneous conception of the culture of an ethnic or racial group, assuming culture to be a fixed characteristic of individuals who belong to a group, and that students who are group members identify with that conception); and substituting cultural for political analysis of inequalities. In regards to the latter mode of simplification, she states "*Substituting cultural for political analysis* involves maintaining silence about the conditions of racism and other forms of oppression that underlie achievement gaps and alienation from school, assuming that attending to culture alone will bring about equity" (p. 571).

When teacher education programs assume that preservice teachers of Color by virtue of their race and ethnicity enter programs with a developed and sophisticated sense of critical consciousness, they are complicit in the marginalization of culturally responsive teaching. They are choosing to neglect taking an inward gaze and critically reflecting on their silence about the conditions of racism and other forms of oppression for preservice teachers of Color enrolled in their programs.

Beginning Commitments and Reasons for Becoming Teachers

The historical and contemporary teaching environment for teachers of Color has been troublesome and shaped by racist and structural inequities (Jackson & Kohli, 2016). When looking specifically at Black teachers, school desegregation efforts of the past led to the displacement of numerous Black teachers (Douglas, 2005; Foster, 1997). Contemporary iterations of pushing Black teachers out of the profession (Buras, 2016) continue to demonstrate the conundrum between the rhetoric and reality of constructing a teacher workforce that mirrors the student demographics. Despite this turbulent history of exclusion, college students of Color still desire to pursue careers in teaching.

In a study that examined the experiences of preservice teachers of Color learning how to teach for social justice with a Black female professor at a PWI (Jackson et al., 2017), five women shared their reasons for choosing teaching as a career. During a focus group interview the following exchange occurred.

> **Laryn:** I was kind of avoiding it, because (pause) I don't know I was really scared. But the more I started doing stuff like around classrooms and working with kids, I decided to embrace my fear and just see if I would really be into it. But growing up I think I always wanted to be a teacher just because of my experience in the classroom. I didn't want other kids to go through what I experienced in the classroom... being the only Black girl in my class and not having anybody to relate to and the teachers not taking time to relate to me.
>
> **Brianna:** I was 15 when I decided this was the path I wanted to take. I am the oldest of 14 cousins, so my whole life I was always babysitting, and entertaining them, watching them, and talking to them. So, I was always around kids- like all the time. So, I started volunteering in a kindergarten class my sophomore year in high school, and I just loved it. I just realized that I didn't want to be anywhere but the classroom. Now, the reason why I want to teach has changed. At first it was just because I loved kids, and I felt comfortable with it. But as I got older, I just realized, like Laryn was saying, there are so few Black teachers, and I want to have an influence and be able to connect with my students, because I've always wanted to teach in an urban setting. So, I just want to be that influence, because I know when I've had Black teachers it's made all the difference in my education. So, I want to be that to other students... In 3rd grade I had my first Black teacher- Ms. E. And to this day, I still have a relationship with her, because I just connected with her so much- like she came to my wedding and she told me I could come be in her classroom...
>
> **Ashley:** I didn't want to be a teacher. I actually wanted to go into art and be a comic book artist or something like that. But my mom was like you need something that will make you some money... And so I thought about it as I went through high school, and I had teachers that really connected with me, and they weren't the same race as me but they connected with me and pushed me in my education. So, I was like if they can do that for me then I can do that for someone else, so I will be teacher. And I like it so far.

Marena: ...I never saw myself as a teacher. Growing up it was never on my radar and so I just went into psychology as a thing to go into in college. My freshman year in college we had to volunteer at an elementary school... and I kind of just fell into it. There was something inside that told me this is where I need to be; this is my path. I don't know why, but this is it. But ever since I switched my major I have loved all my classes. I have loved my professors. It just felt right. So, I've just been following my gut this entire time and just going with it.

Felicia: Well, like most of us at this table I avoided teaching at first. And that was because my mom is a teacher, and so I saw all the hours that she put in and didn't necessarily get the recognition or the pay for it. So, I was like no, I don't want to do that. And when you're 18 it doesn't sound cool to be like your mom. But I actually started out as a psychology major at [university] and did the same field experience (as Marena) at the [elementary school]. And I also started tutoring at [high school] and getting to work with students. And it's something I felt successful at- teaching people and helping them learn material.

Two studies (Miller & Endo, 2005; Szecsi & Spillman, 2012) cited the positive impact of previous teachers as reasons for becoming teachers. This also resonated with both Brianna and Ashley. Interestingly, Brianna's positive experience was with a Black teacher while Ashley's experiences were with teachers of a different racial/ethnicity than her own. Also, similar to the literature is the fact that teaching was not the first career choice for Laryn, Ashley, Marena, and Felicia. In addition, Brianna, Marena, and Felicia talked about having previous experiences with teaching and assisting in classrooms as events that influenced their decisions. Similar to the participants in Szecsi and Spillman's (2012) study, Laryn and Brianna drew upon their previous racialized K-12 schooling experiences and intentionally wanted to be present in the profession for children of Color. While Brianna's initial reason for becoming a teacher hinged on her early experiences with children and her love for children, her reason for teaching changed to a desire to have a positive cultural influence on children of Color. Another interesting contrast is that although Felicia's mother is a teacher, unlike the participants in the studies that cited familial influence (Miller & Endo, 2005; Williams, Graham, McCary-Henderson, & Floyd, 2009), for Felicia, that was an initial deterrent for her because of her observation of thankless hard work.

The reasons the women gave for deciding to become teachers varied and many are evident in the research literature and support diverse reasons for teaching and beginning commitments for preservice teachers of Color. The narratives in the studies illuminate that evident in early or beginning teacher identity for preservice teachers of Color is a strong commitment to teaching, although in some instances inclusive of initial avoidance and hesitation. For some, their decision to move forward with selecting teaching as a career was grounded in desires for better racialized schooling experiences for students of Color; but for others it was simply a matter of seeing teaching as enjoyable or an opportunity for gainful employment. Hence, it is important for teacher education programs to understand that preservice teachers of Color do not enter programs as a homogeneous group with already established and shared commitments about teaching. Just as the research literature is filled with examples of helping the White girls "get it" (Mason, 2016), equally concerted efforts are warranted (albeit for different reasons) for preservice teachers of Color.

Overall, early and beginning teacher identity for preservice teachers of Color is positive. They have favorable beliefs about teaching and being a teacher, despite their macro experiences of marginalization and racism in their K-12 schooling and society at large prior to entering teacher education programs. Their beginning commitments and reasons for becoming teachers (which for many is the starting point of their teacher identity) should be supported, and not essentialized or left unaddressed, in the context of teacher preparation programs. This is especially important, because their attitudes and beliefs about the professional when they enter may come into conflict with what they come to know and experience as professional identity in the context of the teacher preparation program.

Experiences in Teacher Education at PWIs

Using critical race theory in education as an analytical lens, a portion of a review of literature on preservice teachers of Color focused on their experiences in teacher education (Brown, 2014). Brown's findings demonstrate a troubling pattern in the experiences of preservice teachers of Color. That is, many "preservice teachers of Color encounter teacher preparation programs that are marginalizing, isolating and not culturally affirming" (Brown, 2014, p. 334). Other studies (Amos, 2010; Jackson, 2015; Rodriguez & Cho, 2011) outside of Brown's review corroborate this finding and suggest that both White peers and White teacher educators are at the center of creating and sustaining racially marginalized and isolated environments in teacher education programs at PWIs.

For example, in a study of four preservice teachers of Color in an elementary program at a rural PWI, Amos (2010) found themes of frustration, despair and fear that students of Color felt toward their White peers in a multicultural education course. These tensions resulted in the silencing of the preservice teachers of Color and the maintenance of White dominance for the White students. The preservice teachers of Color experienced shock and frustration as they witnessed their White peers' insensitivity to issues of race and ethnicity through joking about race, being insensitive to racial issues, know-it-all attitudes about people of Color, normalizing whiteness, and white bonding behaviors. They experienced despair due to the well-intentioned but discriminatory attitudes and behaviors/comments and naiveté of their White peers in their perceived empathy with people of Color (false empathy). Fear was generated from the defensive and "combative" resistance held and displayed by White students, as well as how the instructor of Color was treated by the White students. They were also fearful of ostracism and to voice their opinions in class.

Rodriguez and Cho (2011) report on a cross-case analysis on seven bi/multilingual preservice teachers of Color at PWIs in the Midwest and Hawaii. The authors illuminate "the similarities between the experiences of linguistically and culturally diverse preservice teachers who have been both 'silent' by choice and 'silenced' by others in academic settings in the U.S. and in their teacher education programs" (Rodriguez & Cho, 2011, p. 499). Their analysis focused on the participants' resistance to labeling practices (e.g. "minority" and "non-native") as well as their developing teacher identity narratives as bi/multilingual teachers. Moreover, the participants resisted simplistic and imposed conceptions of their teacher identities and challenged being positioned as bilingual teachers who were negatively perceived as different from mainstream teachers because of a false perception that native language teachers easily make cultural and linguistic connections with students. Instead they embraced multiple and hybrid conceptions of teacher identity.

In a study of thirty preservice teachers of Color at a PWI in the southeast, Jackson (2015) found preservice teachers of Color perceived a lack of commitment by their programs and professors as affecting their development of culturally responsive pedagogy or lack thereof. Specifically, the preservice teacher of Color felt as though their presence in the teacher education programs was only to benefit the university's image of being an inclusive environment, yet there was no commitment of including their voices, narratives, or interests into the curriculum. Furthermore, the participants perceived their professors as being uncomfortable with and lacking in their knowledge of culturally responsive pedagogy. A lack of care and a sense of dismissiveness on the part of the professors were noted.

Overall, these studies contextualize the experiences of preservice teachers of Color in teacher education programs at PWIs and expose ugly truths about the environments in which teacher identity develops. Since identities develop as a response to daily negotiations in space over time, it is easy to assume that alienating and hostile spaces will negatively impact teacher identities. In the previous section, I posited that early and beginning teacher identity for preservice teachers of Color is positive. Here I give pause to the alarming fact that there is a significant discrepancy between the percentages of preservice teachers enrolled in university-based preparation programs—37% (Dilworth & Coleman, 2014) and the percentage that actually enter the profession—14% (Feistritzer, 2011). While there are various reasons for this discrepancy (i.e., teachers of Color have lower pass rates on credential entrance exams, Ahmad & Boser, 2014), we cannot discount the salience of place in the development of teacher identity for preservice teachers of Color. If their racial identities are constantly assaulted and misrepresented, then that impacts how they see themselves as teachers.

Implications of Teacher Identity, Race, and Place

Miller (2006) notes that for preservice teachers "an identity is coming to be in several spaces at once: the school, the teacher preparatory program, and the other communities of learning that are apprenticing the inchoate teacher" (p. 166). Before entering teacher education, the primary influences on the teacher identity development of preservice teachers of Color are located within their decisions to become teachers (e.g., influential teachers, educators in the family, previous teaching experiences, etc.). Despite some initial hesitation, their overall beliefs about teaching and how they view themselves as future teachers are generally positive. Once they enter teacher education, their beliefs about teaching and teachers are influenced by the environment of the program. Such environments at PWIs have proven to be marginalizing for preservice teachers of Color and are problematic for leading to critically conscious teacher identity development. As noted in Rodriguez and Cho's (2011) study, preservice teachers of Color can and do resist the toxicity of the teacher education environment on their developing teacher identities, but intentional support on the part of programs is warranted. Moreover, focusing such support on critical consciousness equips preservice teachers of Color with tools to both resist racism and build upon their earlier positive sense of teacher identity.

It would be unwise for teacher education programs at PWIs to not consider the significance of their context as impacting critical conscious teacher identity for preservice teachers of Color. Since there is a pattern of teacher education programs at PWIs as being hostile places for learning and void of culturally relevant/responsive/sustaining curriculum and instructional practices for preservice teachers of Color, it is imperative that those leading such programs consult the research literature and expand their efforts. Therefore, if the administrators of teacher education programs at PWIs are unaware, uninformed, or simply unconcerned with paying attention to the development of teacher identity for preservice teachers of Color, then by default they are complicit in perpetuating structural racism.

A troubling occurrence in the literature is the silencing that is manifested in these spaces. A part of developing critical consciousness also entails developing voice. Moreover, voice lends itself to the construction of teacher identity because it is a tool for how individuals author and mediate their socially constructed professional identities (Sisson, 2016). It is not enough to know about education inequity, but teachers have to develop strong voice so they can actively work against it and speak out about it. If preservice teachers of Color are struggling with finding their voice as novices, it is unlikely that they will enter the profession as strong advocates. They should be exposed to the literature and narratives of both preservice (Gomez, Ridriguez, & Agosto, 2008) and veteran teachers of Color (Foster, 1997) who have been in similar contexts. This can serve as a sanity check for them; to let them know they are not alone and others have named such oppression. It can also serve as a means for critical analysis of institutional racism and inequity and making connections between their experiences and the experiences of the PK-12 students they will teach. The narratives of veteran teachers can also serve as role models for positive teacher identity grounded in critical consciousness.

Finally, focusing on building critical consciousness as an integral part of their developing teacher identities allows for preservice teachers of Color to see themselves as empowered teachers with the potential to not only impact students but also change systems of oppression. From this perspective teaching is a means of activism, and the profession of teaching is a vehicle for change.

References

Ahmad, F. Z., & Boser, U. (2014). *America's leaky pipeline for teachers of color: Getting more teachers of color into the classroom.* Washington, DC: Center for American Progress.

Amos, Y. T. (2010). "They don't want to get it!" Interaction between minority and white preservice teachers in a multicultural education class. *Multicultural Education, 17*(4), 31–37.

Barret, A. M. (2008). Capturing the différance: Primary school teacher identity in Tanzania. International Journal of Educational Development, 28, 496–507.

Beauboeuf-Lafontant, T. (1999). A movement against and beyond boundaries: Politically relevant teaching among African American teachers. *Teachers College Record, 100*(4), 702–723.

Boser, U. (2011). *Teacher diversity matters: A state-by-state analysis of teachers of color.* Washington, DC: Center for American Progress.

Britzman, D. (1991). Practice makes practice. Albany: State University of New York Press.

Brown, K. D. (2014). Teaching in color: A critical race theory in education analysis of the literature on preservice teachers of color and teacher education in the US. *Race, Ethnicity and Education, 17*(3), 326–345.

Buras, K. L. (2016). The mass termination of black veteran teachers in New Orleans: Cultural politics, the education market, and its consequences. *The Educational Forum, 80*(2), 154–170.

Chong, S., & Low, E. (2009). Why I want to teach and how I feel about teaching - formation of teacher identity from pre-service to the beginning teacher phase. Education Research Policy and Practice, 8, 59–72.

Cochran-Smith, M., & Zeichner, K. M. (2005). Teachers' characteristics: Research on the demographic profile. In M. Cochran-Smith & K. M. Zeichner (Eds.), *Studying teacher education* (pp. 111–156). Mahwah, NJ: Lawrence Erlbaum Associates, Inc.

Dilworth, M. E., & Coleman, M. J. (2014). *Time for change: Diversity in teaching revisited.* Washington, DC: National Education Association.

Dixson, A. D. (2003). "Let's do this!": Black women teachers' politics and pedagogy. *Urban Education, 38*(2), 217–235.

Douglas, D. M. (2005). *Jim Crow moves North: The battle over northern school segregation, 1865–1954.* New York: Cambridge University Press.

Feistritzer, C. E. (2011). *Profile of teachers in the US 2011.* Washington, DC: National Center for Education Information.

Foster, M. (1997). *Black teachers on teaching.* New York: The New Press.

Frankenberg, E. (2009). The segregation of American teachers. *Education Policy Analysis Archives, 17*(1). Retrieved August 11, 2017 from http://epaa.asu.edu/epaa/v17n1/

Gay, G. (2000). *Culturally responsive teaching: Theory, research and practice.* New York: Teachers College Press.

Gomez, M. L., Rodriguez, T. L., & Agosto, V. (2008). Life histories of Latino/a teacher candidates. *Teachers College Record, 110*(8), 1639–1676.

Jackson, T. O. (2015). Perspectives and insights of preservice teachers of color on developing culturally responsive pedagogy at predominantly white institutions. *Action in Teacher Education, 37*(3), 223–237.

Jackson, T. O., Ballard, A., Drewery, M., Membres, B., Morgan, L., & Nicholson, F. (2017). "Black like me": Female preservice teachers of Color on learning to teach for social justice with a Black female professor. In A. Farinde, A. Allen-Handy, & C. Lewis (Eds.), *Black female teachers: Diversifying the United States' teacher workforce* (pp. 93–113). Bingley, UK: Emerald Publishing Group Limited.

Jackson, T. O., & Bryan, M. L. (2015). Black women professors' evolving teacher identities: Reconciling past, present, and future. In S. Hancock, A. Allen, & C. Lewis (Eds.), *Autoethnography as a lighthouse: Illuminating race, research, and the politics of schooling* (pp. 141–159). Charlotte, NC: Information Age Publishing.

Jackson, T. O., & Kohli, R. (2016). Guest editors' introduction: The state of teachers of color. *Equity & Excellence in Education, 49*(1), 1–8.

Ladson-Billings, G. (1995). Toward a theory of culturally relevant pedagogy. American Educational Research Journal, 32(3), 465–491.

Mason, A. M. (2016). Taking time, breaking codes: Moments in white teacher candidates' exploration of racism and teacher identity. International Journal of Qualitative Studies in Education, 29(8), 1045–1058.

Melnick, S., & Zeichner, K. M. (1997). Enhancing the capacity of teacher education institutions to address diversity issues. In J. E. King, E. R. Hollins, & W. C. Hayman (Eds.), Preparing teachers for cultural diversity. New York: Teachers College Press.

Miller, P. C., & Endo, H. (2005). Journey to becoming a teacher: The experiences of students of color. Multicultural Education, 13(1), 2–9.

Miller, S. J. (2006). Foregrounding preservice teacher identity in teacher education. Teacher Education and Practice, 19(2), 164–185.

Orfield, G., Ee, J., Frankenberg, E., & Siegel-Hawley, G. (2016). Brown at 62: School segregation by race, poverty, and state. Los Angeles: Civil Rights Project/Proyecto Derechos Civiles.

Rodriguez, T. L., & Cho, H. (2011). Eliciting critical literacy narratives of bi/multilingual candidates across U.S. teacher education contexts. Teaching and Teacher Education, 27, 496–504.

Sisson, J. H. (2016). The significance of critical incidents and voice to identity and agency. Teachers and Teaching: Theory and Practice, 22(6), 670–682.

Sleeter, C. E. (2001). Preparing teachers for culturally diverse schools: Research and the overwhelming presence of whiteness. Journal of Teacher Education, 52(2), 94–106.

Sleeter, C. E. (2012). Confronting the marginalization of culturally responsive pedagogy. Urban Education, 47(3), 562–584.

Søreide, G. E. (2007). The public face of teacher identity- narrative construction of teacher identity in public policy documents. Journal of Education Policy, 22, 129–146.

Szecsi, T., & Spillman, C. (2012). Unheard voices of minority teacher candidates in a teacher education program. Multicultural Education, 19(2), 24–29.

The Southern Education Foundation. (2010). A new diverse majority: Students of color in the South's public schools. Atlanta, GA: Author.

U.S. Department of Education. (2016). The state of racial diversity in the educator workforce. Washington, DC: Office of Planning, Evaluation and Policy Development, Policy and Program Studies Service. Retrieved from https://www2.ed.gov/rschstat/eval/highered/racial-diversity/state-racial-diversity-workforce.pdf

Villegas, A. M., & Irvine, J. J. (2010). Diversifying the teaching force: An examination of major arguments. The Urban Review, 42, 175–192.

Williams, E., Graham, A., McCary-Henderson, S., & Floyd, L. (2009). "From where I stand:" African American teacher candidates on their decision to teach. The Educational Forum, 73(4), 348–364.

Zeichner, K. M., Grant, C., Gay, G., Gillette, M., Valli, L., & Villegas, A. M. (2006). A research informed vision of good practice in multicultural teacher education: Design principles. Theory into Practice, 37(2), 163–171.

Chapter 19
The Indispensability and Impossibility of Teacher Identity

Matthew Clarke

Teacher identity has emerged as a key focus of education research, with a considerable body of work on the personal and professional lives of teachers (Beauchamp & Thomas, 2009; Day, Sammons, Stobart, Kington, & Gu, 2007), and with identity increasingly recognised as an essential and invaluable resource in navigating the myriad challenges – policy, pedagogical, personal – confronting teachers on a daily basis (Hong, Greene, & Lowery, 2017). Teacher identity is often conceived as a positive or substantive entity, structured around core beliefs and perceptions and developed through reflection and discussion. Seen from this perspective, our identities embody who and what we are as teachers (Maclean & White, 2007; Settlage, Southerland, Smith, & Ceglie, 2009; Walkington, 2005). Meanwhile, other perspectives emphasise the constructedness of teachers' identities, highlighting the role played by narrative (e.g. Søreide, 2006; Watson, 2006) or discursive (e.g. Clarke, 2006; Devos, 2010) processes in the ongoing construction, formation, and development of teacher identity. What each perspective shares is the view that teacher identity is an indispensable resource that enables teachers to make sense of who they are and what they do and that can be leveraged in the face of struggles (Danielewicz, 2001; MacLure, 1993). As Day, Sammons, Stobart, Kington and Gu note, "teachers' sense of professional and personal identity is a key variable in their motivation, job fulfilment, commitment and self-efficacy" (2007, p. 102).

Whatever we understand by teacher identity, there can be little doubt that, like those of the wider population, teachers' identities are located within the wider temporal, spatial, and political contexts of history, geography, and policy. In particular, teacher identity is intimately linked to notions of professionalism and the process of professionalization, which in itself is closely tied to politics and policy. In recent times, teachers' identities have undergone a transformation since the 1980s as a

M. Clarke (✉)
School of Education, York St John University, York, UK
e-mail: m.clarke@yorksj.ac.uk

consequence of what Connell (2013) refers to as the 'neoliberal cascade'[1] that has swept across education and schooling in many international contexts. Elements of this cascade have included an increase in the level of policy prescriptivism in relation to core aspects of teachers' work, such as curriculum, pedagogy, and assessment, along with heightened levels of audit and accountability (Taubman, 2009). These changes have been described in terms of the 'intensification' of teaching and teachers' work (Burchielli, 2006; Williamson & Myhill, 2008). Intensification has both quantitative and qualitative dimensions, referencing both the increased volume of teachers' workloads and the heightened emotional strains to which they are subjected as a consequence of burgeoning cultures of audit and performativity (Ball, 2003; Clarke, 2013).

We might describe these changes in terms of a move away from an earlier 'inside out' form of professionalism, where the contours of professional identity were largely determined from within the profession by individuals and groups, to forms of 'outside in' professionalism, where the profession is largely reacting and responding to pressures and agendas emanating from policy makers and politicians (Clarke, Michell, & Ellis, 2016; Dawson, 1994). These changes can be linked to a wider shift that has impacted on professionals in a range of professions and occupations from 'occupational' identities, originating within the profession and characterised by relatively high levels of autonomy and trust, as well as by more collegial relationships, to 'organisational' identities that derive from the organisation or institution, are distinguished by lower levels of professional autonomy and trust, and involve hierarchical rather than egalitarian relationships (Evetts, 2009).

Drawing on the work of Castells (2010), we can also think about the above shift in terms of a move from 'legitimizing' identities, aimed at establishing the status and standing of teachers as professionals, to 'resistance' identities, struggling to maintain and protect their professional recognition in the face of media denigration and policy moves, such as school-based teacher education, intended to restore earlier 'craft' notions of teacher professionalism.

Underlying the discussion so far is a question that has been touched on, in relation to the different ways in which teacher identity has been conceptualized, but has not been explicitly addressed. This is the question of what we understand by the term 'identity'. Is identity a thing, a process, both of these at once or something else entirely? This question is taken up below, after which I revisit *teacher* identity in light of this discussion.

---

[1] Neoliberalism is understood here as the reconfiguration of all aspects of experience in economic terms and the application of market-like rationalities of measurement, comparison and evaluation within ever-more sectors and institutions (Brown, 2015; Davies, 2014).

The Power and the Paradoxes of Identity

Identity is a widely-used term, the pervasiveness of which belies its conceptual complexity. In everyday readings, identity is seen as something substantive, coherent, consistent and irreducible. Thus, for instance, the online version of the Oxford English Dictionary defines identity as "the quality or condition of being the same in substance, composition, nature, properties, or in particular qualities under consideration; absolute or essential sameness; oneness".[2] Identity in this sense collocates with words like 'core', 'true' and 'authentic'. Such notions of 'absolute or essential sameness' and continuity over time are often evident in popular- and social-media discussions, in which identity is linked to location and to history, often in exclusive and essentialist ways. From this perspective, identity is a sort of zero-sum game, where some identities are seen to encroach on and threaten others, particularly during times of social change, demographic movement, technological development, or economic upheaval – in other words during normal human existence. Politics thus becomes a process of managing the competing claims of different identities – an assumption reflected in much media commentary on identity issues and not just in right-wing outlets. For instance, the UK's *New Statesman*, typically a publication with a left of centre orientation, declared in 2016 that identities matter and that many of them, including majoritarian identities such as those of white residents of England, are under current threat.[3] Indeed, looking back at the identity-driven political revolutions of 2016 in the USA and the UK it seems clear that, whatever we understand by it, identity is a powerful concept that does significant discursive work with tangible material effects.

Eric Santner describes this popular view as the global consciousness perspective on identity, in which "every stranger is ultimately just like me, ultimately familiar; his or her strangeness is a function of a different vocabulary, a different set of names that can always be translated" (Santner, 2001, p. 5). In other words, encountering the other is a matter of my fully self-transparent identity engaging with another, similarly self-transparent identity, albeit one comprising different 'content'. However, what this view overlooks is the structuralist insight that meaning – including the meaning of any given identity – is always relational insofar as any entity derives its meaning by way of contrast with what it is not in order to make sense – so 'night' requires the contrast with 'day', just as 'right' relies on 'left'. In this sense identity, far from being solely about sameness, is revealed as reliant on difference, with all positive identities haunted and 'contaminated' by the negative presence of their constitutive outside. Thus, the possibility of a full, self-sufficient identity becomes an impossibility. Poststructuralism pushes this insight further by insisting that the overall system of signification is inherently unstable and that any claims made in the name of truth or knowledge are always partial (in both senses of the word) and situated (temporally and spatially). Such a view highlights the historical contingency and hence the fragility of all identities.

---

[2] www.oed.com/view/Entry/91004?redirectForm=identity#eid

[3] http://www.newstatesman.com/politics/uk/2016/12/lesson-2016-identity-matters-even-white-people

Psychoanalytic Theory and Identity

Psychoanalytic theory incorporates these structuralist and poststructuralist insights into the relational, contingent, and fragile nature of identity, but adds the distinctive 'twist' of positing an enigmatic emptiness or void at the core of our being that confounds any aspirations for full self-transparency or disclosure. For psychoanalysis, "the possibility of 'We', of community, is granted on the basis that every familiar is ultimately strange and that, indeed, I am even in a crucial sense a stranger to myself" (Santner, 2001, p. 6). In other words, "what makes the other Other is not his or her spatial exteriority with respect to my being but the fact that he or she is strange, is a stranger, and not only to me but also to him or herself, is the bearer of an internal alterity, an enigmatic density of desire calling for response beyond any rule governed reciprocity" (2001, p. 9). This reading renders identity less a source of agentive power than a fantasmatic structure erected to mask the enigmatic incompleteness and self-division of the human subject. Indeed, one way to read the twin shocks delivered to the political establishment of the UK and the USA by Brexit and the election of Donald Trump respectively, is as the unleashing of deep reservoirs of non-rational, affective intensity directed against the unwelcome spectre of encroaching racial and ethnic diversity among populations whose identities are aligned with, and shaped by, the fantasmatic wholeness and self-sufficiency offered by colonial legacies of whiteness (Binkley, 2017). Understanding this more fully requires a brief foray into Lacanian theory and in particular his notion of the mirror stage.

Lacan's mirror stage offers fruitful material for any consideration of the divided nature of the human subject and, as we shall see below, it has significant potential insights to offer in relation to the struggles and conflicts that seem to comprise teacher identity. Initially conceived as a specific stage in the development of the human infant, the mirror stage is fundamental to Lacan's overall conception of human subjectivity (Evans, 1996). Critically, the mirror stage is both an explanatory narrative and an enduring structure in relation to the human psyche: "the mirror stage (stade du miroir) is not a mere epoch in the history of the individual but a stadium (stade) in which the battle of the human subject is permanently being waged" (Bowie, 1991, p. 21).

The mirror stage involves self-recognition on the part of the human infant when it confronts the specular image perceived in the (literal or figurative) mirror and realises that it is in some way a distinct entity separate from the rest of existence. Prior to this moment of realisation there is only undifferentiated existence with no distinction between self and other. For the infant, the experience of self-recognition is paradoxical, at once exhilarating and perturbing, insofar as its "jubilant" assumption" of the mirror image as its own self is also "the assumption of the armour of an alienating identity" (Lacan, 1977, p. 2 & 5). For on the one hand, identification with the image offers the (illusory) promise of (potential) self-reliance and mastery. Yet on the other hand, this process of external identification entails an alienating separation and distinction between self and other, whereby the external other is also the paradoxical source of the self.

The initial alienation of the mirror stage is compounded on accession to subjecthood through entry into the symbolic. This is the register of law and language, a social system of regulation and signification, prohibition, and recognition. Preceding and exceeding the subject's existence, the symbolic realm of language and discourse henceforth mediates the individual's relations with others and with the world. Critically, for the purposes of our discussion of teacher identity, by barring direct access to the objects of the world and to the other, the symbolic register entails another experience of alienating loss, since entry into the symbolic not only entails prohibitions but also engenders an awareness of objects and experiences the subject does not have access to. To take a simple example, a child listening to stories is exposed to worlds beyond her own, which may engender new yearnings, as may seeing her older siblings taking part in activities and experiences that remain inaccessible to her. This experience of alienating loss is further underscored by the incapacity of language to ever fully or adequately convey the individual's intentions and desires, since, owing to the play of difference, the signifier is never fully present and consequently, no signifier can adequately represent the individual's identity; yet at the same time, paradoxically and frustratingly, the symbolic register often conveys more than the individual intended (Chiesa, 2007).

One consequence of the alienation engendered through the mirror stage and entry into the symbolic register is a pervasive sense of lack whereby something is continually sensed as missing and where our lives and the world are felt to be strangely out of joint. My daughter exemplified this when, as a seven-year old, she asked why she was herself rather than someone else; why had she been born when and where she had rather than at some other time in some other place? These questions ultimately unanswerable – as Lacan noted there is no Other of the Other, providing an ultimate ground; no final cause behind what we refer to as causality (Lacan, 1977). This experience explains the ongoing lure of fantasy, which seduces us into a series of futile attempts to attain an imagined full and harmonious state and to seek the enjoyment that we presume will accompany this state. Such fantasies, which are ubiquitous in political, professional and personal life, typically take one of two opposite but related forms. Specifically, fantasies may be of the 'beatific' variety – "if we leave the European Union we will take back democratic control of our country and regain our greatness as a nation; if we implement this curriculum reform our students' outcomes will significantly improve" – in which the achievement of a specific concrete object is positioned as the key to accessing a more generalized state of well-being. Yet fantasies may also adopt a contrasting 'horrific' form, whereby the non-achievement of an object is regarded as a prelude to disaster – "unless we tackle immigration our social infrastructure will collapse; if we don't raise our country's position in the PISA tables we will never achieve global economic competitiveness". Both type of fantasies, the beatific and the horrific versions, typically pivot around an object – an individual or a group – blamed for hindering our full flourishing or representing an obstacle to the realization of our goals. In political debates, the unemployed, refugees, and asylum seekers are frequently positioned as such objects in the national psyche of many wealthy nations, while insufficiently aspirational students, under-committed teachers or 'coasting' schools are among those occupying such a position in education debates. The key point here, however, is that these scapegoats are unfortunate but necessary figures insofar as the notion of a fully realised state of wellbeing beyond the conflicts, compromises, and contradictions of present social reality is a chimera – something that is constitutively impossible and unattainable for us as fragmented and divided human subjects. The resulting dilemma between the indispensability of fantasy and fantasmatic thinking that Žižek (1997) refers to as the 'plague of fantasies', involving the pursuit of an imagined state of harmonious wholeness on the one hand, and the impossibility of achieving a full identity on the other hand, is one that has implications at any scale, from the individual, to the group to the societal.

Another consequence of our constitutive alienation is an ongoing tension between the ways in which we would like to see ourselves – our preferred self image or ideal ego – and the meanings and practices we assume the Other of the symbolic order of society expects us to accept and adopt – our ego ideal (Lacan, 1991). This ongoing struggle between ideal ego and ego ideal reflects the larger tension in the constitution of the human psyche between the imaginary and symbolic orders and, like the dilemma posed by the lure of fantasy, offers insights into the challenges faced by novice teachers struggling to establish their teacher identities. The following discussion illustrates these points with examples from two recently published studies, both focused on the difficulties and dilemmas involved in constructing teacher identity.

The Seductions of the Imaginary: Heroes and Villains[4]

The position of the student teacher[5] is nothing if not challenging, requiring its occupants to combine two incompatible roles – the term is in many ways oxymoronic (Britzman, 2003) – and to navigate a boundary that can seem disconcertingly fluid and porous but can also prove rigid and impermeable. Critically, passage through this rite is typically mediated by the classroom mentor teacher who is tasked with the responsibility for guiding but also assessing the progress of the novice teacher. In a sense, the mentor teacher holds the novice teacher's future in their hands. It is not surprising, therefore, that many student teachers elevate their mentor teacher to the status of a hero, while others demote them to the level of a villain. Psychoanalytic theory can help explain this tendency.

This discussion in the earlier sections of this chapter highlighted the complexity of identity, explaining how this arises from the conflicted nature of the human psyche. In particular, I noted the tension between the imaginary register, with its tendency to seek out and hold on to perceptual unities, and the symbolic register, characterized by multiplicity and fluidity. The fixity or stasis associated with the imaginary, Lacan's reworking of the Freudian ego, reflects its origins in identification with the external specular image in the mirror stage. The imaginary is thus

---

[4] The discussion in this section draws on Clarke & Sheridan, 2017.

[5] I use the terms 'novice teacher' and 'student teacher' interchangeably in this chapter.

oriented towards the perception and retention of stable and enduring gestalts, unlike the symbolic, which is a fluid configuration comprising ever-shifting and *un*stable signifiers. The imaginary is, in this sense, a conservative force, resistant to growth and change.

The same qualities that characterize the imaginary are also characteristics of one of its main forms of defense: the projection of fantasies (Evans, 1996, p. 60) whereby simplified and reductive readings of reality are maintained at the expense of more complex, but also more demanding and potentially threatening, versions of the world. The division of the world into categories such as 'saints' and 'sinners', good and bad, deserving and undeserving, are just some examples of the fantasmatic structuring of reality. Critically, as Britzman (Britzman, 2009; see also Phelan, 2013) notes, in relation to teacher identity, this tendency towards idealization, frequently returns in novice teachers as a powerful "need to believe". Critically for the purposes of this chapter, the fantasies arising from the need to believe and the accompanying tendency towards idealization seduce us with an appealing yet reductive coherence – 'if I adopt the same language and gestures as my mentor I will achieve her levels of control over the students in class'. Fantasy can thus appear as a source of inspiration through the projection of a graspable vision of the professional teacher identity the novice teacher aspires to adopt and inhabit. Yet unfortunately, the operation of such reductive and simplified visions is likely to serve as a potential source of illusion, inhibiting the growth that would result from engagement with more complex, challenging, and adequate accounts of teaching.

So what might be done to resist the operations of such fantasies? How might mentors and others involved in initial teacher education assist novice teachers in recognizing the complexity of teaching and the dangers and limitations of simplified rather than complex teacher identities? One way in which the operation of fantasies can be challenged is through the operation of the signifier, (i.e., through "a symbolically mediated process of exchange [which] submits the imaginary organization of the ego to a continuous pressure toward re-formation") (Boothby, 1991, p. 159). Such symbolic mediation essentially requires ongoing critical dialogue and discussion as part of mentoring in the context of the practicum component of teacher education and beyond into the early stages of professional practice – the pedagogic equivalent of the psychoanalytic 'talking cure'. As part of this critical dialogue, interpretations and conclusions of events and interactions in professional practice, including the implications of various policies and practices, need to be continually held up for further probing, reflection, and analysis. As a result, searching and questioning, rather than compliant or complacent, teacher identities are repeatedly modelled. But the seductions of imaginary fantasies are not the only challenge confronting the teacher identities of novice teachers. Another challenge arises from tensions between external, institutional or professional demands, and those arising from the novice teachers' aspirations for their professional teacher identity.

Competing Demands: Ego Ideal and Ideal Ego

Many teachers embark on initial teacher education with passionately held views of why they want to teach and the sort of teacher they want to be. Yet teacher identity is never asocial – it is not the manifestation of some inner 'essence' but entails a complex and paradoxical entanglement of the social and individual (Zembylas, 2003). In other words, "to learn to teach, student-teachers need to develop their capacity to balance and understand the competing demands of their desires, consciences, other people and reality" (Boote, 2003, p. 258). This entails recognition that developing a teacher identity requires a capacity to balance, if not reconcile, the desires and demands of self and other. In the terms referred to earlier in this chapter, it requires integrating the 'inside out' view of teaching that may be the source of passionate personal investment in the profession and the 'outside in' approaches that currently dominate initial teacher education, as manifested in the dominant 'standards' and 'competencies' discourses that emphasize the acquisition of discrete skills as the key to 'effective' teaching. This integration work can involve difficult and often painful negotiations between diverse demands including, for instance, official conceptions of what teaching is or should be, the identities of more established and experienced others, and the aspirations and desires of the novice teacher's own emergent professional identity.

A recent article (Clarke et al., 2016) utilized the Lacanian notions of the ideal ego and the ego ideal – two related concepts introduced in the section on identity above – in considering the tensions between outside-in and inside-out perspectives and pressures in learning to teach and how these tensions are managed by individual novice teachers. Exploring interview data from a single case of a novice teacher during a practicum placement, my co-authors and I asked to what extent teacher identity is shaped by symbolic prototypes imposed by the social, to what extent was it shaped by imaginary identifications shaped by internal ideals, aspirations and desires, and to what extent these 'forces' function in a space of productive tension.

For this teacher, Christian, as for many novice teachers on placement, school-based professional experience was the key site where fundamental issues of teacher identity and identification were negotiated, if not resolved. In particular, Christian's professional experience was marked by a struggle between becoming the kind of teacher he thought he wanted to be (his ideal-ego) and the kind of teacher he thought he ought to be (his ego-ideal) in the eyes of his mentor as representative of the school and the wider education system. This professional identity struggle was played out in two common challenges of professional experience – classroom management and professional commitment. In the course of negotiating these areas, Christian sought an answer to a fundamental identity question; 'what kind of teacher am I?' His identity struggle was a dialectic process marked by tensions between opposing images and readings of teaching that might seem to call for some form of resolution. Against this, my co-authors and I argued for the value of sustaining the state of tension as productive of growth and insight – so long as Christian was supported by understanding and encouraging mentors.

In one sense, our analysis of Christian's developing teacher identity and suggestion of maintaining the tension between the conflicting demands of ideal-ego and the ego-ideal may seem counter-intuitive. Indeed, it seems to literally split and de-centre Christian's teacher identity. This may seem counter to popular ways of thinking about identity, which is commonly conceived as a process by which one discovers one's true self (Woodward, 2002). Yet in common with postmodern and poststructuralist approaches, psychoanalysis rejects a vision of a unified subject and suggests that it may be more helpful to talk in terms of identifications, since this suggests that, rather than being an object or 'thing', teacher identity is more helpfully and productively conceived of as a process. As such, teacher identity remains an ongoing and unfinalizable project, as well as being, as we have seen in the examples above, a site of struggle and striving.

Conclusion

Overall then, my argument is that pre-service teachers – and indeed all teachers – are almost inevitably going to experience tensions in their personal and professional identities – whether we frame these as occurring between the aspirations of their ideal-ego and the demands of the ego-ideal, as with Christian, or between the imaginary and symbolic identifications, as with the student teachers in the 'heroes and villains' article discussed above. In both cases the tension reflects that between inside-out and outside-in views of teaching and teachers discussed above. In either instance, merely prioritising one side of the division at the expense of the other is hardly likely to yield a satisfactory long term solution. Specifically, the consequence is likely to be alienation from, and rejection by, the professional community when inside-out perspectives prevail on the one hand; and, on the other hand, depression, inauthenticity and resentment when the compliance with the social demands of outside-in views achieve complete dominance. Instead of either of these equally unattractive options, I suggest the need to recognize that teacher identity remains at once indispensable and impossible. This in turn suggests that teachers and teacher educators need to recognize and engage with the challenge of maintaining a productive tension between the inside-out and outside-in teaching and teacher identity though ongoing critique, dialogue and reflection.

References

Ball, S. J. (2003). The teacher's soul and the terrors of performativity. *Journal of Education Policy, 18*(2), 215–228.

Beauchamp, C., & Thomas, L. (2009). Understanding teacher identity: An overview of issues in the literature and implications for teacher education. *Cambridge Journal of Education, 39*(2), 175–189.

Binkley, S. (2017). *The work of diversity in the neoliberal age of rage: Humiliation and the indebted subject of antiracist governmentality.* Paper presented at Goldsmiths: University of London.

Boote, D. (2003). Teacher educators as belief-and-attitude therapists: Exploring psychodynamic implications of an emerging role. *Teachers and Teaching: Theory and Practice, 9*(3), 257–277.

Boothby, R. (1991). *Freud as philosopher: Metapsychology after Lacan.* New York: Routledge.

Bowie, M. (1991). *Lacan.* Cambridge, MA: Harvard University Press.

Britzman, D. (2003). *Practice makes practice: A critical study of learning to teach* (2nd ed.). Albany, NY: SUNY.

Britzman, D. (2009). *The adolescent teacher: A psychoanalytic contribution to developing education.* Paper presented at the Mathematics Education and Contemporary Theory Conference, Manchester Metropolitan University. http://www.esri.mmu.ac.uk/mect/keynotes_11/dbritzman.pdf

Brown, W. (2015). *Undoing the demos: Neoliberalism's stealth revolution.* Cambridge, MA: MIT Press.

Burchielli, R. (2006). The intensification of teachers' work and the role of changed public sector philosophy. *International Journal of Human Resources Development and Management, 6*(2), 146–160.

Castells, M. (2010). *The power of identity* (2nd ed.). Chichester, England: Wiley-Blackwell.

Chiesa, L. (2007). *Subjectivity and otherness: A philosophical reading of Lacan.* Cambridge, MA: The MIT Press.

Clarke, M. (2006). Beyond antagonism? The discursive construction of 'new' teachers in the United Arab Emirates. *Teaching Education, 17*(3), 225–237.

Clarke, M. (2013). Terror/enjoyment: Performativity, resistance and the teacher's psyche. *London Review of Education, 11*(3), 229–238.

Clarke, M., Michell, M., & Ellis, N. J. (2016). Dialectics of development: Teacher identity formation in the interplay of ideal ego and ego ideal. *Teaching Education*, 1–16.

Clarke, M., & Sheridan, L. (2017). Heroes and villains: The insistence of the imaginary and the novice teacher's need to believe. *Asia-Pacific Journal of Teacher Education, 45*(2), 194–206.

Connell, R. (2013). The neoliberal cascade and education: An essay on the market agenda and its consequences. *Critical Studies in Education, 54*(2), 99–112.

Danielewicz, J. (2001). *Teaching selves: Identity, pedagogy and teacher education.* Albany, NY: SUNY.

Davies, W. (2014). *The limits of neoliberalism: Authority, sovereignty and the logic of competition.* London: Sage.

Dawson, A. J. (1994). Professional codes of practice and ethical conduct. *Journal of Applied Philosophy, 11*(2), 145–153.

Day, C., Sammons, P., Stobart, G., Kington, A., & Gu, Q. (2007). *Teachers matter: Connecting work, lives and effectiveness.* Buckingham, UK: Open University Press.

Devos, A. (2010). New teachers, mentoring and the discursive formation of professional identity. *Teaching and Teacher Education, 26*, 1219–1223.

Evans, D. (1996). *An introductory dictionary of Lacanian psychoanalysis.* London: Routledge.

Evetts, J. (2009). The management of professionalism: A contemporary paradox. In S. Gerwirtz, P. Mahony, I. Hextall, & A. Cribb (Eds.), *Changing teacher professionalism: International trends, challenges and ways forward.* Abingdon: Routledge.

Hong, J., Greene, B., & Lowery, J. (2017). Multiple dimensions of teacher identity development from pre-service to early years of teaching: A longitudinal study. *Journal of Education for Teaching, 43*(1), 84–98.

Lacan, J. (1977). *Écrits: A selection* (A. Sheridan, Trans.). London: Routledge.

Lacan, J. (1991). *The seminar of Jacques Lacan: Book II: The ego in Freud's theory and in the technique of psychoanalysis, 1954–1955* (S. Tomaselli, Trans.). New York: Norton.

Maclean, R., & White, S. (2007). Video reflection and the formation of teacher identity in a team of pre-service and experienced teachers. *Reflective Practice, 8*(1), 47–60.

MacLure, M. (1993). Arguing for your self: Identity as an organising principle in teachers' jobs and lives. *British Educational Research Journal, 19*(4), 311–322.

Phelan, A. (2013). *"The incredible need to believe": Teacher as perpetual pilgrim.* Paper presented at the European Conference for Educational Research, Istanbul.

Santner, E. (2001). *On the psychotheology of everyday life.* Chicago: Chicago University Press.

Settlage, J., Southerland, S. A., Smith, L. K., & Ceglie, R. (2009). Constructing a doubt-free teaching self: Self-efficacy, teacher identity, and science instruction within diverse settings. *Journal of Research in Science Teaching, 46*(1), 102–125.

Søreide, G. E. (2006). Narrative construction of teacher identity: Positioning and negotiation. *Teachers and Teaching: Theory and Practice, 12*(5), 527–547.

Taubman, P. (2009). *Teaching by numbers: Deconstructing the discourse of standards and accountability in education.* New York: Routledge.

Walkington, J. (2005). Becoming a teacher: Encouraging development of teacher identity through reflective practice. *Asia-Pacific Journal of Teacher Education, 33*(1), 53–64.

Watson, C. (2006). Narratives of practice and the construction of identity in teaching. *Teachers and Teaching: Theory and Practice, 12*(5), 509–526.

Williamson, J., & Myhill, M. (2008). Under 'constant bombardment': Work intensification and the teachers' role. In D. Johnson & R. Maclean (Eds.), *Teaching: Professionalisation, development and leadership* (pp. 25–43). Dordrecht, The Netherlands: Springer.

Woodward, K. (2002). *Understanding identity.* London: Arnold.

Zembylas, M. (2003). Interrogating "teacher identity": Emotion, resistance, and self-formation. *Educational Theory, 53*(1), 107–127.

Žižek, S. (1997). *The plague of fantasies.* London: Verso.

Chapter 20
Professional Self-Understanding in Practice: Narrating, Navigating and Negotiating

Geert Kelchtermans

Nobody interested in teachers' work lives and their development throughout their career, can escape taking a stance on the issue of how teachers conceive of themselves as teachers and how that conception relates to their professional practice. Because teaching is first and foremost a practice, at its core there is a person –the teacher-, who, with professional expertise engages in a committed and responsible relationship with others to support them in their learning and development. Practice, then, refers to the embodied behaviours as well as the discursive representations around them (thinking, talking). Since the person of the teacher is inevitably involved in teaching, I take the stance that it is in the educational practice that teachers' sense of themselves, their professional self-understanding emerges and becomes visible: "who I am in how I teach is the message" (Kelchtermans, 2009, p. 257). I'll start by explaining how the personal and the professional intertwine in practice: teachers' self-understanding is at the same time *the result or outcome of experiences in practice as well as a condition for future professional practice.* Taking that stance allows for the unpacking of a number of ambiguities that are inherent to teaching as a profession, as it develops in its context of time (biography) and space (social professional relationships, organizational context of the school, policy environment, curriculum…etc.). I will illustrate the ambiguities referring to a number of different studies I have been involved in over the past decade. I end up concluding that there are three important categories of practices, in which teachers' self-understanding develops, as well as influences their choices for action.

G. Kelchtermans (✉)
Faculty of Psychology and Educational Sciences, University of Leuven, Leuven, Belgium
e-mail: geert.kelchtermans@kuleuven.be

© Springer International Publishing AG, part of Springer Nature 2018
P. A. Schutz et al. (eds.), *Research on Teacher Identity*,
https://doi.org/10.1007/978-3-319-93836-3_20

The Intertwinement of the Personal and the Professional Takes Place in Practice

Teachers' "practice" starts quite early in their lives. In many countries, on enrollment student teachers bring with them more than a decade of experience in schools. As pupils and students they have spent thousands of hours observing and interacting with teachers, in many classrooms and different schools. As a result of this "apprenticeship of observation" (Lortie, 1975), they develop a particular understanding of teaching as a job and –eventually- of themselves as possible future teachers. Once they enroll in teacher education, the development of the self-understanding gets intensified, in particular during internship and practical teacher education. New insights and experiences modify, strengthen, challenge or even dramatically change student teachers' views of themselves in the job, explaining for example the often intense emotions of the praxis shock when entering their career or in later career phases during periods of changing policy and educational reforms (Kelchtermans & Deketelaere, 2016).

Using a narrative-biographical perspective, I have made these processes of sensemaking, as fundamentally contextualized in time and space, the core of my research on teachers' development and work lives during different career phases (initial teacher training, induction, mid-career) (Kelchtermans, 2009, 2017; Kelchtermans & Ballet, 2002; Rots, Kelchtermans & Aelterman, 2012). An important outcome of that research has been the conceptualization of professional development as a learning process, which impacts both teachers' actions and their thinking. Professional development becomes evident in the changes in teachers' pedagogical interventions, or –more generally- in the way they enact their professional practice. Parallel to these changes in action, there are also changes in teachers' thinking and sensemaking or in what I have called teachers' *personal interpretative framework*: "a set of cognitions, mental representations that operates as a lens through which teachers look at their job, give meaning to it and act in it." (Kelchtermans, 2009, p. 260). An essential part of that framework is teachers' sense of themselves as teachers, how they conceive of and represent themselves in their professional practice: their *professional self-understanding*. I prefer to use this term over the concept 'identity', because –although widely used and apparently unequivocal- its meaning actually may differ quite dramatically depending on the epistemological and conceptual stance an author takes, not to mention the essentialist and decontextualized connotations the word still often has.

The systematic interpretative analysis of teachers' career stories or professional biographies, resulted in the identification of five components that together make up teachers' self-understanding: self-image, self-esteem, job motivation, task perception and future perspective (Kelchtermans, 2009). The *self-image* is the descriptive component, the way teachers typify themselves as teachers. Closely related, *self-esteem* is the evaluative component of the self-understanding, reflecting one's appreciation of one's actual job performance (how well am I doing in my job as a teacher?). Thirdly, the normative component –the *task perception*- constitutes a teacher's personal professional agenda: what must I do to be a proper teacher?; what are the duties I have to take on if I want to rightly feel that I am doing well as a teacher?; what do I consider as legitimate tasks to perform and what do I refuse to accept as part of 'my job'? This normative component clearly reflects the idea that teaching and being a teacher is not a neutral, technical endeavor, but implies value-laden choices, moral considerations, and ethical stances. As a fourth component the *job motivation* (or conative component) refers to the motives that make people choose to become a teacher, to stay in teaching or to give it up for another career. The job motivation is strongly determined by the agenda in the task perception as well as by the degree to which the specific working conditions in one's school permit to operate according to that personal normative program. Finally the *future perspective* encompasses teachers' expectations about their future in the job ('how do I see myself as a teacher in the years to come and how do I feel about it?'). This component explicitly also refers to the dynamic character of the self-understanding: it is the result of ongoing processes of interaction and sense-making.

To sum up: self-understanding is the dynamic *result and outcome* of teachers' meaningful interactions with their professional contexts. It is subjective –and even to some degree idiosyncratic- in that it reflects teachers' understanding of themselves, but at the same time reflects intense processes of intersubjective and contextualized sense-making. The five constitutive components of self-understanding can be analytically distinguished, yet always need to be understood as intertwined and interdependent.

Self-Understanding and the Ambiguities in Teaching and Teachers' Work Lives

This conceptualization of professional self-understanding allows to incorporate a number of ambiguities that are inherent in and even constitutive for the teaching job: self-understanding as process and product, as situated between agency and structure, and as caught between intentionality and vulnerability. Each of those ambiguities exemplifies how teachers' understanding of themselves is the result of their experiences in their professional practice, as well as an important determinant of future practices.

Self-Understanding as Both Process and Product

The way teachers conceive of themselves as teachers is on the one hand a particular outcome or *product* of their interactive sense-making at a *particular point in time*: this is how I conceive of myself today. Yet, on the other hand, the *process* of understanding oneself goes on, and the result will look or feel different over time. This double characteristic of being both a process and a product is reflected in the very form of the word "self-understanding" as a gerund. It acknowledges that one can meaningfully represent, reconstruct, and make explicit one's understanding of one-self with a sense of internal coherence, consistency, continuity, and meaningfulness, without getting trapped in a deterministic or essentialist stance. Yet at the same time, the gerund form indicates the ongoing dynamic, development, and changes in one's sense of self as life goes on. Historicity is constitutive for human beings and their self-understanding: they experience and make sense of a presence, while incarnating their lived past (and how they construct or define that), as well as having more or less explicit ideas about themselves in the future (Kelchtermans, 2009).

This was illustrated in our study on how student teachers' decision to actually enter the teacher profession after graduation, was found to be deeply affected by the development of their job motivation (as part of their self-understanding) over time during initial teacher education (Rots, Kelchtermans & Aelterman, 2012). We identified three different patterns: from low to high job motivation, from high non-specific to high specific motivation to work as a teacher and from high to low job motivation. The actual experiences as student teachers –in particular during their practical training and internship- brought them to reconsider and redefine themselves as future teachers. An important determinant for the shifts in job motivation was the need for social recognition as a (future) teacher by significant others. Equally crucial was the quality of the social-professional relationships in the placement schools. I'll come back to both determinants below when I discuss intentionality and vulnerability.

Self-Understanding Between Agency and Structure

It is obvious that the concept of self-understanding acknowledges the part of teachers in constructing their sense of self through active sense-making of their interactions and experiences with others. They perceive situations, interpret them and –more or less consciously- decide on what to do, how to act. The verbs deliberating, judging, and choosing how to act all demonstrate teachers' agency in their job. It is in and through this agency that teachers enact their practice, build their self-understanding, that eventually shows in their practices, both in the sense of an embodied enactment and in the discursive actions (talking and thinking) around it.

However, the inevitable contextualization in time and space of one's self-understanding implies that it can never be merely individual or idiosyncratic. Its meaningfulness also stems from the broader culture (meaning systems), institutional rules, organizational structures etc. in which a person is situated. This was illustrated in our study in Finland which showed that even in an educational policy environment without standards, evaluation systems, and formal job descriptions, students are aware of and influenced by normative cultural definitions or subjectifications of teachers in society (Lanas & Kelchtermans, 2015).

However, even when teachers' understanding of themselves is influenced, informed and to some point determined by the context, there always remains space and leeway for their individual choices, motives, and preferences. An attempt to control and reduce the latter can be found in the radical forms of scripted curricula, where policy makers aimed at a complete banning of teachers' individual judgment and decision-making, reducing them to technical executors of decisions made by others (see for example Achinstein & Ogawa, 2006). As such those policy efforts actually confirm in a negative way the fundamental capability of teachers as sense-making agents: judging a situation, acting accordingly and taking responsibility for those decisions.

Further illustration and evidence for this ambiguity of both autonomy for action and determination by institutional structures and instruments can be found in our studies on the implementation of innovative educational policies. We demonstrated that the actual implementation practices of reforms could only be properly understood by purposefully unravelling the interactions between the teachers and their individual and collective sense-making on the one hand and the institutional and organizational structures and conditions on the other. Teachers' self-understanding was shown to play a central part in this interaction. One study, for example, looked at the implementation of new attainment targets (standards) in the mathematics curriculum for Flemish secondary schools, requiring a more prominent attention to statistics as curriculum content (März, Kelchtermans, Vanhoof & Onghena, 2013). An important finding was that teachers' evaluation and appreciation of the reform policy –and as a consequence their (un)willingness to implement it- reflected their self-understanding (in particular their task perception) as related to the goals of the particular study program they were working in. Interestingly all of them used the same argument ("the interest of the students"), while taking opposite stances towards the reform. Teachers working in a program with stronger mathematics resisted the reform, criticizing that statistics was the least mathematical domain in mathematics and feared that having to spend more time on statistics would leave their students ill-prepared when moving on to university studies that require strong mastery of mathematics (for example engineering, mathematics, economics, etc.). Teachers in the study programs with less mathematics in the curriculum and a more explicit focus on social studies or human sciences welcomed and embraced the reform as it offered them the opportunity to make their subject –mathematics- more relevant and therefore appealing for their students (trigger more motivation and eventually have better study outcomes). The resistance or embracing of the reform reflected a particular self-understanding of the teachers, but showed at the same time how the aims and purpose of the program (structural working condition) as a whole had been integrated in that self-understanding, influencing their choices and decisions in practice. Their individual motivation and task perception was framed and justified by the wider curriculum logic and structures of the program.

Self-Understanding and Responsibility: Intentionality and Vulnerability

Since the "object" of educational practices are human beings -the learning and development of the next generation- teaching cannot simply be reduced to the instrumental issue of combining the most effective means to achieve pre-defined goals (learning outcomes). As an educational practice enacting teaching implies finding oneself in a *relationship of responsibility* for the students that have been entrusted to one's care (Kelchtermans, 2011). It must be clear that this 'responsibility' goes beyond 'accountability'. The latter is prominent in performativity policies, requiring that one proves one's effectiveness (and efficiency) as a teacher by providing evidence that one's professional actions have been productive (e.g., producing added learning-value as shown in the measurement of students' learning outcomes). Of course in itself there is nothing wrong with the ambition to be effective as teachers in stimulating and supporting student learning. Yet, merely framing the educational relationship in terms of effects and output (and for example using them to evaluate and sanction teachers) doesn't do justice to the inevitable moral or ethical dimension in teaching. Caring for the students requires treating them as unique human beings and as such automatically brings the person of the teacher in the relationship. Teaching as an educational practice requires ethical commitment, personal judgment in particular situations, deliberate choice and purposeful or intentional action (Kelchtermans, 2011).

However, the actual context in which teachers need to work, make decisions and take responsibility, is to a large extent predetermined and out of the teachers' control. And yet teachers cannot but act purposefully towards the envisaged goals and outcomes. This creates the third ambiguity of *intentionality and vulnerability* that characterizes teaching. The intentionality is clearly reflected in curriculum goals, lesson plans and deliberate, purposeful interventions by teachers. The vulnerability is not to be understood as a characteristic of the person, nor as an emotional state, but rather as a structural or inherent feature of the teaching job (Kelchtermans, 2009, 2011).

Firstly, an important number of working conditions –all of which are relevant for teachers' enacted practices - are 'found' rather than 'made' by the teachers. Teachers don't have control over a number of working conditions, which strongly determine their practice. For example, teachers normally don't chose who the students are in their classrooms, nor do they pick their colleagues or principal, and it is obvious that the actual school population as well as the other members of the school team, will strongly determine their practice and –as a consequence- the kind of person they can be in that practice. Similar arguments can be made about material infrastructure, contract conditions, policy environment, etc. So, a first source of the *structural vulnerability* in teaching and being a teacher is that lack of control over important working conditions in their school. Secondly, teachers are supposed to act intentionally, trying to achieve particular outcomes. However, they can never really *prove their efficacy* as students' learning is overdetermined by a broad range of factors, not the least their individual motivation and study efforts (both of which eventually are out of the teacher's control). It is obvious that policy environments with high stakes testing and accountability (for example evaluating and sanctioning teachers based on how well their students are doing on tests) create an institutional vulnerability, that deeply affects teachers' self-understanding (self-esteem, motivation, task perception) as well as their practice. Finally, and maybe most fundamentally, in their professional practice teachers cannot but act. They have to make sense of the situations they find themselves in, make reflective judgments, and act on them – yet without ever being sure that they do the right thing. Since those judgements, deliberations, and decisions for action are never merely technical, but by definition imply value-laden choices and have ethical consequences, teachers cannot but feel vulnerable because there is *no uncontestable basis for their judgment or its justification* (Kelchtermans, 2009, 2011). Decisions can and will be questioned by others. In taking up professional responsibility, teachers can only make explicit their choices and the rationale behind them, but without the indisputable authority to justify their actions.

This ambiguity, for example, helps to understand the central importance of the quality of social-professional relationships as a working condition for teachers, as well as teachers' ongoing concern with and striving for social recognition. In our work with beginning teachers (Kelchtermans & Ballet, 2002) we documented how early career teachers actively engage in seeking social recognition from significant others. These others are of course the pupils and their parents, but also colleagues and school leaders. Being acknowledged and valued by them as a proper teacher was a fundamental concern for the beginning teachers and directly related to their developing self-understanding (self-esteem, task perception). Since this recognition remains a gift, something one receives from others, it is never fully achieved and also may be lost at some point. Again, this working condition, which is constitutive for self-esteem and job motivation, escapes teachers' control (vulnerability). Furthermore it is clear that it should not be seen as an indicator for weak personality or lack of intrinsic job motivation, but rather as resulting from a structural feature of the teaching job. Finally, it needs to be stressed that -although the urge to develop a socially recognized self-understanding is most often higher for early career teachers-, it is a concern that continues over the career. Particularly times of educational reform or when teachers move into leadership roles were found to intensify the issue and make it more pressing (see for example, Kelchtermans & Deketelaere, 2016; Kelchtermans, Piot & Ballet, 2011). Every imposed reform or call to implement an educational innovation carries the inevitable implicit (or even explicit) message that what one has been doing so far is not or no longer the best or desirable practice.

These findings help us to think differently about teachers' resistance to change. Although resistance is often viewed as a negative and unprofessional attitude – mostly related to teachers' 'personality' as conservative or lazy-, it is actually the normal reaction of anybody who is highly committed as a person and professional in one's practice. When that practice is questioned, the person enacting it feels automatically questioned in his/her self-esteem, job motivation and task perception. Teachers showing resistance or at least reluctance to simply take on the new normative instructions for their practice is the self-evident first response for committed professionals, who try to live up to their personal beliefs. Achinstein and Ogawa (2006) refer to this as "principled resistance". In our own work we argued that maintaining a socially valued understanding of one-self that is enacted in one's practice, constitutes a crucial working condition for teachers. When that is threatened, they will engage in micro-political action to safe-guard or restore it (see for example, Kelchtermans, 2007; März et al., 2013). In another study (Ballet & Kelchtermans, 2009) we showed how this concern for social recognition, as well as the fit between one's task perception (as the normative component of self-understanding) with the school culture (shared values and norms that guide practices in a particular school) strongly determines teachers' experience of job intensification and how it –eventually- might even contribute to teachers' decisions to leave the profession (Kelchtermans, 2017).

To sum up, professional self-understanding –as it appears in their enacted or discursive practices- always represents *a momentary positioning in the ambiguities that characterize the job:* process and product, agency and structure, intentionality and vulnerability. Self-understanding results from individuals' meaningful interactions with the context, over time. But at the same time, the self-understanding also influences or conditions practical decisions and choices. In other words, conceiving of professional self-understanding as a dynamic process and product, demonstrating teachers' balancing of agency and structure in their practices, while striving for educational goals, but having to deal with the structural vulnerability in their job, constitutes a powerful conceptual tool –for researchers as well as for anybody in charge of educating, training or coaching (student) teachers.

Narrating, Navigating, and Negotiating Professional Self-Understanding

In the former paragraphs I have argued that teachers' self-understanding is always at the same time the result of meaningful interactions with the context and a condition for future practices. Looking back on my research and zooming in on those interactions, I distinguish three types or categories of practices in which the self-understanding is developed, as well as influences teachers' actions and professional choices. As such those categories of action are the places where teachers' self-understanding can emerge and become visible (and be studied): narrating, navigating, and negotiating.

Narrating

Teachers are storytellers. When asked to talk about their job experiences and their work life, teachers often spontaneously choose for narrative language. Storytelling is the natural way through which people make sense of the events, situations, and encounters throughout their lives (Polkinghorne, 1988). The discursive act of narratively sharing anecdotes, metaphorically typifying people or situations, etc. is where the sense-making takes place and the self-understanding is built (Kelchtermans, 2009). Stories are never neutral representations of facts. They inevitably are at the same time descriptive and evaluative (Labov & Waletzky, 1973). They provide the information of time and place, situate the event and picture the characters in the scene to the listener or reader. But at the same time the tone, style, and form of the narration reflects its meaning, how it is (emotionally) experienced by the storyteller: for example irony, hyperbolic language or explicit expression of emotion (indignation, despair, wondering, surprise, anger, curiosity, etc.). The endlessly ongoing storytelling for example in staffrooms, during lunch breaks, but also in more formal staff meetings constitutes the discursive reality and practice in which teachers take a stance, find their place, seek confirmation or express unease and feeling challenged in who they are as teachers.

It is important to stress that a story not only needs a storyteller and a plot in which s/he composes and presents an account of events. Equally essential is the listener or the audience. The act of storytelling only becomes meaningful when there is an audience. As a consequence, however, the audience (listener) influences the meaning that is being constructed through his/her listening, non-verbal reactions, questions or comments. They can confirm the storyteller or challenge (some of) his views, add details or elements to reinforce the sense-making or to enhance nuance and complexity in the account. As such storytelling is a way of engaging with and responding to the world. It implies doing something, making an impact. At the same time storytelling reflects the fundamental subjective and intersubjective nature of teaching as well as the ongoing individual and collective sense-making, the creation, recreation or altering of existing normative narrative structures and meaning systems.

Navigating

However important agency in teaching and in the construction of their self-understanding, it is obvious that its development is not simply a free, voluntaristic construction. One always has to deal with already existing conditions (material, social, cultural). Several working conditions which strongly impact one's practices and self-understanding as a teacher are encountered, rather than chosen or constructed. As such they make up part of the vulnerability and passivity that structurally characterize the teaching job. The expression in English "I found myself…", followed by a verb in gerund, linguistically represents and stresses this reality. One cannot but react, deal with, find a way around these conditions. The more reactive ways of dealing with one's working conditions are metaphorically captured by the term "navigating": like tacking a sailing boat between obstacles (for example, people, regulations, organizational structures and procedures, etc.), trying to find and use the wind to stay on course, or at least to keep the course in line with where one wants to go. In terms of the developing self-understanding this means exploring and getting to know the complex realities of schools, teaching, and being a teacher, and at the same time becoming aware of one's deeply held normative beliefs as a teacher, discovering what really matters in the job, where one's existential loyalties and motives lie and how to preserve them in the given conditions.

Negotiating

While navigating referred to the reactive or adaptive mode of dealing with working conditions and (re)shaping one's self-understanding accordingly, negotiating stresses the (micro)political agency of the teacher, attempts to change the conditions, and their relation to the developing self-understanding. Hoyle (1982) defined micropolitics as "those strategies by which individuals and groups in organisational contexts seek to use their resources of power and influence to further their interests" (p. 88). Political is used here in the broad sense of exerting power, influencing, strategically changing.

Micropolitical activity, I have argued, (Kelchtermans, 2007; Kelchtermans & Ballet, 2002) encompasses teachers' actions to establish, safeguard or restore desirable working conditions, when those are absent, threatened or destroyed. In line with the normative elements in their self-understanding (task perception), teachers have a more or less clear idea of which working conditions they consider desirable or even necessary for them to be able to do their job properly and to be loyal to their beliefs on what makes them good teachers. As such those conditions operate as professional interests. Those conditions can be material, social-professional, organizational and cultural-ideological, but also "self-interests" (Kelchtermans, 2007). This last category refers to the teachers' personal interpretative framework and more in particular to their professional self-understanding. If one can't be the teacher one wants to be, if essential aspects of one's self-understanding are questioned or threatened or if one finds oneself forced to act in ways that differ too widely from one's normative and evaluative beliefs (task perception, self-esteem), teachers will engage in micro-political actions, sometimes even meaning that they quit teaching (Kelchtermans, 2017).

Who I Am in How I Teach Is What Matters

The central thesis I have argued throughout this chapter is that teachers' professional self-understanding is both the result of and a condition for their meaningful professional practices. It is in and through those practices that teachers' understanding of themselves emerges. This practice-based view takes a very different approach to teachers' and their sense of self as professional actors than the 'blueprint'-approach that is most often used by policy makers. The latter implies that organisations and institutions outside the school define what teaching and teachers are and should be. Policy documents, procedures, instruments and regulations contain a whole set of normative demands, claims that are being imposed on teaching and teachers (for example, through lists of competencies, standards, items in central testing, etc.). Although they are launched as scripts for teachers' self-understanding, whether or not and to what extent they actually will influence educational practices, will always depend on teachers sense-making (narrating) about, navigating between and negotiating with them. And for that reason, teachers' actual practices are the place where what really matters in their understanding of themselves emerges and becomes apparent.

References

Achinstein, B., & Ogawa, R. (2006). (In)Fidelity: What the resistance of new teachers reveals about professional principles and prescriptive educational policies. *Harvard Educational Review, 26*(1), 30–63.

Ballet, K., & Kelchtermans, G. (2009). Struggling with workload. Primary teachers' experience of intensification. *Teaching and Teacher Education, 25*, 1150–1157.

Hoyle, E. (1982). Micro-politics of educational organisations. *Educational Management and Administration, 10*(2), 87–98.

Kelchtermans, G. (2007). Macropolitics caught up in micropolitics: The case of the policy on quality control in Flanders. *Journal of Education Policy, 22*, 471–491.

Kelchtermans, G. (2009). Who I am in how I teach is the message: Self-understanding, vulnerability and reflection. *Teachers and Teaching: Theory and Practice, 15*, 257–272.

Kelchtermans, G. (2011). Professional responsibility: Persistent commitment, perpetual vulnerability? In C. Sugrue & T. D. Solbrekke (Eds.), *Professional responsibility: New horizons of praxis* (pp. 113–126). London: Routledge.

Kelchtermans, G. (2017). 'Should I stay or should I go?' Unpacking teacher attrition/retention as an educational issue. *Teachers and Teaching: Theory & Practice.* https://doi.org/10.1080/135 40602.2017.1379793.

Kelchtermans, G., & Ballet, K. (2002). The micropolitics of teacher induction: A narrative-biographical study on teacher socialisation. *Teaching and Teacher Education, 18*, 105–120.

Kelchtermans, G., & Deketelaere, A. (2016). The emotional dimension in becoming a teacher. In J. Loughran & M. L. Hamilton (Eds.), *International handbook on teacher education* (Vol. 2, pp. 429–461). Singapore, Singapore: Springer.

Kelchtermans, G., Piot, L., & Ballet, K. (2011). The lucid loneliness of the gatekeeper: Exploring the emotional dimension in principals' work lives. *Oxford Review of Education, 37*, 93–108.

Labov, W., & Waletzky, J. (1973). Erzählanalyse. Mündliche Versionen persönlicher Erfahrung. In J. IHWE (Ed.), *Literaturwissenschaft und Linguistik* (Vol. 2, pp. 78–126). Frankfurt am Main, Germany: Athenäum.

Lanas, M., & Kelchtermans, G. (2015). "This has more to do with who I am than with my skills": Student teacher subjectification in Finnish teacher education. *Teaching and Teacher Education, 47*, 22–29.

Lortie, D. (1975). *The schoolteacher: A sociological study.* Chicago: University of Chicago Press.

März, V., Kelchtermans, G., Vanhoof, S., & Onghena, P. (2013). Sense-making and structure in teachers' reception of educational reform: A case study on statistics in the mathematics curriculum. *Teaching and Teacher Education, 29*, 13–24.

Polkinghorne, D. (1988). *Narrative knowing and the human sciences.* Albany, NY: State University of New York Press.

Rots, I., Kelchtermans, G., & Aelterman, A. (2012). Learning (not) to become a teacher: A qualitative analysis of the job entrance issue. *Teaching and Teacher Education, 28*, 1–10.

Part VI
A Future Agenda for Research on Teacher Identities

Chapter 21
Research on Teacher Identity: Common Themes, Implications, and Future Directions

Ji Hong, Dionne Cross Francis, and Paul A. Schutz

The empirical and theoretical interest on teacher identity has been rapidly growing over the last two decades. This emerging interest was often attributed to shifting beliefs about the role of teachers. Unlike the traditional notion of teachers as professionals who acquire 'assets' (e.g., knowledge, skills, competencies) and predefined professional standards, current research focuses on the teacher as a whole person and agent who make sense of themselves in their teaching practices (Korthagen, 2004; Porter, Youngs, & Odden, 2001). This holistic approach emphasizes teachers' own meaning making processes within multilayered contexts, non-linear identity development, and its connection to various psychological constructs and contextual dynamics.

Aligned with this, the chapters in this book collectively make compelling arguments for the central role teacher identity plays in understanding teachers' instructional practices, motivation to teach, personal and professional well-being, teaching effectiveness, and career decision-making. Given the complexity of teacher identity, the authors drew from various perspectives and frameworks with the goal of unpacking the nature and core attributes of teacher identity as situated within various school, community, social, and political contexts. Despite this eclectic mix of approaches to teacher identity, there were common themes that connected these

J. Hong (✉)
Department of Educational Psychology, University of Oklahoma, Norman, OK, USA
e-mail: jyhong@ou.edu

D. Cross Francis
Department of Curriculum and Instruction, Indiana University, Bloomington, IN, USA
e-mail: dicross@indiana.edu

P. A. Schutz
Department of Educational Psychology, University of Texas at San Antonio,
San Antonio, TX, USA
e-mail: paul.schutz@utsa.edu

© Springer International Publishing AG, part of Springer Nature 2018
P. A. Schutz et al. (eds.), *Research on Teacher Identity*,
https://doi.org/10.1007/978-3-319-93836-3_21

chapters. Below, we discuss several of these themes and attempt to synthesize the discussions around them highlighting the ways they extend teacher identity research in relation to its theoretical grounding and practical implications for the future.

Agency as a Core Component of Teacher Identity

One recurring theme across several chapters is the acknowledgement of teacher agency as a key attribute of teacher identity. The identification of agency as central to teacher identity is based on the assumption that "human beings are active agents who play decisive roles in determining the dynamics of social life and in shaping individual activities" (Sfard & Prusak, 2005, p.15). Having a sense of control over one's teaching context has also been identified as a key basic psychological need (i.e., need for autonomy) (Ryan & Deci, 2000; Ryan, Huta, & Deci, 2008) and specifically tied to teacher identity. As suggested by Beijaard, Meijer, and Verloop (2004), the formation of a teacher identity involves agency and an active pursuit of one's goals and the self-efficacy to achieve those goals.

This echoes recent studies that identified teacher agency as a central part of teachers' professionalism and identity development, and a key contributor to teachers' professional learning and growth (e.g., Eteläpelto, Vähäsantanen, & Hökkä, 2015; Eteläpelto, Vähäsantanen, Hökkä, & Paloniemi, 2013; Vähäsantanen, 2015). Teacher agency, which has been defined as "intentional regulation of learning and context dependent on-task action strategies steering professional development" (Soini, Pietarinen, Toom, & Pyhältö, 2015, p. 643), implies two key assumptions: (1) teachers have the capabilities to manage their learning and development actively and intentionally, and (2) teachers' professional agency is "not a fixed disposition of an individual teacher, rather, it is constructed situationally in relation to the current context and past personal experiences" (Toom, Pyhältö, & Rust, 2015, p. 616.).

Aligned with these assumptions, chapters in this book foreground the notion that teachers have the capacity to set goals, actively pursue these goals (e.g., need for compentency), and construct their sense of self through meaning-making processes in relation to interactions and experiences with others (e.g., need for relatedness) (Ryan & Deci, 2000). Authors often situated their arguments in relation to the "structure" (e.g., societal, school etc.), which is often disempowering to teachers and tends to create tension due to the pressure of performativity-driven school cultures and accountability-based policies. This is aligned with Gidden's earlier notion, "duality of structure" in that "structures must not be conceptualized as simply placing constraints on human agency, but as enabling" (Giddens, 1976, p. 161). In other words, individual teachers, as active agents, have the ability to make choices and act on those choices within any given set of contextual affordances and constraints. Thus individuals can shape their own lives and environment, while at the same time be influenced by social processes.

In their chapters, authors showed various ways to conceptualize teacher agency and its relationship with teacher identity in the midst of various micro- and macro- contexts. For example, agency was addressed as voicing "narratives of balance" between authority and vulnerability, as ways to deploy motivational filters, which ultimately function as a way to appraise the feasibility and meaningfulness of teaching practices, and as a mediator (e.g., identity-agency) between the environment and the individual teacher's identity, which works to either renegotiate their identities by assimilating with the environment or defend their identities by refusing to assimilate. Authors also highlighted the associations between teacher agency and other psychological constructs (e.g., self-efficacy, resilience, attributional beliefs, and emotions), and the ways they collectively contribute to shape teacher identity. As such, acknowledging its significance in teacher identity development, several of the authors of this volume have explicitly foregrounded agency in their discussions, while it is more tacitly included in others.

Agency stands out as a key construct in teachers' pathways to authoring their professional identities. Depending on whether the elements of the micro- or macro-contexts provide supports or present barriers, teachers' perceived agency serves as a guide, informant, negotiator, or advocate as teachers traverse their teacher education programs, teacher induction, or the teaching career trajectories. We encourage researchers in the field to further unpack the nature, variation, and intensity of the associations between teachers' perceived agency and identity in relation to diverse educational contexts, and identify ways to strengthen and sustain teacher agency, which ultimately contributes to the successful development of teacher identity.

Affective Dimension of Teacher Identity

The second recurrent theme is the central role of emotion in teacher identity development. This aligns well with the perspective that teachers' work is not only a role or the enactment of technical skills, but encompasses involvement of the whole person; and, is akin to Day and Gu's (2010) notion of the "person in the professional", which acknowledges the unavoidable interrelationship between personal identities and professional identities. The emotional nature of teaching and the connection between the cognitive and affective aspects of teaching are emphasized in several chapters in this book.

At the core, these chapters share a central tenet – teaching is fundamentally emotional work. How teachers emotionally regulate and manage teaching-related emotional experiences serve to influence how they come to perceive teaching and who they should be as teachers. Further, teachers' approaches to teaching are influenced by their emotional experiences. Aligned with appraisal theory (Folkman & Lazarus, 1988a, 1988b), if a teacher assesses the person-environment transactions as goal incongruent within particular activity settings, then he or she is more likely to experience unpleasant emotions, which may influence developing beliefs about teacher identity. Within this framework, some authors positioned critical classroom incidents and associated emotional episodes at the center of teachers' identity construction. For example, critical emotional events and attribution beliefs working in concert can provide feedback that facilitate reflection and reappraisal of how successful a teacher may be in pursuing his/her goals. As such, emotions serve as a key informational source in developing his/her sense of self as a teacher.

Authors also discussed the intensification of emotions, mostly unpleasant emotions, resulting from heightened accountability demands and increased managerialism. Micro- and macro- contexts impact the type and intensity of emotions teachers experience, and consequently these experiences inform teachers' actions. In particular, emotional experiences can serve as informants, guiding how teachers renegotiate their identity and resolve identity tensions.

The relational aspect of teaching is also fundamentally emotion-generating as it requires authentic relations of care, taking on the feelings of others as their own, acting on these feelings (professional empathy), and constantly drawing on reserves of emotional energy. As such, teaching is conceptualized as 'emotional work'. This work is intensified if the context does not allow emotions to be experienced and displayed with authenticity, as the experience of emotional labor may have negative consequences in the long term as the interpersonal, caring aspect of teaching may be minimized and teaching may become routine. Although all these emotion-related actions are associated with teaching effectiveness, they can negatively impact a teacher's willingness and ability to build and sustain a positive sense of identity. As such, the chapters in this book consistently recognized and highlighted the affective dimension of teacher identity, especially in relation to student-teacher interactions, job-related tasks, challenging school policy, and social-historical contextual constaints and affordances.

In alignment with the growing body of literature on teachers' emotion, authors in this volume acknowledged that teaching is deeply emotionally laden. Teachers' emotional experiences are not evoked solely by internal psychological interactions; rather, micro- and macro- influences existing within the teachers' environment shape the nature and intensity of the emotional experiences and often the resources available to effectively address the emotion-eliciting event. Given the centrality of emotions in teachers' lives and its susceptibility to contextual factors, future research on teacher identity needs to pay close attention to the ways teachers experience, express, and regulate emotions as they navigate their career pathway, and its influence on their decision-making, interpersonal relationships, the trajectory of their teacher identity development, and the level of commitment they have to the profession overall.

Dynamic Teacher Identity in Changing and Challenging Context

Attending to the social, historical, and cultural influences on teacher identity was a core theme across multiple chapters in this book. Acknowledging the role of context in the shaping of identity provides greater clarity in understanding the diversity with which teachers' identities shift and change over time. In her earlier work, acknowledging the heterogeneous, unbounded, and emergent nature of social context, Holland defined identity as "forms of self-understanding developed through engagement in activities in a lived world" (Holland, Lachicotte, Skinner, & Cain, 1998, p.68). This definition emphasizes the contribution of "action" or "practice" in the development of identity. In other words, identity is developed through practices and activities that are situated in historically contingent, socially enacted, and culturally constructed frames of social life. Given this, the current educational climate of heightened accountability, increased managerialism, and demand for quality teaching in diversified school contexts presents multi-level and multifaceted challenges, which often forces teachers to enact practices that conflict with their beliefs and self-understanding (Day & Hong, 2016; Kelchtermans, 2005). The lack of agency experienced in such inhibiting and restrictive environments may elicit unpleasant emotional experiences which may adversely impact teacher identity development.

Authors in this book addressed various levels of contextual influences on teachers' identity development. At a macro level, several authors addressed the intersectionality of teacher identity and racial identity, or teacher identity and politics. By foregrounding adverse macro- contexts such as the racialized North American context shaped by a culture of white dominance, and policy environments with high stakes testing and accountability, authors discussed the ways pre-service and in-service teachers act, navigate, and negotiate their sense of self as teachers in the midst of competing demands, which makes teacher identity inevitably politicized and transformative. Several chapters in this book also addressed micro-level influences on teachers' identity development such as mentor teachers' impact on pre-service teachers' identity, supervision dialogues and the ways pre-service teachers balance time, content, and salience, which impact their sensed continuity and discontinuity, and creativity cultivating classroom context as a process of identity development. One of the unique contributions of this book is the inclusion of subject-specific micro-level influences, as each subject area requires different knowledge, instructional skills, evaluation standards, and orientations. Chapters in this book showed how subject-specific teachers navigate their pedagogical spaces in classrooms and within schools, and what unique challenges they experience in developing subject-specific teacher identities.

Another valuable perspective authors of this book offered is the changing and developing nature of teacher identity over time. They emphasized the need and importance of longitudinal perspectives to unpack the process of teacher identity development over time, and the ways in which teachers author their identity construction responsive to context. While highlighting the situated nature of teacher identity, some authors in this book pushed the boundary of teacher identity further by conceptualizing identity as a site of conflict and alienation, due to the external location of identity sources, which makes identity "indispensable and impossible". Also, authors extended the concept of teacher identity by arguing for using the term 'self-understanding' instead of 'identity', in order to address some of the ambiguities inherent in the identity construct, such as self-understanding as both process and product, as situated between agency and structure, and as caught between intentionality and vulnerability. These chapters provide a more robust description of teacher identity, pushing for a conceptualization of teacher identity as more than the self-perception or self-image that a teacher has about himself/herself; instead, one that inevitably embodies the dual dynamic of how teachers view themselves and how they are influenced by various social, historical, and cultural contexts. When these two are not synergistically connected, the differences and misalignments are likely to create tensions and identity shifts, fueled by changes over time and contexts.

Chapters in this book consistently highlighted the situated nature of teacher identity and the ways teachers navigate and negotiate their identity in the midst of dynamic contextual influences. In this process, it is important to remember that any changes in teacher identity occur neither easily nor quickly. Constantly changing educational contexts and increasing challenges require teachers to carefully negotiate and adopt new roles, and make decisions about whether and how to incorporate new standards and pratices. In order to capture these complex dynamics, comprehensive longitudinal inquiry on teacher identity, which encompasses multifaceted contexts over time, is needed.

Why Do We Care About Teacher Identity?: Implications & Future Directions

So "why should we care about teacher identity?" The answer to this question involves recognizing that high-quality learning does not occur without high-quality teachers. As such, preparing, developing, and sustaining effective teachers who attend to both the academic and socio-emotional needs of students is paramount (Darling-Hammond & Youngs, 2002; Harris & Rutledge, 2010). "Effective teachers" or "quality teaching" has been the main focus and concern for educators and policy makers over the past 20 years or so. Existing research understands "effective teacher" not as a static outcome, but rather as an ongoing process that changes over time in relation to the context and conditions in which the teacher is embedded. No one is born a good teacher and "being effective" means different things as the professional and personal life context changes. Thus, it is critical to understand the "becoming" of effective teachers within specific contexts and over time. Anchored in teacher identity, the three themes that connect the chapters in this book unpack the "becoming" of effective teachers using various data sources, analytic approaches, and theoretical models. In this last section, we summarize the implications of teacher identity research and suggest future directions.

A key message from chapters in this book, especially as delineated in the third theme above, is the significance of classroom, school, social, cultural, and political contexts in teachers' identity development, and the ways teachers negotiate and balance their sense of self between authority and vulnerability; between narrative and positional identities; between one's own aims and the needs of the workplace;

between continuity and discontinuity; between inside-out and outside-in teaching; and between content area expert and generalist. This dynamic nature of teacher identity development necessitates the importance of empowering teacher agency so that teachers can author their teacher identity narrative with autonomy, motivation, and critical consciousness. As noted above, identity is not automatically ascribed to someone who starts working as a teacher; instead it is a continually developing process through practices and activities (Holland et al., 1998). Thus, identity development requires critically reflecting within situated contexts and on their own responses to the contexts, and actively engaging in dialogues with mentor teachers, teacher educators, peers, professional developers, and school administrators.

In this process, it is important to remember that individual teachers do not act in a social vacuum, and thus the successful negotiation of identity entails not only individual agency, but also collective and collaborative agency. Given the politicized educational climate and accountability demands, voicing one's own teacher identity could mean working against the imposed structure. It is essentially risk taking, as opposing the systemic power structure can be viewed as "deviant". As several authors in this book emphasized, collective efficacy and collaborative agency building is critical for teachers to have the safe and supportive environment they need to feel sufficiently empowered to take risks and practice vulnerability – essential experiences for identity development. As Marcia (1980) addressed, the strength of identity can be acquired "only through vulnerability" (p. 110). Although there are studies that addressed collective efficacy (e.g., Goddard & Goddard, 2001; Goddard, Hoy, & Hoy, 2000; Ross & Gary, 2006) and collective agency (e.g., Day & Hong 2016; Gu, 2014), studies that focused on their connection to teacher identity development are scant. Future research of teacher identity should address the challenges and affordances of building collective efficacy and collaborative agency within the worlds teachers navigate, and its connection to identity development for both pre-service and in-service teachers throughout various trajectories of their career.

Common throughout the chapters in this book is the non-linear and non-universal nature of teacher identity development, which begs the question of how to define "successful" development of teacher identities. In particular, we foreground the importance of paying closer attention to subject-specific teacher identity development. Existing studies on teacher identity tend to generalize teacher development regardless of content areas. However, as chapters in section four of this book showed, different content areas require different expertise, knowledge, pedagogical skills, orientations, and actions. In addition to the broader education landscape in which teachers operate, there are subject-specific micro-worlds they also have to navigate. These micro-worlds present ideal views of the identity the [subject] teacher should have, the set of beliefs she should hold, how she should engage with students, and essentially who she should be in the classroom. Currently, teacher identity research focuses on the "teacher" as educator of the learner, in the discipline-agnostic sense. However, within the discipline-specific field, teachers are considered not just teachers, but "mathematics teachers", "science teachers" etc., with expectations that the identity they develop should embody the teacher qualities that align with high-quality instruction in the discipline– a prescribed [subject] teacher identity. How can we reconcile these seemingly opposing perspectives on teacher identity development? This is another critical question that future research needs to address.

Final Thoughts

Although the chapters in this book, through the use of a range of theoretical approaches, methodologies, and contexts, deconstruct teacher identity in ways that refocus and extend our conceptions of the construct, they also open the door to questions about how to utilize what we know to better scaffold teachers' identity development, create agency-supporting environments and minimize the tensions teachers experience as a result of intersectionality and demands of discipline-focused teaching. We encourage researchers, including authors and readers of this volume to consider the ways in which their work helps us answer these questions and how they potentially inform future research.

References

Beijaard, D., Meijer, P. C., & Verloop, N. (2004). Reconsidering research on teachers' professional identity. *Teaching and Teacher Education, 20*(2), 107–128.

Darling-Hammond, L., & Youngs, P. (2002). Defining "highly qualified teachers:" What does "scientifically-based research" actually tell us? *Educational Researcher, 31*(9), 13–25.

Day, C., & Gu, Q. (2010). *The new lives of teachers* (1st ed.). London: Routledge.

Day, C., & Hong, J. (2016). Influences on the capacities for emotional resilience of teachers in schools serving disadvantaged urban communities: Challenges of living on the edge. *Teaching and Teacher Education, 59*, 115–125.

Eteläpelto, A., Vähäsantanen, K., & Hökkä, P. (2015). How do novice teachers in Finland perceive their professional agency? *Teachers and Teaching: Theory and Practice, 21*(6), 660–680.

Eteläpelto, A., Vähäsantanen, K., Hökkä, P., & Paloniemi, S. (2013). What is agency? Conceptualizing professional agency at work. *Educational Research Review, 10*, 45–65.

Folkman, S., & Lazarus, R. S. (1988a). Coping as a mediator of emotion. *Journal of Personality and Social Psychology, 54*, 466–475.

Folkman, S., & Lazarus, R. S. (1988b). The relationship between· coping and emotion: Implications for theory and research. *Social Science in Medicine, 26*, 309–317.

Giddens, A. (1976). *New rules of sociological method: A positive critique of interpretive sociologies*. London: Hutchinson.

Goddard, R. D., & Goddard, Y. L. (2001). A multilevel analysis of the relationship between teacher and collective efficacy in urban schools. *Teaching and Teacher Education, 17*(7), 807–818.

Goddard, R. D., Hoy, W. K., & Woolfolk Hoy, A. (2000). Collective teacher efficacy: Its meaning, measure, and impact on student achievement. *American Educational Research Journal, 37*(2), 479–507.

Gu, Q. (2014). The role of relational resilience in teachers' career-long commitment and effectiveness. *Teachers and Teaching: Theory and Practice, 20*(5), 502–529.

Harris, D. N., & Rutledge, S. (2010). Models and predictors of teacher effectiveness: A review of the literature with lessons from (and for) other occupations. *Teachers College Record, 112*(3), 914–960.

Holland, D., Lachicotte, W., Skinner, D., & Cain, C. (1998). *Identity and agency in cultural worlds.* Cambridge, MA: Harvard University Press.

Kelchtermans, G. (2005). Teachers' emotions in educational reforms: Self-understanding, vulnerable commitment and micropolitical literacy. *Teaching and Teacher Education, 21*, 995–1006.

Korthagen, F. A. J. (2004). In search of the essence of a good teacher: Towards a more holistic approach in teacher education. *Teaching and Teacher Education, 20*(1), 77–97.

Marcia, J. E. (1980). Identity in adolescence. In J. Adelson (Ed.), *Handbook of adolescent psychology* (pp. 159–187). New York: Wiley.

Porter, A. C., Youngs, P., & Odden, A. (2001). Advances in teacher assessments and their uses. In V. Richardson (Ed.), Handbook of research on teaching (4th ed.). Washington, DC: American Educational Research Association.

Ross, J. A., & Gray, P. (2006). Transformational leadership and teacher commitment to organizational values: The mediating effects of collective teacher efficacy. *School Effectiveness and School Improvement, 17*(2), 179–199.

Ryan, R. M., & Deci, E. L. (2000). Self-determination theory and the facilitation of intrinsic motivation, social development, and well-being. *American Psychologist, 55*(1), 68–78.

Ryan, R. M., Huta, V., & Deci, E. L. (2008). Living well: A self-determination theory perspective on eudaimonia. *Journal of Happiness Studies, 9*, 139–170.

Sfard, A., & Prusak, A. (2005). Telling identities: In search of an analytic tool for investigating learning as a culturally shaped activity. *Educational Researcher, 34*(4), 14–22.

Soini, T., Pietarinen, J., Toom, A., & Pyhältö, K. (2015). What contributes to first-year student teachers' sense of professional agency in the classroom? *Teachers and Teaching: Theory and Practice, 21*(6), 641–659.

Toom, A., Pyhältö, K., & Rust, F. (2015). Teachers' professional agency in contradictory times. *Teachers and Teaching: Theory and Practice, 21*(6), 615–623.

Vähäsantanen, K. (2015). Professional agency in the stream of change: Understanding educational change and teachers' professional identities. *Teaching and Teacher Education, 47*, 1–12.

Printed by Printforce, the Netherlands